BLACK BOOK OF

LOS ANGELES

*The Indispensable Guide to
the City of Angels*

MARLENE GOLDMAN

MAPS BY DAVID LINDROTH INC.

ILLUSTRATED BY
KERREN BARBAS STECKLER

PETER PAUPER PRESS, INC.
WHITE PLAINS, NEW YORK

Special thanks to Panos for enduring long hours during the birth of this book and offering unwavering support, and to my feline family for keeping me company late nights while writing—Joe-Joe, Sofia, Mamacat, and Babyboo.

Thanks to my New York friends—Kurt, Jon, Patti, PJ, and Yvonne—and my N.Y. family, especially my father who took us to L.A. many times as we were growing up.

Also thanks to Mahnaz and my L.A. friends for their help and advice.

Thanks to my S.F. friends at Funky Door Yoga, KUSF and Meetings Media, and to Diane, Steve, Beth, and the rest of my extended travel and yoga families.

The publisher has made every effort to ensure that the content of this book was current at time of publication. It's always best, however, to confirm information before making final travel plans, since telephone numbers, Web sites, prices, hours of operation, and other facts are always subject to change. The publisher cannot accept responsibility for any consequences arising from the use of this book. We value your feedback and suggestions. Please write to: Editors, Peter Pauper Press, Inc., 202 Mamaroneck Avenue, Suite 400, White Plains, New York 10601-5376.

Editor: Vicki Fischer
Proofreader: JCommunications
Illustrations copyright © 2009 Kerren Barbas Steckler

Transportation map © 2009 LACMTA
Neighborhood maps © 2009 David Lindroth Inc.
Designed by Heather Zschock

Copyright © 2009
Peter Pauper Press, Inc.
202 Mamaroneck Avenue
White Plains, NY 10601

ISBN 978-1-59359-839-6
Printed in Hong Kong
7 6 5 4 3 2 1

Visit us at www.peterpauper.com

THE LITTLE
BLACK BOOK OF
LOS ANGELES

CONTENTS

INTRODUCTION 7
  How to Use This Guide 8
  Getting to Los Angeles 9
  Getting Around the City 10
  Seasonal Events 16
  Los Angeles Top Picks 23

CHAPTER 1 24
  Downtown Historic District 28
  Downtown Financial District/Bunker Hill . .37
  Downtown Commercial District and
  Exposition Park 45

CHAPTER 2 54
  Miracle Mile/Mid-City 57
  Hancock Park/Larchmont Village 66
  Koreatown/Westlake 70

CHAPTER 3 76
  Los Feliz/Griffith Park 79
  Silver Lake 84
  Echo Park 89
  Highland Park/Eagle Rock 93

CHAPTER 4 98
  Hollywood 102
  West Hollywood 111
  Beverly Hills/Century City 119

CHAPTER 5 ....*126*
Westwood *129*
Brentwood/Bel-Air *134*
West L.A. *138*
Culver City *142*

CHAPTER 6 ....*148*
Malibu/Pacific Palisades *152*
Santa Monica *158*
Venice *165*
Marina del Rey *171*

CHAPTER 7 ....*176*
South Bay—Manhattan Beach,
Hermosa Beach, Redondo Beach *180*
San Pedro/Palos Verdes *186*
Long Beach *192*
Catalina Island *198*
Disneyland *200*
South Los Angeles/Leimert Park *202*

CHAPTER 8 ....*206*
Studio City/Western Valley *209*
North Hollywood/Universal City *215*
Burbank/Glendale *220*

CHAPTER 9 224
  Pasadena/San Gabriel Valley 226

INDEX 235

TRANSPORTATION MAP 257

If they can't do it
in California, it can't be done
anywhere.

—TAYLOR CALDWELL

INTRODUCTION

I t's America's Queen of Glamour—a sculpted, sun-kissed beauty slipping into her Manolos for a cruise down Sunset Strip in a turbocharged Maybach.

But beneath the Botox- and silicon-enhanced fantasy lies the true Los Angeles, a cultural milieu that transcends celluloid image—an amalgam of mini-cities connected by a web of freeways and boulevards.

Nearly 10 million *Angelenos* weather daily torrents of traffic and Tinseltown gossip, not to mention wildfires, earthquakes, and mudslides, yet they remain, held by the promise of this magical city: With the right connections, opportunity will knock.

In addition to its historical ties to the film industry, Los Angeles is considered a manufacturing capital and one of the birthplaces of the Internet. Culturally, world-class museums and art spaces like the Getty Center are found in nearly every neighborhood, whether Gallery Row in rejuvenated Downtown, or Norton Simon in Pasadena.

Surf seekers are drawn to bustling beaches like Santa Monica and quiet enclaves like Hermosa Beach. International shoppers empty bank accounts on Rodeo Drive or bargain hunt on Santee Alley. Burgeoning neighborhoods such as Highland Park lend as much interest as fabled Beverly Hills.

The City of Angels is a kaleidoscope of palm-studded boulevards, floodlit Hollywood venues, historic sights, and Pacific vistas. Let this *Little Black Book* help you experience it all!

HOW TO USE THIS GUIDE

We have included fold-out maps for each chapter, organized by neighborhood sections, with color-coded keys to help you find places listed in the text. **Red** symbols indicate **Places to See**: landmarks and arts and entertainment. **Blue** symbols indicate **Places to Eat & Drink**, including restaurants, bars, and nightlife. **Orange** listings indicate **Where to Shop**. **Green** symbols tell **Where to Stay**.

Price keys for restaurants and hotels:

Restaurants
Cost of an appetizer and main course without drinks

($)	Up to $25
($$)	$25-$45
($$$)	$45-$70
($$$$)	$70 and up

Hotels
Cost per night

($)	$50-$125
($$)	$125-$250
($$$)	$250-$400
($$$$)	$400 and up

GETTING TO LOS ANGELES

Los Angeles International Airport *(LAX, 310-646-5252, www.lawa.org/lax)* is about 17 miles southwest of Downtown. The fastest way in and out of this chaotic hub is by taxi or shared van. **Prime Time Shuttle** *(310-536-7922, www.primetimeshuttle.com)* and **SuperShuttle** *(800-258-3826, www.supershuttle.com)* operate out of LAX and serve southern California counties. Expensive cabs and SuperShuttle head Downtown, or rent a car. Another option: **FlyAway** *(www.lawa.org/flyaway)*, a bus service linking Downtown and LAX; it runs 24 hours, with prime-time frequency about every 30 minutes. The bus stops at Downtown Union Station, Westwood, and the private Van Nuys Airport *(VNY)* in the San Fernando Valley. Mass transit options take significantly longer, but are available.

The airport's free **G Shuttle** services the Metro Rail Green Line at Aviation Station, while the free  **C Shuttle** hits Metro Bus Center *(800-266-6883)* for city buses to Los Angeles. Other public Bus Center buses: Culver City Bus Lines, Santa Monica Big Blue Bus, and Torrance Transit. **Bob Hope Airport** *(BUR, 818-840-8840, www.bobhopeairport.com)* in Burbank serves the San Fernando and San Gabriel valleys, and is a relaxed alternative to LAX. **Bob Hope Airport Train Station**, an Amtrak and Metrolink rail station, is served by Amtrak's Pacific Surfliner from San Luis Obispo to San Diego, and Metrolink's Ventura County Line from Los Angeles

Union Station to Montalvo. **Long Beach Airport** *(LGB, 562-570-2600; www.longbeach.gov/airport)* serves Long Beach, south of Downtown. The Blue Line train from Downtown to the Transit Mall Station in Long Beach connects with the Long Beach Transit Bus Route 111 to the airport *(www.mta.net, 800-COMMUTE)*. **John Wayne Airport** *(SNA, 949-252-5200, www.ocair.com)* serves Orange County, useful for anyone going to Disneyland. **LA/Ontario International Airport** *(ONT, 909-937-2700, www.lawa.org/ont)*, 35 miles east of Downtown, is located in the Inland Empire.

Amtrak *(800-872-7245, www.amtrak.com)* services Los Angeles at the city's downtown Union Station. **Metrolink** *(800-371-5465, www.metrolinktrains.com)* links Los Angeles County with Orange County, Ventura County, San Bernardino County, Riverside County, San Diego County, and other locations.

Greyhound Bus *(www.greyhound.com)* makes a number of stops in L.A., including the main Los Angeles Greyhound Station *(1716 E. 7th St., 213-629-8401)*.

GETTING AROUND THE CITY

Driving

It's no surprise that the city that invented the freeway remains obsessed with its cars. L.A.'s freeways, shuttling some 12 million vehicles a day, were designed to help speed drivers. But, in a city that boasts the highest-per-capita car population in the world, the busy thoroughfares, especially the **San Diego Freeway (405)**, turn into parking lots come rush hour. **La Cienega Boulevard** is a better choice. L.A.'s rush hour lasts longer than most, from approximately 7AM–10AM and 3PM–8PM. Surface roads can be a faster option. Slower but more scenic: the **Pacific Coast Highway** *(PCH)*, which lends access to beach communities. The driver's best companion: the ***Thomas Guide***, though it can be a bear to use while behind the wheel. For instant traffic updates, check the **Sigalert** Web site *(www.sigalert.com)*. Drive defensively—*Angelenos* are not known for driving etiquette.

Taxis

Destinations in Los Angeles are far-flung, and cab fares are high; even short jaunts cost $10 or more. A surcharge is added to fares originating at LAX. Except in the heart of Downtown, cabs will usually not pull over when hailed. Cabstands are located at airports, at Downtown's Union Station, and at major hotels. Or call in advance: **Checker Cab** *(310-330-3720)*, **Yellow Cab** *(310-808-1000)*, or **United Independent Taxi** *(213-483-7660)*.

Public Transportation

Los Angeles does offer an extensive public transportation system, including a light rail and subway **Metro** system *(800-COMMUTE, www.metro.net)*. The **Metro Blue Line** *(light rail)* runs north and south between Long Beach and L.A. The **Metro Green Line** *(light rail)* runs east and west between Norwalk and Redondo Beach. The **Metro Red Line** *(subway)* meets the Blue Line in L.A. and provides service through Downtown, the Mid-Wilshire area, Hollywood, and the San Fernando Valley, where it meets the **Metro Orange Line** *(rapid bus transit)*, running from North Hollywood to the Warner Center in Woodland Hills. The **Metro Purple Line** *(subway)* runs between Union Station, Wilshire Boulevard, and Western Avenue. The **Metro Gold Line** *(light rail)* connects with the Red Line at Union Station and runs to Pasadena. A 2009 six-mile extension, with eight new stations, extends to East Los Angeles. **Metro Expo Line** will connect Downtown Los Angeles with Culver City.

Most of the city's 300-plus bus routes are operated by the **Metropolitan Transportation Authority** (MTA), with white-and-orange buses. The fare is $1.25 (45¢ for seniors); transfers last an hour. Weekly Metro passes are available for $14 at Metro Customer Centers and local convenience and grocery stores. Three-dollar day and other passes are also available. Passes are good on Commuter Express, DASH Downtown, Community Connection, and Metro MTA rail and bus routes.

The **City of Los Angeles Transportation** *(LADOT, www. ladottransit.com)* operates the **DASH** *(Downtown Area Short Hop)* shuttle system, with six bus routes through Downtown. Buses depart every five to 10 minutes weekdays *(6:30AM–6PM)*, and every 15 minutes Sa–Su *(10AM–5PM)*. Routes:

- Route A–Little Tokyo to City West
- Route B–Chinatown to Financial District
- Route C–Financial District to South Park
- Route D–Union Station to South Park
- Route E–City West to Fashion District
- Route F–Financial District to Exposition Park/USC

DASH serves Hollywood, Los Feliz, and Mid-City and operates a commuter express. **Community Connection** services San Pedro, Long Beach, and Griffith Park, among other destinations. **Commuter Express** covers Culver City, Westwood, Brentwood, Glendale, Burbank, the San Fernando Valley, and other locations. **Holly Trolly** runs between Highland and Vine in Hollywood *(Th–Sa 6:30PM–2:30AM)*. Municipal buses include **Big Blue Bus** *(www.bigbluebus.com, 310-451-5444)*, serving Santa Monica, Malibu, Venice, and Downtown (via express). In West Hollywood, the **Cityline** *(800-447-2189)* shuttle operates weekdays *(9AM–4PM)* and Saturday *(10AM–7:30PM)*, stopping at shops and restaurants.

City Tours

For one price, the **Go Los Angeles Card** offers access to over 35 attractions, including Universal Studios, the *Queen Mary*, shops, and restaurants, plus a guidebook. *(617-671-1001, www.golosangelescard.com)*

LAStageTIX.com offers half-price tickets to over 100 musicals, plays, concerts, and other live performances. Tickets are released and posted online every Tuesday. *(http://lastagetix.com)*

 L.A. City Tours takes you past 45 homes of the stars, from John Travolta to Britney Spears. Five-hour tours include Beaches, Downtown, Hollywood, Mulholland Drive, Beverly Hills, Rodeo Drive, Bel-Air, and Sunset Strip. *(6806 Hollywood Blvd., 323-960-0300, www.lacitytours.com)*

Los Angeles Conservancy offers Art Deco tours and tours of City Hall, Downtown, Little Tokyo, Union Station, Broadway theaters, and the Biltmore Hotel. *(523 W. 6th St., 213-623-2489, www.laconservancy.org)*

Los Angeles Sightseeing Tours offers the City Tour by Air, which flies over Hollywood, Downtown, and beaches. *(310-458-0257, www.lasightseeing.net)*

Hollywood Trolley Tour offers a narrated tour of Tinseltown landmarks, including Paramount Studios and CBS, as well as movie filming locations. *(323-463-3333, www.starlinetours.com)*

L.A. Tours operates general tours of the city, from Downtown and the Music Center to Disneyland. *(323-460-6490, www.latours.net)*

Red Line Tours offers guided walking tours through Hollywood, departing daily from the Stella Adler Academy & Theatres. *(6773 Hollywood Blvd., 323-402-1074, www.redlinetours.com)*

Beverly Hills Civic Center Public Art Walking Tour is a self-guided tour of Beverly Gardens Park and several galleries. *(310-550-7963, www.beverlyhills.org)*

Echo Park Historical Society offers three walking tours— Echo Park Lake, Elysian Park, and Echo Park Stairways. *(323-860-8874, www.HistoricEchoPark.org)*

Undiscovered Chinatown Tour, a 2-½-hour walking tour, uncovers Chinatown's history and treasures. *(first Sa of every month, 213-680-0243, www.chinatownla.com)*

Hollywood Pro Bicycles rents all kinds of bikes with tour maps. *(6731 Hollywood Blvd., 323-466-5890, www.hollywoodprobicycles.com)*

Celebrity Helicopters offers themed trips, ranging from a Celebrity Home Tour to a flyby of the L.A. coastline. Night tours available. *(877-999-2099, www.celebheli.com)*

Off 'N Running Tours takes joggers on guided runs, from

four to 12 miles. *(310-246-1418, www.offnrunning tours.com)*

Beverly Hills Trolley runs 40-minute art and architecture tours, departing from the corner of Rodeo Drive and Dayton Way. *(310-285-2442, www.beverlyhills.org, on the hour, 11AM–4PM)*

Spirit Cruises runs harbor bay sails that pass the *Queen Mary*, whale-watching tours, and more. *(562-495-5884 or 310-548-8080, www.spiritdinnercruises.com)*

SEASONAL EVENTS:

Winter-Spring

Tournament of Roses Parade. January 1. Inaugurated in 1890, the Rose Parade still dazzles with fanciful floats, music, and equestrian pageantry, topped off by the Rose Bowl football game itself. Pasadena. *(626-449-4100, www.tournamentofroses.com)*

Doo Dah Parade. January. Tournament of Roses Parade spoof includes superheroes and political pundits. Pasadena. *(626-205-4029, www.pasadenadoodahparade. info)*

Chinese New Year and Golden Dragon Parade. Late January/early February. Dragon dancers and martial artists take to the street. Chinatown. *(213-617-0396, www.lachinesechamber.org)*

Pan African Film and Art Festival. February. The world's largest African-American film festival features 100-plus films. Crenshaw. *(323-295-1706, www.paff.org)*

Queen Mary Scottish Festival. February. Break out the kilt for this Scottish culture celebration. Long Beach. *(562-499-1650, www.queenmary.com)*

Academy Awards. February. This is the biggie for the movie biz. Kodak Theatre, Hollywood. *(310-247-3000, www.oscars.org)*

Mardi Gras. Late February/early March. Angelenos turn it up for Fat Tuesday on Olvera Street. Downtown. *(213-625-7074)*

Los Angeles Marathon. First Sunday in March. L.A. steps out of the vehicle. Downtown Los Angeles. *(310-444-5544, www.lamarathon.com)*

WestWeek. March. Interior designers unite. Pacific Design Center, West Hollywood. *(310-657-0800, www.pacificdesigncenter.com)*

Cherry Blossom Festival Southern California. First weekend in April. Take in Taiko drumming, martial arts, samurai warriors, and Japanese food. Little Tokyo. *(626-683-8243, www.cherryblossomfestivalsocal.org)*

Blessing of the Animals. April. Humans and furry and feathered friends descend on Olvera Street for the country's oldest animal blessing, dating to 1930. Downtown. *(213-485-6855, www.olvera-street.com)*

Toyota Grand Prix. Mid-April. Start your engines. Presented by the Grand Prix Association. Long Beach. *(562-981-2600, www.gplb.com)*

LA Times Festival of Books. Late April. Touted as the country's largest celebration of the written word. UCLA campus, Westwood. *(213-237-7335, www.latimes.com/extras/festivalofbooks)*

Indian Film Festival. Late April. Indian film minus the Bollywood factor. ArcLight Cinemas. Hollywood. *(310-364-4403, www.indianfilmfestival.org)*

Fiesta Broadway. April–May. Join in the largest Cinco de Mayo festival in the world, attracting over 500,000, including top Latino performers. Downtown. *(310-914-0015, www.fiestabroadway.la)*

Venice Art Walk. Second half of May. This self-guided art walk through galleries and private studios of 50 up-and-coming artists benefits the Venice Family Clinic. Venice Beach. *(310-392-9255, www.venicefamilyclinic.org)*

VC Filmfest: Los Angeles Asian-Pacific Film & Video Festival. May. Visual Communications' eight-day event features nearly 150 films and videos. Various venues, West Hollywood and Downtown. *(213-680-4462, www.vconline.org)*

Long Beach Lesbian & Gay Pride Parade and Festival. Mid- to late-May. More than 100 floats and live entertainment hit Shoreline Park. Long Beach. *(562-987-9191, www.longbeachpride.com)*

Last Remaining Seats. Wed. nights May–June. LA Conservancy showcases restored film classics at historic Downtown theaters, often with live music. *(213-623-2489, www.laconservancy.org)*

Summer

Playboy Jazz Festival. Mid-June. Hollywood Bowl. Los Angeles. *(310-450-1173, www.playboy.com)*

Christopher Street West Festival & Parade. Mid-June. One of the world's largest gay and lesbian pride events culminates with a Sunday parade. West Hollywood. *(323-969-8302, www.lapride.org)*

Los Angeles Film Festival. Late June. More than 175 international and American independent films and shorts air. *(866-345-6337 or 310-432-1240, www.lafilmfest.com)*

Outfest Gay and Lesbian Film Festival. July. Pick from 300 films, shorts, and documentaries. Venues in West Hollywood, Hollywood, Downtown. *(213-480-7088, www.outfest.org)*

Lotus Festival. July. Celebrate with Pacific Island and Asian music and dance. Echo Park Lake. *(213-485-8743, www.laparks.org/grifnet/lotus.htm)*

Beach Festival. End of July. It's the U.S. Open of Pro-Surfing. Huntington Beach. *(714-969-3492, www.surfcityusa.com)*

International Surf Festival. August. Sandcastle contests, volleyball tournaments, and paddleboard championships reign. Hermosa, Redondo, and Manhattan beaches. *(310-376-0951, www.surffestival.org)*

Nisei Week Japanese Festival. August. Since 1934, this weeklong celebration has honored *Nisei*—second-generation Japanese-Americans—with food, dance, taiko drumming, and a parade. Japanese American Cultural and Community Center Plaza, Little Tokyo. *(213-687-7193, www.niseiweek.org)*

African Marketplace and Cultural Faire. Mid-August– Labor Day. This culture and arts celebration focuses on those from Africa and of African descent. Rancho La Cienega Park. *(323-293-1612, www.africanmarket place.org)*

Long Beach Jazz Festival. Mid-August. Jazz greats perform with a lagoon backdrop. *(562-424-0013, www. longbeachjazzfestival.com)*

Fall

Mexican Independence Day. September. Celebration lasts a week with rides, crafts, and other revelry. Olvera Street. *(213-485-6855, www.olvera-street.com)*

Los Angeles City Birthday Celebration. September. Honor the 1781 founding of the City of Angels. El Pueblo Historical Monument. *(213-485-8372, www.lacity.org)*

Emmy Awards. September. The National Academy of Television Arts & Sciences hosts. Shrine Auditorium. *(212-586-8424, www.emmyonline.org)*

Silver Lake Film Festival. September. See independent narrative features and documentaries, as well as short films. *(323-953-8340, www.silverlakefilmfestival.org)*

Port of Los Angeles Lobster Festival. September. It's the world's largest lobster extravaganza. San Pedro. *(310-798-7478, www.lobsterfest.com)*

TarFest. Late September. Celebrate emerging film, music, and art. Miracle Mile. *(323-964-7100, www.tarfest.com)*

Watts Towers Day of the Drum Festival. September. Drum performances as well as gospel, jazz, and R&B dominate. *(www.trywatts.com)*

Abbot Kinney Festival. End of September. Music, dance, arts, crafts, and over 300 vendors dazzle. Venice. *(310-396-3772, www.abbotkinney.org)*

21

LA Shorts Fest. September/early October. Hundreds of short films are featured. *(323-461-4400, www.lashorts fest.com)*

Grand Avenue Festival. Late September/early October. Performances are staged in the Walt Disney Concert Hall and other Downtown venues. *(213-972-7611, www.grandavenuefestival.org)*

Hollywood Film Festival. October. Screenings, workshops, and film premieres delight. *(310-288-1882, www.hollywoodawards.com)*

 West Hollywood Halloween and Costume Carnival. October. Nearly a half-million people turn out for costume competition and live performances. West Hollywood. *(800-368-6020)*

Día de Los Muertos. November. Day of the Dead livens up Olvera Street. *(213-485-6855, www.olvera-street.com)*

AFI Fest. November. The American Film Institute's annual event is L.A.'s longest-running film festival. *(866-AFI-FEST, www.afi.com)*

Griffith Park Light Festival. November–December. Griffith Park lights up for the holidays. *(213-473-0800, www.griffithobservatory.org)*

chapter 1

DOWNTOWN HISTORIC DISTRICT

DOWNTOWN FINANCIAL DISTRICT/
BUNKER HILL

DOWNTOWN COMMERCIAL DISTRICT
AND EXPOSITION PARK

LOS ANGELES TOP PICKS

TOP PICK!

Los Angeles offers an abundance of one-of-a-kind attractions, neighborhoods, and experiences for visitors. Here are 11 of the top picks, not to be missed!

- ★ La Brea Tar Pits *(see page 58)*
- ★ Griffith Park *(see page 80)*
- ★ Hollywood Walk of Fame *(see page 103)*
- ★ Rodeo Drive *(see page 119)*
- ★ Getty Center *(see page 134)*
- ★ Santa Monica Pier *(see page 158)*
- ★ Venice *(see page 165)*
- ★ RMS *Queen Mary* *(see page 193)*
- ★ Disneyland *(see page 200)*
- ★ Norton Simon Museum *(see page 228)*
- ★ Huntington Library and Gardens *(see page 229)*

DOWNTOWN HISTORIC DISTRICT
DOWNTOWN FINANCIAL DISTRICT/ BUNKER HILL
DOWNTOWN COMMERCIAL DISTRICT AND EXPOSITION PARK

Places to See:

1. El Pueblo de Los Angeles Historic Monument
2. Sepulveda House
3. Avila Adobe
4. Chinese Historical Society of Southern California
5. Union Station
6. City Hall
7. Criminal Courts Building
8. Los Angeles Times Building
9. Cathedral of Our Lady of the Angels
10. Geffen Contemporary at the Museum of Contemporary Art
11. Japanese American National Museum
12. Japanese American Cultural and Community Center
13. Chinese American Museum
14. Mexican Cultural Institute
39. Angels Flight Railway
40. Bunker Hill Steps
41. U.S. Bank Tower
42. Richard Riordan Central Library
43. Wells Fargo History Museum
44. Music Center
45. REDCAT
46. MOCA Grand Avenue
65. Bradbury Building
66. Oviatt Building
67. Eastern Columbia Building
68. Pershing Square
69. Ray Charles Memorial Library
70. Exposition Park
71. Natural History Museum of Los Angeles County
72. California African-American Museum
73. Los Angeles Memorial Coliseum & Sports Arena
74. Staples Center
75. Nokia Theatre L.A. Live
76. University of Southern California
77. USC Fisher Museum of Art

25

78. Museum of Neon Art
79. Brewery Arts Colony
80. FIDM Museum and Galleries
81. California Science Center

Places to Eat and Drink:
15. Philippe the Original
16. Traxx Restaurant and Bar
17. R23
18. Sushi-Gen
19. Sushi Go 55
20. Honda-Ya
21. Shabu Shabu House Restaurant
22. Sam Woo Bar-B-Q Restaurant
23. Phoenix Bakery
24. Mountain Bar
25. Weiland Brewery
47. Engine Company No. 28
48. Water Grill
49. Ciudad
50. Noe Restaurant and Bar
51. Patina
52. Rooftop Bar at the Standard
53. The Edison
54. Redwood Bar & Grill
55. Library Bar
82. Cicada
83. Zucca
84. Liberty Grill

85. The Palm
86. Clifton's Brookdale Cafeteria
87. The Original Pantry Café
88. Bordello Bar
89. Broadway Bar
90. Golden Gopher
91. Seven Grand

Where to Shop:
26. Dynasty Center
27. Chinatown Plaza
28. Realm
29. Choose Chinatown
30. Japanese Village Plaza Mall
31. Mikawaya
32. Fugetsu-Do
33. Popkiller Second
34. Freaks Vintage Clothing
35. Flock Shop
56. Caravan Book Store
57. 7+ Fig at Ernst & Young Plaza
92. Los Angeles Fashion District
93. Los Angeles Flower District
94. Jewelry District
95. Michael Levine
96. FIDM Museum Shop

Where to Stay:
36. Kyoto Grand Hotel & Gardens

37. Miyako Hotel
38. Best Western Dragon
    Gate Inn
58. Millennium Biltmore Hotel
59. The Standard,
    Downtown LA
60. Hilton Checkers Hotel
61. Omni Los Angeles
    Hotel at California Plaza

62. Westin Bonaventure Hotel
63. O Hotel
64. Ritz Milner Hotel
97. Radisson Hotel
    Los Angeles Midtown
    at USC
98. Figueroa Hotel
99. Inn at 657

Perhaps there is no life
after death…
there's just Los Angeles.

—RICK ANDERSON

DOWNTOWN HISTORIC DISTRICT

Metro Lines: Red, Purple, Blue, Gold

*Bus lines: 2, 4, 10, 33, 42, 45, 48, 55, 60, 68,
78, 79, 81, 83, 84, 90, 91, 92, 94, 333,
355, 376, 378, 381, 394*

DASH: Route A, B, Lincoln Heights-Chinatown

Metro Rapid Line: 704, 714, 728, 745, 760, 770

• SNAPSHOT •

Downtown Los Angeles is a work in progress. Not more
than a decade ago, the area was deserted and best
ignored after dark. Today, Downtown is beginning to
flourish with an urban renewal of monumental propor-
tions. Historic theaters and buildings are being transformed into posh new restaurants, performance venues,
and art spaces. The area is an ethnic gumbo, including
Chinatown, Little Tokyo, and a center for the city's
Latino community. It's also home to the Civic Center as
well as a burgeoning Arts District.

PLACES TO SEE

Landmarks:

El Pueblo de Los Angeles Historic Monument (1) *(bounded by Spring St., Cesar E. Chavez Ave., Arcadia/Alameda Sts., 213-628-1274, www.lasangelitas.org)* is a 44-acre historic park near the site of L.A.'s original pueblo, founded in 1781. Considered a living museum, the monument is home to 27 historic buildings; 11 are open to the public either as businesses or museums. Fiestas and parades are the norm in **El Pueblo de Los Angeles Plaza**, where Angelenos celebrate Cinco de Mayo, Día de los Muertos, and Mexican Independence Day. The pedestrian center of the monument, **Olvera Street**, known by locals as *La Placita*, became a re-created Mexican marketplace in 1930. Today it's filled with handicraft shops and the smell of taquitos. Landmarks include the 1887 **Sepulveda House (2)** *(W-12 Olvera St., 213-628-1274, M–Sa 10AM–3PM)*, now a visitor center. Schedule free walking tours of Olvera Street, or watch an 18-minute film, *Pueblo of Promise*. **Avila Adobe (3)** *(10 Olvera St., daily 9AM–4PM)*, the oldest house in L.A., was built by mayor Francisco Avila in 1818 and has operated as a museum since 1976. Though not as extensive as the Chinatowns in New York or San Francisco, Los Angeles traces its first Chinese settlement to 1852 at the site of today's Union Station. By 1870, an identifiable **Chinatown** *(www.chinatownla.com)* had evolved, mostly men in the laundry or produce industries. Chinatown blossomed at the turn of the century, expanding from 200 to 3,000 inhabitants, filling streets and alleys. But after years of decline, the Supreme Court condemned the old Chinatown area in the early 1900s, razed it, and built the Union Station rail terminal. The **Chinese Historical Society of Southern California (4)** *(411/415 Bernard St., 323-222-1918, www.chssc.org, W–F 11AM–3PM, Su noon–4:30PM)* displays artifacts and photos of the 1880s houses. Today, Chinatown spills over with immigrants from Vietnam and Cambodia, while the city's Chinese community mostly lives in Monterey Park and the San Gabriel Valley. Where the original Chinatown once stood, the 1939 **Union Station (5)** *(800 N. Alameda St.)* now serves as an active rail station for Amtrak, Metrolink, and the Metro Rail. Considered the last of America's great railway stations, it's been the backdrop for movies, that show off its Art Deco and Spanish Colonial flavors, courtyards, and

 52-foot ceilings. Bordered by 1st, 3rd, Los Angeles, and Alameda streets, **Little Tokyo**, or J-town, remains one of three Japantowns in the U.S. Today, the bulk of the L.A. Japanese community resides elsewhere, but Little Tokyo remains its cultural center.

During the '70s and '80s, artists took over long abandoned warehouses, breathing life into the deserted district. Northeast of Little Tokyo, L.A.'s **Civic Center** houses a number of administrative buildings, including the 1928-built **City Hall (6)** *(200 N. Spring St.)*, standing 454 feet high. The concrete in its tower is said to be made with sand from each of California's 58 counties and water from its 21 historical missions. A 27th-floor observation level is open to the public. The **Criminal Courts Building (7)** *(210 W. Temple St., M–F 8:30AM–4:30PM)*, built in 1925, the seat of several state and municipal courts, is where the 1995 O.J. Simpson trial was held. Built in 1935, the **Los Angeles Times Building (8)** *(202 W. 1st St., 213-237-5000, www.latimes.com)* was once the tallest building in the western United States. Don't miss the Globe Lobby, with its 10-foot-high murals and exhibit showcasing the first century of the Times. Far from subtle, the **Cathedral of Our Lady of the Angels (9)** *(555 W. Temple St., 213-680-5200, www.olacathedral.org, M–F 6:30AM– 6PM, Sa 9AM–6PM, Su 7AM–6PM)*, designed by Spanish architect José Rafael Moneo, spans over five acres. The 12-story building can accommodate more than 3,000 worshippers. On site are a plaza, gardens and waterfalls, a gift shop, conference center, and a mausoleum, the final resting spot for Gregory Peck.

Arts & Entertainment:

The **Geffen Contemporary at the Museum of Contemporary Art (10)** *(152 N. Central Ave., 213-626-6222, www.moca.org, M 11AM–5PM, Tu–W closed, Th 11AM–8PM, F 11AM–5PM, Sa–Su 11AM–6PM, free Th 5PM–8PM)*, funded largely in part by the David Geffen Foundation, is a bare-bones interior fashioned by Frank Gehry, from an old warehouse in Little Tokyo. MOCA samples are on display as well as a variety of avant-garde displays. Also in Little Tokyo, the **Japanese American National Museum (11)** *(369 E. 1st St., 213-625-0414, www.janm.org, Tu–W, F, Sa–Su 11AM–5PM, Th 11AM–*

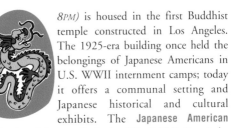

8PM) is housed in the first Buddhist temple constructed in Los Angeles. The 1925-era building once held the belongings of Japanese Americans in U.S. WWII internment camps; today it offers a communal setting and Japanese historical and cultural exhibits. The **Japanese American Cultural and Community Center (12)** *(244 S. San Pedro St., 213-628-2725, www.jaccc.org)* owns and operates the Center Building, which houses the **George J. Doizaki Gallery**. It also runs the Japanese Cultural Room, the 880-seat Aratani/Japan America Theatre, the JACCC Plaza designed by Isamu Noguchi, and the tranquil James Irvine Garden. **Gallery Row** *(Main/Spring Sts. from 2nd St. to 9th St., www.galleryrow.org)* emerged in 2003 with a wide variety of galleries.

Located near **El Pueblo de Los Angeles Historic Monument**, the **Chinese American Museum (13)** *(425 N. Los Angeles St., 213-485-8567, www.camla.org, Tu–Su 10AM–3PM)* focuses on the Chinese-American experience, with artifacts donated by locals. In the new Chinatown, artists have helped revitalize the area with an array of galleries, namely along Chung King Road and Gin Ling Way. The **Mexican Cultural Institute (14)** *(125 Paseo de la Plaza, 213-624-3660, www.angelfire.com/ca/mexicopara siempre, Tu–F 9:30AM–4PM, Sa–Su 11AM–4PM)* offers a Spanish-language literature collection and traditional Mexican handicrafts.

PLACES TO EAT & DRINK
Where to Eat:

For a slice of old L.A., sit at one of the communal tables at **Philippe the Original (15) ($)** *(1001 N. Alameda St., 213-628-3781, www.philippes.com, daily 6AM–10PM)*, established in 1908 by Philippe Mathieu, who claimed to have invented the French-dipped sandwich. Location is key to **Traxx Restaurant and Bar (16) ($$)** *(800 N. Alameda St., 213-625-1999, www.traxxrestaurant.com, M–F 11:30AM–2:30PM; M–Th 5:30PM–9PM, F 5:30PM–9:30PM, Sa 5PM–9:30PM)*, serving California small plates and full-sized entrées in the heart of Union Station. **R23 (17) ($$)** *(923 E. 2nd St., 213-687-7178, www.r23.com, M–F 11:30AM–2PM, M–Sa 5:30PM–10PM)*, just east of Little Tokyo in the Arts District, brings a touch of Manhattan chic to Downtown L.A., including Frank Gehry–designed chairs and gallery-style artwork. But the fresh fish and diverse menu eclipse all else. Enduring the wait for one of L.A.'s top sushi spots, **Sushi-Gen (18) ($$)** *(422 E. 2nd St., 213-617-0552, M–F 11:15AM–2PM, 5:30PM–10PM, Sa 5PM–10PM)*, is rewarding. **Sushi Go 55 (19) ($)** *(Mitsuwa Plaza, 333 S. Alameda St., 213-687-0777, www. sushigo55.com, M–F 11:15AM–2:15PM, 5:30PM–10PM, Sa–Su 11:30AM–2:30PM, 5PM–10PM)* is a local favorite and excels at its lunchtime menu. Media darling **Honda-Ya (20) ($)** *(Mitsuwa Plaza, 333 S. Alameda St., 213-625-1184, M–Sa 5:30PM–1AM, Su till midnight)* garners acclaim for creative *iza-kaya* (small portions of pub food) plates and *yakitori.*

Expect to wait for the privilege of cooking your meal at popular **Shabu Shabu House Restaurant (21) ($)** *(127 Japanese Village Plaza Mall, 213-680-3890, M–F 11:30AM–2:30PM, 5:30PM–10PM)*. For late-night greasy spoon Chinese barbecue, try **Sam Woo Bar-B-Q Restaurant (22) ($)** *(803 N. Broadway, 213-687-7238, daily 9AM–1AM)*, with specialties like kung pao squid or seafood sizzling rice. **Phoenix Bakery (23) ($)** *(969 N. Broadway, 213-628-4642, www.phoenixbakeryinc.com, daily 9AM–9PM)*, Chinatown's oldest and largest, is known for strawberry whipped cream cakes.

Bars & Nightlife:

Not exactly a nightlife hub, Downtown's historic area does pump up the volume at **Mountain Bar (24)** *(475 Gin Ling Way, 213-625-7500, www.themountainbar.com, Tu–Su 6:30PM–2AM)*, with two levels of music in the heart of Chinatown and monthly art shows. Choose

 from one of two happy hours at **Weiland Brewery (25)** *(400 E. 1st St., 213-680-2881, www.weilandbrewery.net, M–F 11AM–2AM, Sa–Su 5PM–2AM)*, evening or late night, with house brews like India Pale Ale and pub grub.

WHERE TO SHOP

The many cultures of Downtown's Historic District makes for an around-the-world shopping experience. Chinatown is crammed with family-run shops, galleries, and trinket stores. **Dynasty Center (26)** *(800 N. Broadway)*, the largest of Chinatown's shopping centers, packs in bargain shops owned by immigrants from Laos, Cambodia, and Vietnam. Chinatown Plaza (27) *(930 N. Broadway)* is one of the oldest plazas, dating back to 1938. You'll find good deals on gold jewelry, plus everything from jade and porcelain to herbs and teas. Also check out the 50-foot high Golden Pagoda.

Central Plaza *(bounded by N. Broadway, North Hill, Bernard/College Sts.)* harbors a few dia- 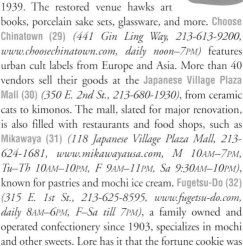 monds in the rough, including Realm (28) *(425 Gin Ling Way, 213-628-4663, www.realmhome.com, daily 11AM– 7PM),* a former Chinese restaurant and bar developed by the Hong family in 1939. The restored venue hawks art books, porcelain sake sets, glassware, and more. Choose Chinatown (29) *(441 Gin Ling Way, 213-613-9200, www.choosechinatown.com, daily noon–7PM)* features urban cult labels from Europe and Asia. More than 40 vendors sell their goods at the Japanese Village Plaza Mall (30) *(350 E. 2nd St., 213-680-1930),* from ceramic cats to kimonos. The mall, slated for major renovation, is also filled with restaurants and food shops, such as Mikawaya (31) *(118 Japanese Village Plaza Mall, 213-624-1681, www.mikawayausa.com, M 10AM–7PM, Tu–Th 10AM–10PM, F 9AM–11PM, Sa 9:30AM–10PM),* known for pastries and mochi ice cream. Fugetsu-Do (32) *(315 E. 1st St., 213-625-8595, www.fugetsu-do.com, daily 8AM–6PM, F–Sa till 7PM),* a family owned and operated confectionery since 1903, specializes in mochi and other sweets. Lore has it that the fortune cookie was invented here. Popkiller Second (33) *(343 E. 2nd St., 213-625-1372, www.popkiller.us, daily 11AM–11PM, F–Sa till midnight)* houses Japanese imported clothes and accessories, plus an art gallery. They offer a vintage shop on Sunset Boulevard. Also selling vintage, plus denim, rocker T-shirts, and Western boots is Freaks Vintage Clothing (34) *(826 E. 3rd St., 213-628-1234, myspace.com/freaksvintage, Su–Th noon–7PM, F–Sa till 8PM).* Flock Shop (35) *(943 N. Broadway, 213-229-9090, www.flockshopla.com, W–Su noon–7PM)* carries consignment items and new designs by local artists.

WHERE TO STAY

Kyoto Grand Hotel & Gardens (36) ($$) *(120 S. Los Angeles St., 213-629-1200, www.kyotograndhotel.com),* formerly New Otani Hotel and Garden, boasts a third-floor half-acre Japanese garden, a health spa offering Shiatsu massage, and a few Japanese suites. The hotel is still home to Thousand Cranes *(213-253-9255, www.thousandcranes restaurant.com, M–F, Su 11:30AM–3PM, daily 5PM– 10PM)* sushi restaurant. A good value: Miyako Hotel (37) ($-$$) *(328 E. 1st St., 213-617-2000, www.miyako inn.com),* which has its own spa amenities and four floors of Tokyo Executive Suites. Standard rooms are small but comfortable. Best Western Dragon Gate Inn (38) ($$) *(818 N. Hill St., 213-617-3077, www.dragongate inn.com)* offers a no-frills option.

DOWNTOWN FINANCIAL DISTRICT/ BUNKER HILL

Metro Lines: Red, Purple, Blue

Bus Lines: 14, 16, 18, 26, 30, 51, 52, 53, 55, 60, 62, 70, 71, 76, 78, 79, 96, 316, 350, 352, 376, 378

DASH: Route A, B, C, E, F

Metro Rapid Line: 704, 714, 728, 745, 760, 770

• SNAPSHOT •

Though not quite Manhattan, the cluster of skyscrapers in the Bunker Hill area and Financial District looks more like a true city center than other Downtown areas. First developed in the late 1800s, Bunker Hill was prime real estate, lined with opulent Victorian houses for L.A.'s upper class. Following WWI, with the arrival of streetcars and city sprawl, the elite moved west to new communities. In time, the neighborhood was deemed a slum, and in the 1950s, the Bunker Hill Redevelopment Project set out to raze its Victorians rather than restore them. In their place came nondescript plazas and towering buildings. The parallel Financial District, also an amalgam of office buildings, banks, and hotels, is expanding its horizons with new luxury lofts, condos, restaurants, and bars.

PLACES TO SEE
Landmarks:
Angels Flight Railway (39) *(351 S. Hill St., 213-626-1901, www.angelsflight.com)* claims to be the shortest railway in the world. The funicular was built in 1901 to transport passengers up the steep incline between Downtown and Bunker Hill. It closed in 1969 during redevelopment. The second Angels Flight, maintained and operated by the Angels Flight Railway Foundation, reopened nearby in 1996 and closed again in 2001 after a fatal accident. There are plans for it to reopen. The **Bunker Hill Steps (40)** *(5th St. bet. Grand Ave./Figueroa St.)* often referred to as the **Spanish Steps**, were designed by Lawrence Halprin in 1990. The 103 steps wind around the base of the First Interstate World Center and link Hope Street to Fifth Street. The **U.S. Bank Tower (41)** *(633 W. 5th St.)*, the former Library Tower, is California's tallest structure at 1,018 feet. Its famous 1989 office building has been used in several movies, including *Speed* and *The Day After Tomorrow*. The 9/11 Commission reported it had been an Al-Qaeda terrorist

target. At the bottom of the Bunker Hill Steps is the 1926 **Richard Riordan Central Library (42)** *(630 W. 5th St., 213-228-7000, www.lapl.org, M–Th 10AM–8PM, F–Sa 10AM–6PM, Su 1PM–5PM)*, with one of the largest book and periodical collections in the country. The **Wells Fargo**

History Museum (43) *(333 S. Grand Ave., 213-253-7166, www.wellsfargohistory.com, M–F 9AM–5PM)* showcases the company's history, with an original Concord Coach and sculptures by Jean Dubuffet, Louise Nevelson, and Robert Graham.

Arts & Entertainment:

At the heart of Downtown's Business District is the 11-acre **Music Center (44)** *(135 N. Grand Ave., 213-972-7211, www.musiccenter.org)*, home to the **Dorothy Chandler Pavilion**, **Ahmanson Theatre**, **Mark Taper Forum**, and **Walt Disney Concert Hall**. Resident companies include the Los Angeles Philharmonic and Los Angeles Opera. Free tours of the campus are available *(daily 10AM–2PM)* from the Symphonians, volunteer docents. The **Walt Disney Concert Hall** was designed by renowned architect Frank Gehry, who fashioned its steel exterior to resemble a ship with sail at full mast. The structure's centerpiece, a 2,265-seat auditorium in which the audience surrounds the orchestra, was designed to look like the ship's hull. Resident performers include the **Los Angeles Philharmonic** *(323-850-2000, www.laphil.com)* and the **Los Angeles Master Chorale** *(213-972-7282, www.lamc.org)*. The **Dorothy Chandler Pavilion** debuted in 1964 with Zubin Mehta conducting the Los Angeles Philharmonic. Today the Pavilion is the home of the **Los Angeles Opera** *(213-972-7219, www.losangelesopera.com)* and Music Center Dance. Also at the center is the **Ahmanson Theatre**, presenting Broadway shows and major productions; its stage has hosted the likes of Elizabeth Taylor and Katharine Hepburn. It currently boasts the largest theatrical subscription base on the West Coast, and it is one of three venues for **Center Theatre Group** *(213-628-2772, www.centertheatregroup. org)*. Focusing more on new plays, the award-winning

Mark Taper Forum also hosts productions by the Center Theatre Group. Sharing the same complex as the Disney Concert Hall is the Roy and Edna Disney/CalArts Theater, better known as **REDCAT (45)** *(631 W. 2nd St., 213-237-2800, www. redcat.org)*, presenting cutting-edge performances, experimental films, and art from up-and-coming talent. **MOCA Grand Avenue (46)** *(250 S. Grand Ave., 213-626-6222, www.moca-la.org, M, F 11AM–5PM, Tu–W closed, Th 11AM–8PM, Sa–Su 11AM– 6PM)*, part of the Museum of Contemporary Art, is one of Downtown's architectural masterpieces, designed by Arata Isozaki. It houses underground galleries as well as the flagship **MOCA Store** and **Patinette Café**. The **Grand Avenue Project** is a massive redevelopment that will potentially transform Downtown civic/cultural districts, with new entertainment venues, restaurants, and retail, mixed with a hotel and housing units.

PLACES TO EAT & DRINK
Where to Eat:

The business district has a number of historic and defining restaurant choices. Housed in a 1912-era firehouse, **Engine Company No. 28 (47) ($$)** *(644 S. Figueroa St., 213-624-6996, www.engineco.com, lunch M–F from 11:15AM, dinner daily from 5PM)* is styled after a classic New York grill, with mahogany booths and a granite bar. American comfort foods can be topped with a 911 fudge brownie sundae. Presentation, service, and other formalities distinguish **Water Grill (48) ($$$)** *(544 S. Grand Ave., 213-891-0900, www.water grill.com, M–Tu 11:30AM–9PM, W– Sa 11:30AM–10PM, Su 4:30PM– 9PM).* Seafood connoisseurs delight

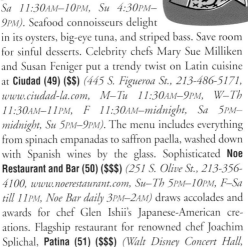

in its oysters, big-eye tuna, and striped bass. Save room for sinful desserts. Celebrity chefs Mary Sue Milliken and Susan Feniger put a trendy twist on Latin cuisine at **Ciudad (49) ($$)** *(445 S. Figueroa St., 213-486-5171, www.ciudad-la.com, M–Tu 11:30AM–9PM, W–Th 11:30AM–11PM, F 11:30AM–midnight, Sa 5PM– midnight, Su 5PM–9PM).* The menu includes everything from spinach empanadas to saffron paella, washed down with Spanish wines by the glass. Sophisticated **Noe Restaurant and Bar (50) ($$$)** *(251 S. Olive St., 213-356-4100, www.noerestaurant.com, Su–Th 5PM–10PM, F–Sa till 11PM, Noe Bar daily 3PM–2AM)* draws accolades and awards for chef Glen Ishii's Japanese-American creations. Flagship restaurant for renowned chef Joachim Splichal, **Patina (51) ($$$)** *(Walt Disney Concert Hall, 141 S. Grand Ave., 213-972-3331, www.patina group.com, lunch Tu–F 11:30AM–1:30PM, dinner Tu–Sa 5PM–9:30PM, Su 4PM–9:30PM)* serves haute cuisine inside Frank Gehry's architectural masterpiece.

Bars & Nightlife:

Seal any jaunt to Downtown L.A. with a drink at the **Rooftop Bar at the Standard (52)** *(The Standard Hotel, 550 S. Flower St., 213-892-8080, www.standardhotels.com, daily noon–1:30AM)*, offering cityscape views and  throngs of tourists and scenesters. Amenities include a heated swimming pool, dance floor, outdoor fireplace, and vibrating water beds. Housed in L.A.'s former first power plant, **The Edison (53)** *(108 W. 2nd St., 213-613-0000, www. edisondowntown.com, W–F 5PM–2AM, Sa 6PM–2AM)* resembles a speakeasy, with swanky decor and handcrafted cocktails. A gastropub with a maritime theme, **Redwood Bar & Grill (54)** *(316 W. 2nd St., 213-680-2600, www.theredwoodbar.com, M–F 11AM–2AM, Sa–Su 5PM–2AM)* serves a full menu of tasty grub like fish and chips and turkey pot pie, along with a variety at the bar. Adjacent to the Central Library, the **Library Bar (55)** *(630 W. 6th St., 213-614-0053, www.librarybarla.com, M–F 3PM–2AM, Sa–Su 7PM–2AM)* offers sophistication without the attitude. Sink into a cozy couch with a tome from the bar's own floor-to-ceiling library.

WHERE TO SHOP

Established in 1954 on what was then known as Booksellers Row, Caravan Book Store (56) *(550 S. Grand Ave., 213-626-9944, M–F 11AM–6PM, Sa noon–5PM)* bills itself as the last antiquarian bookstore in Downtown, featuring rare books, first editions, and out-of-print titles. Downtown's main outdoor shopping locale, **7+Fig at Ernst & Young Plaza (57)** *(735 S. Figueroa St., 213-955-7150, www.7fig.com, M–F 10AM–7PM, Sa 10AM–6PM, Su noon–5PM)* spotlights brand names like Ann Taylor, Macy's, and Godiva.

WHERE TO STAY

During its heyday, **Millennium Biltmore Hotel (58) ($$)** *(506 S. Grand Ave., 213-624-1011, www.millennium hotels.com)* was the favorite of presidents and Hollywood stars. The opulent 1923 Italian Renaissance hotel is also home to the **Gallery Bar**, famed for its martinis. Set in an André Balazs–renovated fifties office building, **The Standard, Downtown LA (59) ($$$)** *(550 S. Flower St., 213-892-8080, www.standardhotels.com)* adds a whimsical touch to the hotel experience with funky, colorful decor. The posh, boutique-style **Hilton Checkers Hotel (60) ($$–$$$)** *(535 S. Grand Ave., 213-624-0000, www.hiltoncheckers.com),* dating from 1927, has had enough renovations to hide her age. Its **Checkers Restaurant** is a hit with gourmands, while the rooftop pool and bar lends views over Downtown. Located atop Bunker Hill, the **Omni Los Angeles Hotel at California Plaza (61) ($$$)** *(251 S. Olive St., 213-617-3300, www.omnihotels.com)* boasts elegant, spacious rooms and suites, as well as an on-site spa. **Noe Restaurant** also resides here. Business travelers and conventions do well at the **Westin Bonaventure Hotel (62) ($$$)** *(404 S. Figueroa St., 213-624-1000, www.westin.com/bonaventure),* L.A.'s largest, topping out at 35 stories and over 1,000 rooms. Its atrium houses over 40 restaurants and shops. The historic **O Hotel (63) ($$)** *(819 S. Flower St., 213-623-9904, www.ohotelgroup.com)* was reinvented in 2007 with 68 uber-modern rooms and an on-site health spa. Have a drink or Mediterranean-style tapas at their **O Bar & Kitchen ($$)** *(daily 6AM–10:30AM M–F 11AM–11PM, Sa–Su 5PM–11PM)*. The smaller-scale boutique **Ritz Milner Hotel (64) ($)** *(813 S. Flower St., 213-627-6981, www.milner-hotels.com)* dating from 1925, has been refurbished, and is a budget option.

DOWNTOWN COMMERCIAL DISTRICT AND EXPOSITION PARK

Metro Line: Blue

Bus Lines: 2, 4, 10, 18, 28, 30, 31, 33, 37, 40, 42, 45, 48, 55, 62, 66, 70, 71, 76, 78, 79, 81, 83, 90, 91, 92, 94, 96, 302, 330, 333, 355, 366, 376, 378, 381, 394

DASH: Route King-East, Southeast, Pico Union Echo Park, C, D, E, F

Metro Rapid Line: 704, 714, 728, 745, 760, 770, 940

• SNAPSHOT •

Home to L.A.'s Broadway theater district, Fashion District, Los Angeles Coliseum, Staples Center, and Exposition Park, the southern portion of Downtown is a hodgepodge of commercial activity, historic buildings, and heavily trafficked events. One of the city's most talked about developments, the L.A. Live residential and entertainment district, is opening in phases. Serious bargain shoppers do well in this area, while theater buffs are taking heart that some long-neglected structures are beginning to breathe new life.

PLACES TO SEE
Landmarks:

Commissioned by mining magnate Lewis Bradbury and designed by George Wyman, the **Bradbury Building (65)** *(304 S. Broadway, 213-626-1893, M–F 9AM–6PM, Sa–Su 9AM–5PM)* was a sight to behold in its day. The must-see highlight of the 1893 structure: its nearly 50-foot-high Victorian interior court, featuring marble stairs, open-cage elevators, and intricate iron railings. The lobby level is open to the public. Another Downtown gem, the **Oviatt Building (66)** *(617 Olive St., 310-286-2989, www.oviatt.com)* is credited as the first Art Deco building in Los Angeles. The Penthouse—with French marble and more than 30 tons of Rene Lalique chandeliers and art glass—was built for haberdasher James Oviatt, whose shop occupied the ground floor. Today the 13th-floor penthouse is booked for parties. Tours of the building are available *(Tu noon–5PM, Th 2PM–8PM)*. It's hard to miss the 13-story turquoise terra-cotta **Eastern Columbia Building (67)** *(849 S. Broadway, www.easterncolumbialofts.com)*, once the headquarters of the Eastern Columbia Outfitting Company. The blue-and-gold trimmed building now houses condos. **Pershing Square (68)** *(532 S. Olive St., 213-847-4970, www.laparks.org/pershingsquare)* was originally named La Plaza Abaja when dedicated in 1866. Used by the militia in WWI for receptions, the park was renamed Pershing Square in 1918 after the WWI general. The area was renovated and rededicated in the '90s and is now an outdoor concert and event venue.

Ray Charles Memorial Library (69) *(2109 W. Washington Blvd.)* is opening in 2009 on the site of his historic Los Angeles studio. The three-story building will be a library, exhibit space, educational center, and working studio.

Arts & Entertainment:

Formerly an open-air market named Agricultural Park, **Exposition Park (70)** *(bounded by Figueroa St., King Blvd., Vermont Ave., and Exposition Blvd., www.nhm.org/expo/expopark.htm)* was renamed in 1910 when it was converted into a cultural center. Staking its claim as the first cultural institution to open in Los Angeles, the **Natural History Museum of Los Angeles County (71)** *(900 Exposition Blvd., 213-763-DINO, www.nhm.org, free on first Tu of every month, M–F 9:30AM–5PM, Sa–Su 10AM–5PM)* debuted in 1913 and is the largest natural and historical museum in the western U.S. Included in the more than 35 million specimens and artifacts are fossils, dinosaurs, historical objects—even some Hollywood memorabilia. Permanent exhibits at the **California African-American Museum (72)** *(600 State Dr., 213-744-7432, www.caamuseum.org, Tu–Sa 10AM–5PM, Su 11AM–5PM)* include arts and artifacts depicting the migration from the west coast of Africa to the West Coast of America. **Los Angeles Memorial Coliseum & Sports Arena (73)** *(3911/3939 S. Figueroa St., 213-747-7111, www.lacoliseum.com)* exist in tandem. The Coliseum is home to the University of Southern California football team and has hosted two Olympiads, as well as JFK's 1960 Democratic presidential candidate acceptance speech. The **Staples Center (74)** *(1111 S. Figueroa St., 213-742-7340, www.staplescenter.com)* is home to five professional sports teams, including the NBA's **Los Angeles Lakers** and **Los Angeles Clippers**, and the NHL's **Los Angeles Kings**. Another massive development is the **L.A. Live District**; when it's complete, it will be a four-million-square-foot, residential/entertainment district adjacent to the Staples Center. **Nokia Theatre L.A. Live (75)** *(777 Chick Hearn Ct., 213-763-6030, www.nokiatheatrelalive.com)*, a concert and awards show venue, and 40,000-square-foot **Nokia Plaza** debuted in 2007, while Club Nokia, the Grammy Museum, the Conga Room, Lucky Strike Bowling, and 12 new restaurants will flesh out the district over the next couple of years. The campus of the **University of Southern California (USC) (76)** *(bounded by S. Figueroa St., Vermont Ave., Exposition Park, and W. Jefferson Blvd., 213-740-2311, www.usc.edu)* also houses a number of venues,

including the **Arnold Schoenberg Institute** for music performances, and the **USC Fisher Museum of Art (77)** *(823 Exposition Blvd., 213-740-4561, www.fishermuseumofart.org, Tu–Sa noon–5PM)*, the first city museum devoted exclusively to fine art. Downtown is also home to **Broadway's Historic Theater District**, the largest historic theater district in the country. Each of the 1920s-era movie palaces have met different fates: Some transformed into retail outlets; others, into movie houses. The **Los Angeles Conservancy** *(213-623-2489)* provides walking tours of the district and has helped in its preservation, as has the L.A. Historic Theatre Foundation *(213-999-5067, www.lahtf.org).* **Museum of Neon Art (78)** *(136 W. 4th St., 213-489-9918, www.neon mona.org, Th–Sa noon– 8PM,*

Su noon–5PM) exhibits electric media and offers bus cruises on Saturday nights that tour Downtown and Hollywood. The **Brewery Arts Colony (79)** *(2100 N. Main St., 323-342-0717, www.breweryartwalk.com)* touts itself as the biggest artist colony in the country. It offers a twice annual open studio weekend, **Brewery Art Walk**, during which over 100 resident artists participate. Part of the Fashion Institute of Design and Merchandising, **FIDM Museum and Galleries (80)** *(919 S. Grand Ave., 213-236-1397, www.fashionmuseum.org, M–F 9AM–5PM, Sa 9AM–4PM)* boasts a collection of over 12,000 costumes—including film and theater costumes—accessories, and textiles from the 18th century through the present day.

Kids:

Thanks to a $130 million renovation and expansion, the **California Science Center (81)** *(Exposition Park, 39th and Figueroa Sts., 323-724-3623, www.californiasciencecenter.org, daily 10AM–5PM),* formerly the California Museum of Science and Industry, is almost like new. Part of Exposition Park *(see page 47),* the center is readying a new pavilion, **World of Ecology**, that will house live animals, plants, and hands-on exhibits. The Center is also home to an **IMAX Theater** *(213-744-7400)*.

PLACES TO EAT & DRINK
Where to Eat:

Many a wedding has been held at **Cicada (82) ($$$–$$$$)** *(617 S. Olive St., 213-488-9488, www.cicadarestaurant. com, M–Sa 5:30PM–9PM, Su 6PM–9PM)*, an old-school Art Deco space in the **Oviatt Building**, with 30-foot ceilings that look straight out of a Hollywood set. In fact, scenes from *Pretty Woman* were filmed here. The busy Patina Group owns hot spot **Zucca (83) ($$)** *(801 S. Figueroa St., 213-614-7800, www.patina group.com, lunch M–F 11:30AM– 2:30PM; happy hour M–F 4PM–6PM; dinner M–Th 5PM–9:30PM, F–Sa 5PM–11PM)* which draws kudos for Chef Joachim Splichal's wood-fired Neapolitan pizza, fresh pastas, and fish. Also on the Patina list is **Nick & Stef's Steakhouse ($$$)** *(330 S. Hope St., 213-680-0330, www.patinagroup.com, M–F 11:30AM–2:30PM, happy hour 3:30PM–7:30PM, 5:30PM– 9:30PM, F 5:30PM–10:30PM, Sa 5PM–10:30PM, Su 4:30PM–8:30PM)*, once again under Splichal's guidance. Pre-theater goers can nosh from the prime rib cart or dig into something more creative, such as braised American kobe ravioli. Craving a burger before that Lakers game? Make a beeline for **Liberty Grill (84) ($-$$)** *(1037 Flower St., 213-746-3400, www.liberty-grill.com, M–F 11AM– 4PM, Su–Th 4PM–9PM, F–Sa 4PM–10PM)*. For a more upscale pre-courtside meal, old-school **The Palm (85)**

($$$) *(1100 S. Flower St., 213-763-4600, www.thepalm. com, M–F 11:30AM–3PM, M–Th 3PM–10PM, F 3PM– 11PM, Sa 5PM–11PM, Su 5PM–9:30PM)* specializes in attentive service, prime-aged steaks, and jumbo lobsters. **Clifton's Brookdale Cafeteria (86) ($)** *(648 S. Broadway, 213-627-1673, www.cliftonscafeteria.com, daily 6:30AM– 7:30PM)* has been serving comfort food since 1931. Its interior is designed to resemble a redwood forest, replete with 20-foot waterfall cascading into a stream that runs through the dining room. **The Original Pantry Café (87) ($)** *(877 S. Figueroa St., www.pantrycafe.com, 213-972-9279, daily 24 hours)* opened in 1924 and has served celebrities and politicians. Recover from the big night out here with buckwheat pancakes, hash browns, or ham-and-cheese omelets.

Bars & Nightlife:

Bordello Bar (88) *(901 E. 1st St., 213-687-3766, www. bordellobar.com, 6PM–2AM)* was home to the oldest bar and brothel in Downtown L.A. and once housed the popular Little Pedro's Blue Bongo. Live music ranges from jazz to ska to Latin blues to burlesque. The Downtown bar scene is dominated by nightlife developer 213, which created three bars in separate historic buildings. **Broadway Bar (89)** *(830 S. Broadway, 213-614-9909, www.the broadwaybar.net, Tu–F 5PM–2AM, Sa 8PM–2AM)* a glamorous cocktail lounge set in a 24-block Beaux Arts/Gothic Revival building. For a livelier night out, try **Golden Gopher (90)** *(417 W. 8th*

St., 213-614-8001, www.goldengopherbar.com, daily 8PM–2AM), with something for everyone, such as vintage video games and a jukebox. At **Seven Grand (91)** (515 W. 7th St., 213-614-0737, www.sevengrand.la, M–F 5PM–2AM, Sa 7PM–2AM), set in the historic Brock & Co. Jewelers building, throw down one of 125 premium Irish whiskeys or other spirits, or play pool under the gaze of taxidermic animal heads.

WHERE TO SHOP

Los Angeles Fashion District (92) (7th/Main/ San Pedro Sts., 213-488-1153, www.fashion district.org, daily 10AM–5PM) is the spot to shop till you drop. Racks of clothing and accessories from wholesalers and retailers span 90 blocks. **Tip:** Saturdays some wholesale-only stores will sell to the public. **Urban Shopping Adventures** (213-683-9715, www.urbanshoppingadventures.com) offers guided shopping tours of the district that include bottled water, a shopping bag, and discounts. For those who don't mind designer knockoffs, such as faux Coach handbags or Armani sunglasses, and who thrill at the prospect of two miles of bargain hunting, **Santee Alley** is it. Also part of the Fashion District is the Los Angeles Flower District (93) (700 block of Wall St., 213-627-2482 or 213-622-1966, www.laflowerdistrict.com, M, W, F 8AM–2PM, Tu, Th, Sa 6AM–noon), the country's largest flower market, dating from 1913, when Japanese flower growers and sellers launched it a few blocks from its current location. Nothing in L.A. glitters quite like the Jewelry District

(94) *(Hill St. bet. 5th/8th Sts., 213-622-3335, www. lajd.net, M–Sa 9AM–6PM)*, with some 3,000 retailers hawking everything from diamond rings to precious gems. A few are wholesale only, but most offer retail savings from 50 to 70 percent. The sea of fabrics at **Michael Levine (95)** *(919/920 Maple Ave., 213-622-6259, www.mlfabric.com, M–F 9AM–5:30PM, Sa 9AM–4PM, Su 11AM–4PM)* has designers and dressmakers chomping at the bit. One store specializes in clothing materials and the other in upholstery and drapery fabrics. The **FIDM Museum Shop (96)** *(919 S. Grand Ave., 213-624-1200, www.thefidmmuseum store.org, M–F 10AM–5PM)* sells quirky accessories like vintage kimono ties and unique gifts.

WHERE TO STAY

Business travelers will find the **Radisson Hotel Los Angeles Midtown at USC (97) ($$)** *(3540 S. Figueroa St., 213-748-4141, www.radisson.com/losangelesca_midtown)* a convenient option. Leisure travelers take advantage of its affordable, spacious rooms. **Figueroa Hotel (98) ($-$$)** *(939 S. Figueroa St., 213-627-8971, www.figueroa hotel.com)* is a slice of Casablanca with its Moroccan decor. Lounge at the poolside **Verandah Bar** for a cocktail or two. The words *Downtown* and *cozy* seem an unlikely pair, but **Inn at 657 (99) ($$)** *(657 W. 23rd St., 213-741-2200, www.patsysinn657.com)* brings them together with its gardens and B&B setting.

chapter 2

MIRACLE MILE/MID-CITY

HANCOCK PARK/LARCHMONT VILLAGE

KOREATOWN/WESTLAKE

MIRACLE MILE/MID-CITY HANCOCK PARK/LARCHMONT VILLAGE KOREATOWN/WESTLAKE

Places to See:

1. LA BREA TAR PITS ★
2. Page Museum
3. Farmers Market
4. Los Angeles County Museum of Art
5. Craft & Folk Art Museum
6. A+D Architecture and Design Museum
7. Petersen Automotive Museum
8. Los Angeles Museum of the Holocaust
9. CBS Television City
10. ACME Comedy Theater
11. The Silent Movie Theater
12. Merry Karnowsky Gallery
13. 6150 Wilshire Boulevard
48. Getty House
49. House of Davids
50. Wilshire Ebell Theatre
63. Bullocks Wilshire
64. MacArthur Park
65. Park Plaza Hotel
66. Wiltern
67. Korean American Museum

★ *Top Pick*

Places to Eat & Drink:

14. Ortolan
15. AOC
16. Campanile
17. Little Door
18. Hatfield's
19. Cobras & Matadors
20. Canter's Deli
21. Angelini Osteria
22. Izakaya by Katsu-ya
23. Merkato
24. Meals by Genet
25. Milk
26. Joan's on Third
27. El Rey
28. Little Bar
29. The Dime
30. Molly Malone's
31. The Mint
32. Tom Bergin's Tavern
51. Prado
52. Le Petit Greek
53. Girasole
54. Village Pizzeria
55. Larchmont Village Wine Spirits & Cheese
68. Pacific Dining Car

69. Blue Velvet
70. ChoSun Galbee
71. Tommy's Original World
    Famous Hamburgers
72. Papa Cristo's Taverna
73. El Cholo
74. Chunju Han-il Kwan
75. Soot Bull Jeep
76. Taylor's Steak House
77. Langer's Delicatessen
78. R Bar
79. Miss T's Barcade
80. The Prince
81. Brass Monkey
82. Dan Sung Sa

39. Cook's Library
40. Traveler's Bookcase
41. Beige
42. The Way We Wore
43. Flight Club
56. Noni
57. Pickett Fences
58. Petticoats
59. Sonya Ooten Gem Bar
60. Chevalier's Books
61. Larchmont Village
    Farmers' Market
83. Mobius
84. Koreatown Plaza
85. Koreatown Galleria

Where to Shop:

33. Beverly Center
34. The Grove
35. Zipper
36. Polka Dots & Moonbeams
37. Satine Boutique
38. Scout

Where to Stay:

44. Sofitel Los Angeles
45. Élan Hotel
46. The Orlando
47. Farmer's Daughter Hotel
62. Dunes Inn Wilshire
86. Ramada Wilshire Center

MIRACLE MILE/MID-CITY

Metro Rail: Red, Purple

Bus lines: 16, 20, 28, 30, 31, 212, 217, 218, 312, 316, 330, 333, 335

DASH: Wilshire Center/Koreatown, Hollywood/Wilshire, Fairfax

Metro Rapid Bus: 710, 714, 720, 728, 780, 920

• SNAPSHOT •

Mid-Wilshire extends from La Cienega Boulevard on the west, Melrose Avenue on the north, Hoover Street on the east, and the Santa Monica Freeway on the south. The area boomed in the 1920s when developer A. W. Ross transformed it into a commercial district rivaling downtown Los Angeles. The stretch now called Miracle Mile was "America's Champs-Élysées" until the 1960s, when freeways led folks to newer westside suburbs. Today it's home to museums and galleries, as well as the La Brea Tar Pits. Neighboring Mid-City West is home to the Fairfax District and Little Ethiopia. Fairfax encompasses the Farmers Market, the Grove, and shop-lined streets; Little Ethiopia

spans Fairfax Avenue between Olympic and Pico boulevards. Fairfax became the center of L.A.'s Jewish community in the 1940s. Holocaust survivors and Russian immigrants settled here, opening synagogues and businesses. Many kosher butchers, bakeries, and shops remain, especially along Fairfax between Beverly and Melrose.

PLACES TO SEE

Landmarks:

TOP PICK!

The ★**LA BREA TAR PITS (1)** *(5801 Wilshire Blvd., www.latarpits.org)* ooze from the underbelly of Hancock Park, much as they did in prehistory. This famous fossil site (which bubbles not with tar, but asphalt, the lowest grade of crude oil) trapped then preserved an amazing diversity of Ice Age plants and animals, including saber-toothed cats, mastodons, and more. Nearly 400 species of mammals, amphibians, birds, and fish have gotten stuck in the sludge, many of them extinct today. **Pit 91** is excavated each summer; a free viewing station provides a peek, plus a short film documenting the discoveries is also shown *(W–Su 1AM–4PM late June–early Oct.)*. Watch through windows at the **Page Museum (2)** *(5801 Wilshire*

Blvd., 323-934-7243, M–F 9:30AM–5PM, Sa–Su 10AM– 5PM) as fossils are cleaned and repaired in its laboratory.

The **Farmers Market (3)** *(6333 W. 3rd St., 323-933-9211, www.*

farmersmarketla.com, M–F 9AM–9PM, Sa 9AM–8PM, Su 10AM–7PM), an L.A. institution since 1934, features more than 100 shops, restaurants, grocers, and a landmark clock tower.

Arts & Entertainment:

The permanent collection of the **Los Angeles County Museum of Art (4)**, or **LACMA** *(5905 Wilshire Blvd., 323-857-6000, www.lacma.org, M, Tu, Th noon–8PM, F noon–9PM, Sa–Su 11AM–8PM, closed W)*, exceeds 100,000 works, including European, contemporary, U.S., Latin American, and Islamic art, plus an immense Korean art collection, and a Japanese art pavilion. **Tip:** The museum is in the midst of a multi-million-dollar re-do of its 20-acre campus; renowned architect Renzo Piano is collaborating in creating new galleries, gardens, and public spaces. The first phase includes the 72,000-square-foot **Broad Contemporary Art Museum**. Consult Web site for visitor updates before you go.

Also on **Museum Row**: the **Craft & Folk Art Museum (5)** *(5814 Wilshire Blvd., 323-937-4230, www.cafam.org, Tu, W, F 11AM–5PM, Th till 7PM, Sa–Su noon–6PM)* with exhibits ranging from puppetry to katagami to Venetian glass to voodoo art. The **A+D Architecture and Design Museum (6)** *(5900 Wilshire Blvd., 323-932-9393, www.aplusd.org, Tu–F 10AM–6PM, Sa–Su 11AM–5PM)* spotlights architectural, landscape, interior, fashion, and product design. L.A.'s requisite automobiles have a place all their own at **Petersen Automotive Museum (7)** *(6060*

Wilshire Blvd., 323-930-2277, www.petersen.org, Tu–Su 10AM–6PM). The collection encompasses more than 150 rare and classic vehicles. Its **May Family Children's Discovery Center** provides hands-on fun. **Los Angeles Museum of the Holocaust (8)** *(6435 Wilshire Blvd., 323-651-3704, www.lamuseumoftheholocaust.org, M–Th 10AM–5PM, F 10AM–2PM, closed Sa, Su noon–4PM, free),* the country's oldest such museum, was founded in 1961 by Holocaust survivors.

Come on down for tapings of *The Price Is Right* at historic **CBS Television City (9)** *(7800 Beverly Blvd., 323-575-2458, www.cbs.com),* built in 1952. **ACME Comedy Theater (10)** *(135 N. La Brea Ave., 323-525-0202, www. acmecomedy.com)* is known for sketch and improv. Built in 1942 by John and Dorothy Hampton, **The Silent Movie Theatre (11)** *(611 N. Fairfax Ave., 323-655-2510, www.silentmovietheatre.com)*  was restored to its original, vintage 1940s Art Deco design. The theater calendar is in the hands of Cinefamily, an organization of movie lovers. Locals pack **Merry Karnowsky Gallery (12)** *(170 S. La Brea Ave., 323-933-4408, www.mkgallery.com, Tu–Sa noon–6PM)* on opening night receptions. **Miracle Mile Art Walk** *(3rd Sa of each month)* includes over 40 galleries; half are located along Wilshire. **6150 Wilshire Boulevard (13)** is filled with art spaces.

PLACES TO EAT & DRINK
Where to Eat:

Chef Christophe Émé, hubby of actress Jeri Ryan, lends his touch to French cuisine at **Ortolan (14) ($$$)** *(8338 W. 3rd St., 323-653-3300, www.ortolanrestaurant.com, M 6PM–10PM, Tu–F 6PM–11PM, Sa 5:30PM–11PM, Su 5:30PM–10PM)*. Try the seared Napa Valley escargot starter or signature pork confit. **AOC (15) ($$)**, for Appellation d'Origine Contrôlée *(8022 W. 3rd St., 323-653-6359, www.aocwinebar.com, M–F 6PM–11PM, Sa 5:30PM–11PM, Su till 10PM)*, launched the small-plates trend here. Film-biz bigwigs favor the charcuterie's prosciutto di parma or the cheese menu's roasted dates, parmesan, and bacon. **Campanile (16) ($$$)** *(624 S. La Brea Ave., 323-938-1447, www.campanilerestaurant. com, lunch M–F 11:30AM–2:30PM, dinner M–W 6–10PM, Th–Sa 5:30–11PM, Sa–Su brunch 9:30AM–1:30PM)*, in a space built by Charlie Chaplin, is lauded for its Monday three-course dinners and Thursday "Grilled Cheese Nights." Romantics reserve tables at **Little Door (17) ($$$)** *(8164 W. 3rd St., 323-951-1210, www.thelittledoor.com, Su–Th 6PM–10:30PM, F–Sa 6PM–11:30PM, wine bar F–Sa 6PM–1AM)*, the perfect backdrop for the French-Moroccan menu. Quinn and Karen **Hatfield's (18) ($$$)** *(7458 Beverly Blvd., 323-935-2977, www.hatfields restaurant.com, M–Th 6PM–10PM, F–Sa till 10:30PM)* has a fine-tuned menu, including options such as mint-crusted rack of lamb, pan roasted duck breast, or slow baked Tasmanian ocean trout. Don't miss Karen's chocolate–peanut butter truffle cake. Trendies pack boisterous **Cobras & Matadors (19) ($$)** *(7615 Beverly Blvd., 323-932-6178, Su–Th 5PM–11PM, F–Sa 6PM–midnight)*, a Spanish-style tapas spot. It's BYOB, but there's a wine merchant close by. **Canter's Deli (20) ($)** *(419 N. Fairfax Ave., 323-651-2030, www.cantersdeli.com, 24 hours)* has been doling out matzo ball soup and pastrami on rye since 1931. **Angelini Osteria (21) ($$-$$$)** *(7313 Beverly Blvd., 323-297-0070, Tu–F noon–2:30PM, Tu–Su 5:30PM–10:30PM)* delivers with its simple country Italian flavors, whether it's mouth-watering spinach lasagna or pumpkin tortellini. Izakaya dishes and well-prepared sushi at a reasonable cost help fill the white walls and wooden tables at **Izakaya by Katsu-ya (22) ($$)** *(8420 W. 3rd St., 323-782-9536, M–Sa noon–2:30PM, M–Th 5:30PM–11PM, F–Sa till 11:30PM, Su till 9:30PM)*. Expect to wait for a table at this lively spot.

In **Little Ethiopia**, try **Merkato (23) ($)** *(1036-½ Fairfax Ave., www.ethiopianmerkato.com, 323-935-1775, daily 11AM–11PM)* for vegetarian eggplant or beef with spiced butter and chiles. Visit refined **Meals by Genet (24) ($)** *(1053 S. Fairfax Ave., www.mealsbygenet.com, 323-938-9304, W–Su 5:30PM–10PM)* for steak tartar or chicken sautéed in onions and green chiles.

Last stops before the tummy tuck include **Milk (25) ($)** *(7290 Beverly Blvd., 323-939-6455, www.themilkshop.com, Su–Th 8AM–10PM, F–Sa till 11PM)*, serving coffee-toffee crunch shakes, and cupcake fave **Joan's on Third (26) ($)** *(8346 W. 3rd St., 323-655-2285, www.joansonthird.com, M–Sa 8AM–8PM, Su till 6PM)*.

Bars & Nightlife:

Art Deco **El Rey (27)** *(5515 Wilshire Blvd., 323-936-6400, www.theelrey. com)* features live music; its lineup weighs heavy on indie rock. Seeking scene-free respite? Try friendly **Little Bar (28)** *(757 S. La Brea Ave., 323-937-9210, www.littlebarlounge.com, daily 5PM–2AM, opens earlier Sa–Su for sports events)*, pouring soju shooters and green tea martinis. **The Dime (29)** *(442 N. Fairfax Ave., 323-651-4421, daily 7PM–1:30AM)* squeezes Big Apple chic into a tiny space. A young crowd comes for DJs and just-hip-enough vibe. **Molly Malone's (30)** *(575 S. Fairfax Ave., 323-935-1577, www.mollymalonesla.com, daily 10AM–2AM)* has been owned and operated by the same Irish family for over 30 years. Featured in films such as *Leaving Las Vegas, Patriot Games*, and other flicks, today its live music ranges from bluegrass to reggae. Live-music venue **The Mint (31)** *(6010 W. Pico Blvd., 323-954-9400, www.themintla. com, hours vary)* has weathered L.A.'s tastes since 1937. Performers have included Stevie Wonder, Ray Charles, Ben Harper, and Macy Gray. L.A.'s oldest Irish pub, **Tom Bergin's Tavern (32)** *(840 S. Fairfax Ave., 323-936-7151, www.tombergins.com, daily 11:30AM–2AM)* dates to 1936. Some say its horseshoe-shaped bar inspired old TV favorite, *Cheers*.

WHERE TO SHOP

Midtown shopping is anchored by the **Beverly Center (33)** *(8500 Beverly Blvd., 310-854-0071, www.beverly*

center.com, M–F 10AM–9PM, Sa 10AM–8PM, Su 11AM–6PM), with **Macy's**, **Bloomingdale's**, **Louis Vuitton**, **Steve Madden**, and more, plus a multiscreen **movie theater**. Ride the trolley at outdoor mall The Grove (34) *(189 The Grove Dr., 323-900-8080, www.thegrovela.com, M–Th 10AM–9PM, F–Sa till 10PM, Su 11AM–8PM)*, adjacent to the Farmers Market *(see page 58)*. Keep an eye out for celeb shoppers as you enjoy the dancing fountain and glockenspiel.

Boutique-packed **Third Street** *(bet. La Cienega Blvd./La Brea Ave.)* is shopping central. Zipper (35) *(8316 W. 3rd St., 323-951-9190, www.zippergifts.com, M–Sa 11AM–7PM, Su noon–5PM)* showcases modern designs and accessories for home, office, and entertaining. Fashionistas, designers, and film folk suit up at Polka Dots & Moonbeams (36) *(8367/8381 W. 3rd St., 323-*

651-1746; 323-655-3880, www. polkadotsandmoonbeams.com, M–Sa 11AM–7PM, Su 11AM–6PM). Satine Boutique (37) *(8117 W. 3rd St., 323-655-2142, www.satineboutique. com, M–F 11AM–7PM, Sa 10AM–7PM, Su noon–6PM)* earns respect for its sophisticated selection of women's designers, including shoes by Chloe and Stella McCartney, Catherine Holstein dresses, and Vanessa Bruno tops.

Guys and girls shop retro threads and current designs at Scout (38) *(7920 W. 3rd St., 323-658-8684, www.scoutla.com, daily 11AM–8PM, Su noon–7PM)*. Foodies sift the shelves at Cook's Library (39) *(8373 W. 3rd St., 323-655-3141, www.cookslibrary.com, M 1PM–5PM, Tu–Sa 11AM–6PM)*. Explore Traveler's Bookcase (40) *(8375 W. 3rd St., 323-655-0575, www.travelbooks.com, 10AM–7PM)* for travel tomes and guidebooks.

Along **Beverly Boulevard** *(bet. Martel/La Brea Aves.)*, boutique Beige (41) *(7274 Beverly Blvd., 323-549-0064, www.beigestore.com, M–Sa 11AM–7PM, Su noon–5PM)* showcases local and international designers. At The Way We Wore (42) *(334 S. La Brea Ave., 323-937-0878, www.thewaywewore.com, Tu–Sa 11AM–7PM, Su noon–6PM)*, higher-end secondhand threads pack the racks.

In **Fairfax**, consignment shop Flight Club (43) *(503 N. Fairfax Ave., 323-782-8616, www.flightclubla.com, M–Sa 12:30PM–7PM, Su till 6PM)* carries Nikes, Vans, Adidas, and more, including collector and limited editions.

WHERE TO STAY

Sofitel Los Angeles (44) **($$$)** *(8555 Beverly Blvd., 310-278-5444, www.sofitel.com)* comes with all the sexy trimmings, including a destination nightclub and restaurant. Sleek Élan Hotel (45) **($$)** *(8435 Beverly Blvd., 323-658-6663, www.elanhotel.com)* appeals with boutique-style intimacy. With its location, lounge, wireless, and dining, **The Orlando (46) ($)** *(8384 W. 3rd St., 323-658-6600, www.theorlando.com)* offers excellent value. Unwind amid cool country kitsch at the **Farmer's Daughter Hotel (47) ($)** *(115 S. Fairfax Ave., 323-937-3930, www.farmersdaughterhotel.com)*.

Bus lines: 14, 16, 210

DASH: Hollywood/Wilshire, Larchmont Shuttle

Metro Rapid Bus: 710, 714

• SNAPSHOT •

With its lawns and large mansions, upscale Hancock Park remains largely residential. Officially bounded by Melrose and Wilshire, as well as Highland and Rossmore, the district was developed in the 1920s by the Hancock family, who profited from Rancho La Brea oil wells along today's Miracle Mile. Pioneer L.A. families, bearing bigwig names like Huntington, Doheny, and Van Nuys, flocked here. African Americans and Jews were once banned from buying property in the area, but that changed in 1948 when Nat King Cole purchased a house. Today, Hancock Park, which is home to a large Orthodox Jewish population, often  refers to a more expanded region, including Windsor Square, another well-preserved residential zone from Wilshire to Beverly, and from Arden Boulevard to Van Ness Avenue. The commercial center, dubbed Larchmont Village, lies along Larchmont Boulevard.

PLACES TO SEE
Landmarks:

The **Getty House (48)** *(605 S. Irving Blvd., www.getty house.org)*, located in Windsor Square, was built in 1921 for an estimated $83,000. It was purchased in 1959 by Getty Oil Company and donated to the city in 1975. Some 20 years later, the Getty House Foundation restored the building, and it became the official residence of the Los Angeles mayor. The Tudor-style home is used for official city functions and community and children's programs. Another home of note, **Youngwood Court** is known as the **House of Davids (49)** *(corner of W. 3rd and S. Muirfield Rd.)*; its unconventional owner displays some 20 small-scale replicas of Michelangelo's David, and the owner does up the house for Christmas.

Arts & Entertainment:

Wilshire Ebell Theatre (50) *(4401 W. 8th St., 323-939-1128, www.ebellla.com/operating)* opened its doors in 1927 with the West Coast premiere of Sigmund Romberg's operetta *Desert Song*; it also hosted Amelia Earhart's final appearance as well as Judy Garland's first audition. The venue features everything from gospel choirs to Persian plays and is used for filming.

PLACES TO EAT & DRINK
Where to Eat:

Prado (51) ($$) *(244 N. Larchmont Blvd., 323-467-3871, www.pradola.com, M–F 11:30AM–3PM, 5:30PM–10PM, Sa–Su 4:30PM–10:30PM)* pleases eye and palate with its colorful decor and mix of Latin, American, and Caribbean cuisines. Originally from the Peloponnesus, the Houndalas family infuses **Le Petit Greek (52) ($-$$)** *(127 N. Larchmont Blvd., 323-464-5160, www.lepetit greek.com, daily 11:30AM–4PM, 5:30PM–10PM)* with traditional delights such as moussaka and filo-wrapped chicken Olympia. People-watch from the outdoor patio. Tiny **Girasole (53) ($$)** *(225-½ N. Larchmont Blvd., 323-464-6978, W–F noon–3PM, Tu–Sa 5:30PM–10PM)* brings a touch of Italy to Larchmont with spinach gnocchi, pumpkin ravioli, and Venetian specialties like *bresaola*—cured beef. A contender for best L.A. pizza, **Village**

Pizzeria (54) ($) *(131 N. Larchmont Blvd., 323-465-5566, www.village pizzeria.net, M–Th, Su 11:30AM–9:30PM, F–Sa till 10PM)* features handspun, homemade pies. Locals line up for gourmet lunch sandwiches at **Larchmont Village Wine Spirits & Cheese (55) ($)** *(223 N. Larchmont Blvd., 323-856-8699, M–Sa 11AM–5PM)*.

WHERE TO SHOP

Noni (56) *(225 N. Larchmont Blvd., 323-469-3239, www.noniboutiquela.com, M–Sa 11AM–7PM, Su till 5PM)* offers men's and women's clothes bearing such labels as **Anna Sui**, **Louis Verdad**, and **Vivienne Westwood**. Pickett Fences (57) *(214 N. Larchmont Blvd., 323-467-2140, www.pickettfences.com, 10:30AM–6PM, Su 11AM–5PM)* hawks denim, stationery, shoes, and bags. The shop sources wardrobes for TV and film and provides private celeb shopping. **Cosabella** lingerie and other sexy lines are squeezed into tiny Petticoats (58) *(115 N. Larchmont Blvd., 323-467-7178, www.petticoatslingerie.com, M–Sa 10:30AM–6PM, Su 11AM–5PM)*. The  motto at Sonya Ooten Gem Bar (59) *(238 N. Larchmont Blvd., 323-462-4453, www.sonyaooten.com, Tu–F 10:30AM–6PM, Sa noon–7PM, Su noon–5PM)* is no artificial ingredients allowed, whether they be base metals or faux gemstones. The designs here include hand-crocheted gold earrings, quartz earrings, and bracelets of silk and leather. It's easy to while away an afternoon at browsable independently owned Chevalier's Books (60) *(126 N. Larchmont Blvd., 323-465-1334, M–Sa 10AM–6PM, Su 11AM–5PM)*. Kids have their own space here, too. Larchmont Village Farmers' Market (61) *(209 Larchmont Blvd., 818-591-8161, www.ccfm.com, Su 10AM–2PM)* spotlights local produce growers and vendors offering everything from handmade sweaters to bath balms to natural honey.

WHERE TO STAY

Classic roadside motel Dunes Inn Wilshire ($) (62) *(4300 Wilshire Blvd., 323-938-3616, www.dunesla.com)* provides the basics plus a pool for a bargain, considering its central location.

KOREATOWN/WESTLAKE

Metro Rail: Red, Purple

Bus lines: 14, 16, 18, 20, 21, 66, 204, 207, 366, 603

DASH: Wilshire Center/Koreatown

Rapid Bus: 714, 720, 728, 754, 757

• SNAPSHOT •

The Han'gul signs mark the boundaries of L.A.'s sprawling Koreatown; bordered by Wilshire and Pico boulevards and North Western and North Vermont avenues, it roughly spans four square miles. Unlike the tourist strips of Downtown's Olvera Street or Chung King Road in Chinatown, Koreatown is the real deal, jammed with bingsu shops, barbecue, all-night tofu houses, and karaoke studios. Olympic Boulevard serves as its main street, but bars and eateries are found everywhere. Koreatown includes Wilshire Center, one of L.A.'s oldest communities. This once-wealthy area declined in the 1960s as did its property values, sparking an influx of Korean immigrants in search of bargain housing; decades later, Koreatown was the target of looters during 1992's Rodney King riots. Revitalization is evident today; the district is gaining status as a culinary and nightlife hub, and it's strongly influencing the Westlake district to its east. Another former upscale 'hood,

Westlake faded when freeways led the populace to newer western suburbs. Demographics shifted; today Westlake, home to Filipinos and Central Americans, is the most densely populated community in L.A. Though changes are afoot, crime is still a concern. Westlake is frequented for several dining institutions, but it's best to take care here.

PLACES TO SEE
Landmarks:

The fabled Art Deco **Bullocks Wilshire (63)** *(3050 Wilshire Blvd.)* building, with its green-tarnished, copper-topped tower, was once an exclusive department store, serving customers such as Alfred Hitchcock and Marlene Dietrich. Decades later, Bill Clinton and other politicos were photographed here, but by the late 1980s, the store was well past its prime. Southwestern Law School rescued the building; it now houses their library *(www.swlaw.edu/campus/building)*. Westlake's most famous spot, palm tree–lined **MacArthur Park (64)** *(2230 W. 6th St., www.laparks.org/dos/parks/facility/macArthur Pk.htm)* was immortalized in the eponymous 1968 song by Jimmy Webb, which translated to a Donna Summer hit 10 years later. Originally Westlake Park (the name change honored General Douglas MacArthur), the lake-centered space, created in the 1880s, was flanked by upscale hotels; a century later it was a haven for drug dealers. Despite improvements, the park struggles to keep crime in check. Lavish **Park Plaza Hotel (65)** *(607 S.*

Park View), a former Elks Club, was built in 1925; today it's a popular event venue and movie location. Flicks filmed here include *Bugsy*, *Barton Fink*, and *The Mask*.

Arts & Entertainment:

Dating from the Golden Age of Hollywood, the dazzling **Wiltern (66)** *(3790 Wilshire Blvd., 213-380-5005, www.wiltern.com)* was slated for demolition in the 1970s, but the Los Angeles Conservancy helped rescue the Art Deco delight. It's hosted top live performers, from Prince to David Bowie, since its reopening. The **Korean American Museum (67)** *(3727 W. 6th St., 213-388-4229, www.kamuseum.org, M–F 11AM–6PM, Sa till 3PM)* showcases Korean-American art and culture. Operated by the Korean Ministry of Culture, Sports, and Tourism, the **Korean Cultural Center** *(5505 Wilshire Blvd., 323-936-7141, www.kccla.org, M–F 9AM–5PM, Sa 10AM–5PM)* offers exhibits, art, films, language classes, and a library.

PLACES TO EAT & DRINK
Where to Eat:

Pacific Dining Car (68) ($$$) *(1310 W. 6th St., 213-483-6000, www.pacificdiningcar.com, daily 24 hours)*, dating from 1921, was once a haunt for the likes of Mae West. Today, business types, Japanese visitors, and occasional Hollywood bigwigs hobnob while dining on steaks and chops. Though the location sounds unsexy (part of a former Holiday Inn that's now a residential housing development called "the Flat"), über-modern **Blue Velvet (69) ($$$)** *(750 S. Garland Ave., 213-239-0061,* *www.bluevelvetrestaurant.com, M–F 11:30AM–2:30PM, 5:30PM–10:30PM, Sa–Su 5:30PM–10:30PM, bar daily 5:30PM–close)* is stylishly chic, with a sophisticated menu. Enjoy a fireside drink by the pool. The most Westernized of Koreatown's eateries, **ChoSun Galbee (70) ($$-$$$)** *(3330 W. Olympic Blvd., 323-734-3330, www.chosungalbee.com, daily 11AM–11PM)* excels at *galbee* (short ribs) and *bulgogi* (marinated beef), among other barbecue options. Prices run more than its peers, but you pay for the atmosphere.

Tommy's Original World Famous Hamburgers (71) ($) *(2575 Beverly Blvd., 213-389-1682, www.original tommys.com, daily 24 hours)* has pleased Angelenos with artery-clogging chili burgers for over 50 years. Nobody goes hungry at **Papa Cristo's Taverna (72) ($)** *(2771 W. Pico Blvd., 323-737-2970, www.papacristos.com, Tu–Sa 10AM–8PM, Su 9AM–4PM)*; tables groan with falafel, kebabs, and dolmades. Venerable **El Cholo (73) ($)** *(1121 S. Western Ave., 323-734-2773, www.elcholo.com, M–Sa 11AM–10PM, Su 11AM–9PM, Su brunch 10AM–1PM)* has served everyone from Gary Cooper to Madonna to Jack Nicholson; expect great green corn tamales and lethal margaritas. One of K-town's hidden gems, **Chunju Han-il Kwan (74) ($)** *(3450 W. 6th St., 213-480-1799, M–Su 8:30AM–11PM)* serves up heaping portions of banchan and *bu dae chi gae* (noodle and meat soup). Take a long deep breath at **Soot Bull Jeep (75) ($$)** *(3136 W. 8th St., 213-387-3865, daily 11AM–11PM)*, where smoke from charcoal-fueled fire pits and the smell of barbecue fill the air. Decor takes a backseat to the cuisine, as locals line up for a chance to cook their own meats.

Traditional **Taylor's Steak House (76) ($$)** *(3361 W. 8th St., 213-382-8449, www.taylorssteakhouse.com, M–F 11:30AM–4PM; M–Th, Su 4PM–9:30PM, F–Sa 4PM–10:30PM)* is a white-linen, red-leather-booth, steaks-and-chops institution.

A hearty hot pastrami sandwich has been the lifeline for **Langer's Delicatessen (77) ($)** *(704 S. Alvarado St., 213-483-8050, www.langersdeli.com, M–Sa 8AM–4PM)* since its 1947 opening. Though almost forced out of business in the crime-addled '90s, the MacArthur Park subway line has helped this institution flourish once again.

Bars & Nightlife:

You need a password to enter dimly lit hotspot **R Bar (78)** *(3331 W. 8th St., 213-387-7227, M–Sa 7PM–1AM)*. Expect stiff drinks, an indie-rock jukebox, and comfy couches. For just a quarter a try, **Miss T's Barcade (79)** *(371 N. Western Ave., 323-465-5045, M–F 5PM–2AM, Sa 8PM–2AM)* entertains with arcade games like Galaga and Centipede. (Look for the neon PacMan "ghost" in the window.) Located in the former Windsor Hotel, and a film location for the movie *Chinatown*, **The Prince (80)** *(3198 W. 7th St., 213-389-2007, daily 4PM–2AM)* retains British pub ambiance while serving Korean specialties. Karaoke-ites, including occasional celebs, croon to punk and country at **Brass Monkey (81)** *(3440 Wilshire Blvd.,*

213-381-7047, M–Su 10AM–2AM). **Dan Sung Sa (82)** *(3317 W. 6th St., 213-487-9100, daily 4PM–2AM)* is a smoky, old-school dive. Walls are lined with faded Korean newspapers and movie posters.

WHERE TO SHOP

Mobius (83) *(3300 W. 6th St., 213-385-9200, www.shop mobius.com, M–Su noon–10PM)* sells select books, artworks, and Japanese toys, such as C.i.Boys, Gloomy Wobblers, and Cactus Friends. Mega Koreatown Plaza (84) *(928 S. Western Ave. at 9th St., 213-382-1234, www.koreatownplaza.com)* has more than 80 shops and eateries selling food, music, jewelry, and clothing. Koreatown Galleria (85) *(3250 W. Olympic Blvd., 323-733-6000, www.koreatowngalleria.com)* offers over 70 shops, a food gallery, and market.

WHERE TO STAY

Ramada Wilshire Center (86) ($) *(3900 Wilshire Blvd., 213-736-5222, www.ramada.com)* offers free Internet access, continental breakfast, and other amenities at value prices.

chapter 3

LOS FELIZ/GRIFFITH PARK

SILVER LAKE

ECHO PARK

HIGHLAND PARK/EAGLE ROCK

LOS FELIZ/GRIFFITH PARK
SILVER LAKE
ECHO PARK
HIGHLAND PARK/EAGLE ROCK

Places to See:

1. GRIFFITH PARK ★
2. Griffith Observatory
3. Autry National Center
4. Travel Town Museum
5. Barnsdall Art Park
6. Los Angeles Zoo
23. Metro Gallery
24. Ghettogloss
25. Thinkspace Gallery
48. Echo Park Lake
49. Baxter Stairway
50. Elysian Park
51. Dodger Stadium
67. Charles F. Lummis Home and Garden
68. Heritage Square Museum
69. Debs Park
70. Southwest Museum of the American Indian
71. Los Angeles Police Historical Society Museum
72. Center for the Arts Eagle Rock

Places to Eat & Drink:

7. Fred 62
8. Mexico City
9. Yuca's
10. Palermo Ristorante Italiano
11. Bigfoot Lodge
12. The Griffin
13. Dresden Room
14. Vinoteca Farfalla
15. Drawing Room
16. The Roost
17. Good Luck Bar
26. Blair's
27. Cliff's Edge
28. Café Stella
29. Edendale Grill
30. Alegria on Sunset
31. Malo
32. Gingergrass
33. The Kitchen
34. Pazzo Gelato
35. Spaceland
36. Akbar
37. 4100 Bar

★ *Top Pick*

38. Tiki-Ti
39. Cha Cha Lounge
52. Taix
53. Restaurant 15
54. Masa of Echo Park
55. Elf Café
56. El Compadre
57. Brite Spot
58. Short Stop
59. The Echo
60. Gold Room
73. Casa Bianca Pizza Pie
74. Oinkster
75. Auntie Em's Kitchen
76. Café Beaujolais
77. The York
78. Little Cave
79. Footsie's
80. Mr. T's Bowl
81. The Chalet

Where to Shop

18. Wacko
19. Y-Que Trading Post
20. Squaresville
21. Oou

22. Skylight Books
40. Dean
41. Pull My Daisy
42. Clover
43. Yolk
44. Monkeyhouse Toys
45. Bar Keeper
46. Rockaway Records
61. Show Pony
62. Luxe de Ville
63. Flounce Vintage
64. Lemon Frog Shop
65. Sirens and Sailors
82. Owl Talk
83. Lily Simone
84. Eagle Rock Underground
85. Regeneration
86. Imix Book Store

Where to Stay

47. Holiday Inn Express Hotels
    & Suites
66. America's Best Value Inn
87. Best Western Eagle
    Rock Inn
88. Eagle Rock Motel

LOS FELIZ/GRIFFITH PARK

Metro Rail: Gold

Bus lines: 94, 180, 181, 394, 603

DASH: Los Feliz

Rapid Bus: 780

• **SNAPSHOT** •

Sandwiched between Griffith Park and Barnsdall Art Park, Los Feliz has been a haven for artists, filmmakers, and superstars for decades. Its humble beginnings were as Rancho Los Feliz, one of the first land grants in California, given to Corporal Jose Vicente Feliz. A number of owners followed, including Colonel Griffith J. Griffith, who donated over half of the ranch to the city, which turned it into Griffith Park. Other sections of the *rancho* were developed into the communities of Los Feliz and Silver Lake. Los Feliz was home to several movie studios, including the first Walt Disney studio, which is now a supermarket, and D. W. Griffith's studio, which for a time was the ABC Television Center. Today, Los Feliz is a mecca for funky shops, restaurants, and bars, mostly on Hillhurst and Vermont streets.

PLACES TO SEE

Landmarks:

TOP PICK!

L.A.'s primary respite from freeways and concrete is 41,000-acre ★**GRIFFITH PARK (1)** *(4730 Crystal Springs Dr., 323-913-4688, www.lacity.org/rap/dos/parks/griffithpk, daily 6AM–10PM)*, the largest municipal park in the country. The park was named for a mining tycoon, who donated 3,000 acres to the city in 1896. Within its borders are a bird sanctuary, a nature museum, the Greek Theatre, a 1926-era merry-go-round, two 18-hole golf courses, athletic fields, and basketball and tennis courts. The

Griffith Observatory (2) *(2800 E. Observatory Rd., 213-473-0800, www.griffithobs.org, Tu–F noon–10PM, Sa–Su 10AM–10PM)* debuted in 1935 on the southern slope of Mount Hollywood in the park. The original 12-inch Zeiss refracting telescope remains the centerpiece of the newly expanded observatory, which reopened in 2006 after a $93 million renovation. **Tip:** Parking is limited, but there is public access via shuttles and from the Metro Red Line. Get a taste of pioneer history at **Autry National Center (3)** *(4700 Western Heritage Way, 323-667-2000, www.autrynationalcenter.org, Tu–Su 10AM–5PM)*, featuring memorabilia of actor Gene Autry. Peruse the outdoor antique railroad car collection at **Travel Town Museum (4)** *(5200 Zoo Dr., 323-662-5874, www.traveltown.org, M–F 10AM–4PM, Sa–Su 10AM–5PM)* in Griffith Park. Kids love the mini train rides. **Barnsdall Art Park (5)** *(4800 Hollywood Blvd., 323-*

660-4254, www.barnsdallartpark.com, daily noon–5PM), on Olive Hill, is the site of Frank Lloyd Wright's **Hollyhock House** *(323-644-6269, www.hollyhockhouse. net, W–Su hourly tours 12:30PM–3:30PM)*, which owner Aline Barnsdall donated to the city. Barnsdall also gave her land to the city to be used as a public art park. View exhibitions in its **Municipal Art Gallery**, **Gallery Theater**, and **Junior Arts Center**.

Kids:

Located within Griffith Park, the Los Angeles Zoo (6) *(5333 Zoo Dr., 323-644-4200, www. lazoo.org, daily 10AM–5PM)* is  home to 1,200 animals on its 113 acres. New attractions include a golden monkey exhibit; future plans call for a pachyderm forest and a rain forest of the Americas.

PLACES TO EAT & DRINK
Where to Eat:

Fred 62 (7) ($) *(1850 N. Vermont Ave., 323-667-0062, www.fred62.com, daily 24 hours)* is the quintessential diner with its kitsch decor and kitchen-sink-style menu, ranging from tofu chilaquile for breakfast to turkey meat loaf for dinner. For authentic Mexican fare, **Mexico City (8) ($)** *(2121 Hillhurst Ave., 323-661-7227, daily noon–10PM)* serves up killer mole, while **Yuca's (9) ($)** *(2056 Hillhurst Ave., 323-662-1214, www.yucasla.com, M–Sa 11AM–6PM)*, an L.A. institution, simmers with specialties from the Yucatan. **Palermo Ristorante Italiano (10) ($)** *(1858 N. Vermont Ave., 323-663-1178, www.palermorestaurant.net, M 11AM–10:30PM, W–Th,*

Su 11AM–midnight, F–Sa 11AM–1AM) is the spot for a genuine trattoria experience.

Bars & Nightlife:

Bigfoot Lodge (11) *(3172 Los Feliz Blvd., 323-662-9227, www.bigfootlodge.com, daily 5PM–2AM)* transports

patrons to the Sasquatch National Forest, where drinks like Girl Scout Cookie and Toasted Marshmallow are served to indie, punk, and garage music. **The Griffin (12)** *(3000 Los Feliz Blvd., 323-644-0444, M–F 5PM–2AM, Sa–Su 8PM–2AM)* has become a favorite Eastside hang with its European beers, eclectic jukebox, smoking patio, and cool vibe. Swank retro-style **Dresden Room (13)** *(1760 N. Vermont Ave., 323-665-4294, www.the dresden.com, M–Su 9PM–2AM)* branded itself on L.A.'s bar map with its cameo in the movie *Swingers*. Marty and Elayne are the star attractions, belting out covers of Bee Gees songs and other fun tunes. Wine bar **Vinoteca Farfalla (14)** *(1968 Hillhurst Ave., 323-661-8070, www.vinotecafarfalla.com, Su–Th 4:30PM–midnight, F–Sa 4:30PM–1AM)* pours over 45 wines by the glass. **Drawing Room (15)** *(1800 Hillhurst Ave., 323-665-0135, daily 6AM–2AM)* is a neighborhood dive with cheap drinks that pack a punch. Or dig into free popcorn at country-flavored **The Roost (16)** *(3100 Los Feliz Blvd., 323-664-7272, daily 10AM–2AM)*. Asian themed **Good Luck Bar (17)** *(1514 Hillhurst Ave., 323-666-3524, M–F 7PM–2AM, Sa–Su 8PM–2AM)* boasts a varied jukebox and talented mixologists.

WHERE TO SHOP

Wacko (18) *(4633 Hollywood Blvd., 323-663-0122, www.soapplant.com, M–W 11AM–7PM, Th–Sa 11AM–9PM, Su noon–6PM)* is a go-to zany gift center for everything from Catholic school salt-and-pepper shakers to

William Shakespeare action figures. For offbeat T-shirts and other oddities, head to Y-Que Trading Post (19) *(1770 N. Vermont Ave., 323-664-0021, www.yque.com, Su–Th 11AM–8PM, F–Sa 11AM–midnight)*. Vintage duds lure hipsters to Squaresville (20) *(1800 N. Vermont Ave., 323-669-8464, Su–M noon–7PM, Tu–Sa 11AM–8PM)*. Discover retro treasures and independent designers at Oou (21) *(1764 N. Vermont Ave., 323-665-6263, M–Sa 11AM–7PM, Su noon–6PM)*, including vintage sunglasses. Explore a piece of literary heaven at Skylight Books (22) *(1818 N. Vermont Ave., 323-660-1175, www.skylightbooks.com, daily 10AM–10PM)*, known for its collection of fiction and books on L.A., as well as alternative literature.

Bus Lines: 2, 4, 92, 175, 302, 304, 201, 603

Rapid Bus: 704

• SNAPSHOT •

Long a bastion for L.A.'s artistic set, Silver Lake also touts its ethnic diversity and active gay and lesbian community. The district gets its moniker from Silver Lake Reservoir, named after Herman Silver, a member of L.A.'s first Board of Water commissioners. Renowned

1920s–1930s architects Richard Neutra, R.M. Schindler, and John Lautner built residences in Silver Lake, many still standing. Much later, the neighborhood became a hub for L.A.'s independent rock scene and home to the likes of Henry Rollins, Tom Waits, Beck, and members of the Red Hot Chili Peppers. Today you'll find boutiques, art galleries, international restaurants, and some of the city's best bars and live venues here. Its center lies at Sunset Junction, where West Sunset Boulevard and Santa Monica Boulevard intersect.

PLACES TO SEE
Arts & Entertainment:
Spacious **Metro Gallery (23)** *(1835 Hyperion Ave., 323-663-2787, www.metrogallery.org, W–Sa noon–7PM)*

represents local, national, and international talent in various media, including painting, photography, and sculpture. **Ghettogloss (24)** *(2380 Glendale Blvd., 323-912-0008, www.ghettogloss.com, M–F 9AM–6PM, Sa–Su noon–4PM)* is part fine art gallery, part retail store, showcasing local indie designers and artists. **Thinkspace Gallery (25)** *(4210 Santa Monica Blvd., 323-913-3375, www.sourharvest.com, Th–Su 1PM–6PM)* is a collaborative effort representing up-and-coming artists.

PLACES TO EAT & DRINK
Where to Eat:
The hand-picked wine list at **Blair's (26) ($$-$$$)** *(2903 Rowena Ave., 323-660-1882, www.blairsrestaurant.com, lunch daily 11:30AM–5PM, dinner Su–Th 5PM–10PM, F–Sa till 11PM)* accents the refined menu, which varies from risotto to grilled New York steak. **Cliff's Edge (27) ($$)** *(3626 Sunset Blvd., 323-666-6116, www.cliffsedge cafe.com, M–Sa 6PM–closing, Sa–Su 11AM–3PM)* sets the scene for its Mediterranean delights with a candlelit interior and romantic, tree-shaded outdoor patio. Indulge in decadent French cuisine at **Café Stella (28) ($$-$$$)** *(3932 W. Sunset Blvd., 323-666-0265, daily 6PM–11PM)*, perfect spot for a first date. Housed in a former fire station, **Edendale Grill (29) ($$)** *(2838 Rowena Ave., 323-666-2000, www.eden dalegrill.com, Su–W 5PM–midnight, Th–Sa 5PM–2AM, Su brunch 10AM–3PM)* features American-style upscale cuisine. Stay late for cocktail lounge **Mixville Bar**, located in the fire truck bay. Locals

swear by **Alegria on Sunset (30) ($)** *(3510 Sunset Blvd., 323-913-1422, www.alegriaonsunset.com, M–Th 11AM–10PM, F 11AM–11PM, Sa 10AM–11PM)* for authentic Mexican fare. Hipster hang **Malo (31) ($)** *(4326 W. Sunset Blvd., 323-664-1011, www.malorestaurant.com, M 6PM–10PM, Tu–Th 6PM–11PM, F 6PM–midnight, Sa 9AM–midnight, Su 9AM–10PM)* garners acclaim for its burnt habanero and crème salsa and its margaritas. Locals order ground beef and pickle tacos. Vietnamese noodle bowls and lemongrass chicken are just two divine options at **Gingergrass (32) ($)** *(2396 Glendale Blvd., 323-644-1600, www.gingergrass.com, daily 11:30AM–3PM, 5PM–10PM, F–Sa till 10:30PM)*. Brunch in Silver Lake can be quite the scene. Pear pancakes and herb baked eggs are two reasons **The Kitchen (33) ($)** *(4348 Fountain Ave., 323-664-3663, www.thekitchen-silverlake.com, M–Th 5PM–midnight, F till 1AM, Sa 11AM–1AM, Su till 10PM)* fills up on weekends. To satisfy a sweet tooth, head to **Pazzo Gelato (34) ($)** *(3827 W. Sunset Blvd., 323-662-1410, www.pazzogelato.net, Su–Th 11AM–11PM, F–Sa till midnight)* and experiment with mango cayenne or lemoncello mint.

Bars & Nightlife:

One of L.A.'s top indie music venues, **Spaceland (35)** *(1717 Silver Lake Blvd., 323-661-4380, www.clubspaceland.com, nightly 8:30PM–2AM)* is known for breaking new acts. Gays, straights, locals, and West Hollywood's exceedingly hip hit the dance floor at **Akbar (36)** *(4356 W. Sunset Blvd., 323-665-6810, www.akbarsilverlake.com, nightly 7PM–2AM)*. You'll find top-shelf bartenders, a sultry interior, and a rockin' jukebox, all under the gaze of a giant Buddha at **4100 Bar (37)** *(1087 Manzanita St., 323-666-4460, nightly 8PM–2AM)*. Tiny **Tiki-Ti (38)** *(4427 W. Sunset Blvd., 323-669-9381, www.tiki-ti.com, W–Sa 6PM–1AM)* boasts more than 80 tropical

drinks and a roomful of island-style tchotchkes. Kitschy **Cha Cha Lounge (39)** *(2375 Glendale Blvd., 323-660-7595, www.chachalounge.com, nightly 5PM–2AM)* plays up its low-key hip factor with cheap pints, a foosball table, and photo booth.

WHERE TO SHOP

King of all things leather, **Dean (40)** *(3918 W. Sunset Blvd., 323-665-2766, www.deanaccessories.com, M–Sa 11AM–7PM, Su till 6PM)* specializes in handmade bags, watches, and accessories. Silver Lake institution **Pull My Daisy (41)** *(3908 W. Sunset Blvd., 323-663-0608, www.pullmydaisystore.com, M–Sa 11AM–7PM, Su till 6PM)* caters to all budgets with handmade clothing, jewelry, and gifts. Need a last-minute gift? **Clover (42)** *(2756 Rowena Ave., 323-661-4142, www.cloversilverlake.com, M–Sa 10AM–7PM, Su noon–6PM)* has it all, including art books and one-of-a-kind clothes. Visit the gallery upstairs. Colorful **Yolk (43)** *(1626 Silver Lake Blvd., 323-660-4315, www.yolk-la.com, Tu–F 11AM–7PM, Sa 10AM–7PM, Su noon–5PM)* stocks funky kitchenware, toys, and other items. **Monkeyhouse Toys (44)** *(1618-½ Silver Lake Blvd., 323-662-3437, www.monkeyhousetoys. com, Tu–Sa noon–6PM, Su till 5PM)* features everything from children's art books to *Where the Wild Things Are* hand puppets. The focus is on handmade art and toys. Looking for unbreakable wineglasses? Bar Keeper (45) *(3910 W. Sunset Blvd., 323-669-1675, www.barkeepersilver lake.com, M–Tu noon–6PM, W–Sa 11AM–7PM, Su 11AM–6PM)* comes to the rescue with bar necessities, new and vintage. Collectors head to Rockaway Records (46) *(2395 Glendale Blvd., 323-664-3232, www.rock away.com, daily 11AM–7PM)* to stock up on vinyl, posters, and memorabilia.

WHERE TO STAY

Holiday Inn Express Hotels & Suites (47) ($$) *(250 Silver Lake Blvd., 213-639-1920, www.hiexpress.com)* offers basic comfort, plus complimentary continental breakfast and heated pool.

Bus Lines: 2, 4, 10, 55, 60, 92, 94, 200, 302, 365, 394, 603

DASH: Pico Union/Echo Park

Rapid Bus: 704

• SNAPSHOT •

Once home to farms and ranches, Echo Park now spills over with galleries, boutiques, Victorian mansions, and the park itself, for which the district was named. Turn back the clock a century and the neighborhood, at the time named Edendale, was the Hollywood of the day, home to silent film producers and studios, and linked to Downtown by the Pacific Electric Railway. But service stopped following the construction of the Hollywood Freeway (101), and the area went through a downward cycle. Community activism in the early '80s helped save historic homes in nearby Angelino Heights, and in the '90s, other civic groups stepped up to improve safety and quality of life in Echo Park.

PLACES TO SEE
Landmarks:

Echo Park's central feature, **Echo Park Lake (48)** *(751 Echo Park Ave., 213-847-3281)* bursts into color every summer with its pink lotus bed and is the largest planting of lotuses outside Asia. Also located here is the **Angelus Temple**, a Foursquare Gospel church based on the Mormon Tabernacle in Salt Lake City. The best views in Echo Park are from its stairways, namely the **Baxter Stairway (49)** *(Baxter St. three blocks E. of Echo Park Ave.)* with more than 230 steps leading to neighboring Elysian Park. East of Echo Park Lake, you'll spot a colorful row of Victorians along **Carroll Avenue** in neighboring Angelino Heights. The city's second largest park, **Elysian Park (50)** *(835 Academic Rd., 213-485-5054, daily 5AM–10PM)* is also one of the oldest, dedicated in 1886. **Dodger Stadium (51)** *(1000 Elysian Park Ave., 1-866-Dodgers, losangeles. dodgers.mlb.com)* lies on the boundary of Elysian Park.

PLACES TO EAT & DRINK
Where to Eat:

Family-owned **Taix (52) ($$)** *(1911 W. Sunset Blvd., 213-484-1265, www.taixfrench.com, M–Th 11:30AM–10PM, F 11:30AM–11PM, Sa noon–11PM, Su noon–9PM)* is known for its French country flavors and tureens of soup. The mac and cheese at **Restaurant 15 (53) ($-$$)** *(1320 Echo Park Ave., 213-481-0454, www.restaurant 15.com, M–Th 5PM–11PM, F–Sa 5PM–midnight)* is worth the trip, as is the three-course tasting menu (just $15). Chicago-style deep-dish pizza requires about a half hour of prep at **Masa of Echo Park (54) ($)** *(1800 W. Sunset Blvd., 213-989-1558, www.masaofechopark.com, M–Th 11AM–11PM, F 11AM–midnight, Sa 8AM–*

midnight, Su 8AM–11PM). Call ahead or experiment with local draft beers while you wait. Save room for warm croissant bread pudding. A healthier option is **Elf Café (55) ($$)** *(2135 W. Sunset Blvd., W–Su 6PM–11PM),* which uses organic ingredients in its Mediterranean-style cuisine. **El Compadre (56) ($)** *(1449 W. Sunset Blvd., 213-250-4505, daily 11:30AM–1AM)* excels with chips and salsa. Sip a flaming margarita while listening to the live mariachi music. Local standby **Brite Spot (57) ($)** *(1918 W. Sunset Blvd., 213-484-9800, M–Tu 7AM–11PM, W–Su 7AM–4AM)* fills a niche for diner-style breakfasts and late-night eats.

Bars & Nightlife:

Former cop hangout gone trendy dive, **Short Stop (58)** *(1455 Sunset Blvd., 213-482-4942, daily 5PM–2AM)* packs in neighborhood 20-somethings as well as overly hip Westsiders, all making a beeline for the photo booth. **The Echo (59)** *(1822 W. Sunset Blvd., 213-413-8200, www.attheecho.com)* may not be much on atmosphere, but innovative DJs and under-the-radar live performers more than compensate. What lies beneath— **Echoplex** *(entrance at 1154 Glendale Blvd.),* which exceeds its partner in size and presents a steady lineup of indie bands. Intimidating at first, **Gold Room (60)** *(1558 W. Sunset Blvd., 213-482-5259, M–F 11AM–2AM, Sa–Su 8AM–2AM)* draws a largely local, Mexican crowd, for bargain beers and tequila shot combos. Dive into free popcorn and peanuts and hope for the occasional mariachi band.

WHERE TO SHOP

Part art gallery, part fashion boutique, Show Pony (61) (1543 Echo Park Ave., 213-482-7676, www.iloveshow pony.com, W–Sa noon–6PM, Su noon–5PM) dons a mix of vintage duds and handmade clothing by local artists. Luxe de Ville (62) (2157 W. Sunset Blvd., 213-353-0135,

www.luxedeville.com, M–Sa noon–7PM, Su noon–5PM) also blends vintage togs with funky designs from the likes of Imaginary Foundation and Rockett Clothing. Accessories like jewelry and sunglasses are king. Flounce Vintage (63) (1555 Echo Park Ave., 213-481-1975, www.flouncevintage.com, Tu–Su 11:30AM– 6:30PM) leans heavily toward feminine, spanning fashion from Victorian to the '70s. Lemon Frog Shop (64) (1202 N. Alvarado St., 213-413-2143, daily 11:30AM–7:30PM) has a plethora of recycled retro— from shoes to dresses to charm jewelry. Seraph Cosmetics, an organic makeup line, is also sold here. Sirens and Sailors (65) (1104 Mohawk St., 213-483-5423, www.sirensandsailors.com, M–Sa noon–7PM, Su till 6PM) features a mix of offbeat local and emerging East Coast designers.

WHERE TO STAY

America's Best Value Inn (66) ($) (811 N. Alvarado St., 213-413-0050, www.americasbestvalueinn.com) offers 25 basic rooms.

HIGHLAND PARK/EAGLE ROCK

• SNAPSHOT •

Bohos and artists looking to expand beyond uber-hip Silver Lake, Echo Park, and Los Feliz borders are heading east to outer edges. The area of Northeast L.A., or NeLA, is gaining in popularity for its arts and nightlife scenes, especially the neighborhoods of Highland Park and Eagle Rock. This burgeoning area was once filled with sycamore trees, native plants, and the Arroyo Seco, a tributary of the Los Angeles River. Silent film stars and social elite flocked to the Highlands  around the turn of the century, but flood issues spurred the stream's damming and building of first freeway Arroyo Seco Parkway. Over the years, demographics changed, with the elite heading to Western L.A., replaced by a Latino and Filipino population. Filmmakers still favor Highland Park's hillside setting and historic homes, as well as neighboring Eagle Rock, featured in *Reservoir Dogs* and *Top Gun*. For years, Eagle Rock, named for a large rock formation, the shadow of which resembles a bird, was a hotbed for the hot rod culture. Today, Colorado Boulevard is a hub for bars and restaurants, while Figueroa Street is Highland Park's main thoroughfare.

PLACES TO SEE
Landmarks:

Though many of Highland Park's historic homes were razed between the '50s and '70s, it still has a diverse collection. One of the most notable is the turn-of-the-century stone and concrete **Charles F. Lummis Home and Garden (67)** *(200 E. Ave. 43, 323-222-0546, free tours F–Su noon–4PM)*, home of the *Los Angeles Times*'s first city editor and founder of the Southwest Museum (see below). Eight other landmark mansions were relocated for preservation purposes to the **Heritage Square Museum (68)** *(3800 Homer St., 323-225-2700, www.heritage square.org, F–Su noon–5PM)*, including the colorful 1887-built **Hale House**. The **Longfellow-Hasting House** is one of fewer than 500 remaining octagonal structures built in the United States. **Debs Park (69)** *(4235 Monterey Rd., 213-847-3988, daily dawn to dusk)* boasts over 250 acres of hiking trails. The **Audubon Center** at Debs Park is the society's first urban nature center.

Arts & Entertainment:

The **Southwest Museum of the American Indian (70)** *(234 Museum Dr., 323-221-2164, autrynationalcenter.org)* is under renovation. Part of the **Autry National Center**, the museum is home to one of the world's most important Native American collections, with some 250,000 items. Galleries are closed, but the museum store and some exhibition halls are open on weekends *(noon–5PM)*. Plans are to find a larger space and refurbish the current building for cultural use. The **Los Angeles Police Historical Society Museum (71)** *(6045 York Blvd., 323-344-9445, www.laphs.com, M–F 10AM–4PM, third Sa of the month 9AM–3PM)* is housed in Highland Park's former police station, dubbed Old Number 11. Its collection focuses on the LAPD history, including old uniforms and weapons. **Center for the Arts Eagle Rock (72)** *(2225 Colorado Blvd., 323-226-1617, www.centerarts eaglerock.org)* presents performances by Argentinean guitarists, poetry readings, ballet productions, and more.

PLACES TO EAT & DRINK
Where to Eat:

Follow the neon to Eagle Rock's **Casa Bianca Pizza Pie (73) ($)** *(1650 Colorado Blvd., 323-256-9617, www.casabiancapizza.com, Tu–Th 4PM–midnight, F–Sa 4PM–1AM)*, a  traditional pizza parlor, replete with red-checkered tablecloths. The institution still draws a crowd for thin-crust pies topped with sausage or other specialties. Those in-the-know sink into pastrami with cheese or barbecue pulled-pork sandwiches at **Oinkster (74) ($)** *(2005 Colorado Blvd., 323-255-6465, www.oinkster.com, M–Th 11AM–10PM, F–Sa 11AM–11PM, Su 11AM–9PM)*, in a '50s Dairy Queen. Start the day at **Auntie Em's Kitchen (75) ($)** *(4616 Eagle Rock Blvd., 323-255-0800, www.auntieemskitchen.com, M–F 8AM–7PM, Sa–Su 8AM–4PM)* with buttermilk pancakes. Amid all the pizza and barbecue, French beacon **Café Beaujolais (76) ($$)** *(1712 Colorado Blvd., 323-255-5111, Tu–Th 5PM–9PM,*

F–Su till10PM) serves coq au vin and escargot. Highland Park's **The York (77) ($)** *(5018 York Blvd., 323-255-9675, www.theyorkonyork.com, daily 5PM–2AM, Sa–Su brunch 10:30AM–2:30PM)* serves pub grub with its on-tap and bottled beers.

Bars & Nightlife:
Ghoulish **Little Cave (78)** *(5922 N. Figueroa St., 323-255-6871, www.littlecavebar.com, daily 5PM–2AM)* dons all shades of dark, from its cave decor to black, vodka-based Count choc-ula and Bat-tini cocktails. **Footsie's (79)** *(2640 N. Figueroa St., 323-221-6900, daily 4PM–2AM)* steps into New Orleans territory with its bourbon selection and lounge atmosphere. Locals come for cheap beers and the varied jukebox. **Mr. T's Bowl (80)** *(5621-½ N. Figueroa St., 323-256-7561, mrtsbowl. tripod.com, daily 1PM–2AM)* first opened in 1929 as a garage and later became a bowling alley. Today, L.A.'s underground fills the divelike space with live music. Eagle Rock pours a stiff drink under the dim lights of **The Chalet (81)** *(1630 Colorado Blvd., 323-258-8800, daily 7PM–2AM)*, a local artists' chill-out spot. An eclectic jukebox spins everything from funk to indie rock.

WHERE TO SHOP
It's impossible to walk out of tiny Owl Talk (82) *(5060 Eagle Rock Blvd., 323-258-2465, www.owltalk.com, M–Th 11AM–7PM, F–Sa 11AM–6PM, Su 11AM–3PM)* empty-handed. Vintage '60s beaded dresses and pillbox hats are just some of the treasures. For casual designs from trendsetting artists, Lily Simone (83) *(5022 Eagle*

Rock Blvd., 323-254-0530, www.shoplilysimone.com, Tu–F 11AM–7PM, Sa 11AM–6PM, Su 11AM–4PM) carries styles from Mike & Chris, Splendid, and Ella Moss, among others. Selling urban street clothing by day, Eagle Rock Underground (84) (4690 Eagle Rock Blvd., 323-551-6983, Tu–Su noon–7PM) showcases local DJs and artists by night. Go green at Regeneration (85) (1649 Colorado Blvd., 323-344-0430, www.shopregeneration.com, Tu–Su noon–6PM), with everything from lanterns of recycled cans to eco-friendly shoes. Imix Book Store (86) (5052 Eagle Rock Blvd., 323-257-2512, www.imixbooks. com, M–Sa 11AM–7PM, Su till 4PM) specializes in political, social, and historical titles.

WHERE TO STAY
Basic lodging options in NeLA include Best Western Eagle Rock Inn (87) ($-$$) (2911 Colorado Blvd., 323-256-7711, www.bestwestern.com) and the Eagle Rock Motel (88) ($) (7041 N. Figueroa St., 323-256-5106, www.eaglerockmotel.com).

chapter 4

HOLLYWOOD

WEST HOLLYWOOD

BEVERLY HILLS/CENTURY CITY

HOLLYWOOD
WEST HOLLYWOOD
BEVERLY HILLS/CENTURY CITY

Places to See:

1. Hollywood Sign
2. HOLLYWOOD WALK
   OF FAME ★
3. Hollywood and Vine
4. Capitol Records Tower
5. Hollywood Forever
   Cemetery
6. Paramount Studios
7. Hollywood Reservoir
8. RockWalk
9. Grauman's Chinese Theater
10. El Capitan Theatre
11. Egyptian Theater
12. Kodak Theatre
13. Pantages Theatre
14. ArcLight Cinemas
15. Hollywood Museum
16. Hollywood Bowl
48. Sunset Strip
49. Sunset Plaza
50. Santa Monica Boulevard
51. Avenues of Art & Design
52. Pacific Design Center
53. MAK Center for Art &
    Architecture
54. Kantor/Feuer Gallery

55. The Improv
98. RODEO DRIVE ★
99. Greystone Mansion
100. Century City
101. Paley Center for Media
102. Gagosian Gallery
103. Ace Gallery
104. Museum of Tolerance

★ *Top Pick*

Places to Eat & Drink:

17. Providence
18. the hungry cat
19. Yamashiro
20. Musso & Frank Grill
21. Osteria Mozza
22. Pizzeria Mozza
23. M Café de Chaya
24. Grub
25. Pink's Hot Dogs
26. Roscoe's House of
    Chicken and Waffles
27. Mashti Malone's Ice Cream
28. The Music Box
29. The Knitting Factory
30. La Velvet Margarita Cantina
31. Three Clubs
32. L'Scorpion

33. The Well
34. Pig N' Whistle
35. Burgundy Room
36. Frolic Room
37. Tiny's K.O.
56. Sona
57. comme Ça
58. The Foundry on Melrose
59. Lucques
60. Koi
61. All' Angelo
62. Table 8
63. Dan Tana's
64. Griddle Café
65. Urth Caffé
66. House of Blues
    Sunset Strip
67. Troubadour
68. Whisky A Go-Go
69. Bar Marmont
70. Skybar
71. Hyde
72. Area
73. Villa
74. The Abbey
75. O-Bar
76. Bar Lubitsch
77. Lola's
105. Spago
106. CUT
107. The Ivy
108. Urasawa
109. Matsuhisa
110. Mastro's Steakhouse

111. La Cachette
112. Craft
113. Nate 'N Al
114. Sprinkles Cupcakes
115. blue on blue
116. Polo Lounge
117. Nic's Beverly Hills

Where to Shop:
38. Hollywood & Highland
39. Amoeba
40. Larry Edmunds
41. Frederick's of Hollywood
42. Hollywood Toys and
    Costumes
78. Tracey Ross
79. Fred Segal
80. Curve
81. Maxfield
82. Paul Smith
83. Jet Rag
84. Decades
85. Bodhi Tree Bookstore
86. Book Soup
87. A Different Light
    Bookstore
88. Japan LA
89. Kidrobot
98. Rodeo Drive
118. Two Rodeo
119. Harry Winston
120. Dolce & Gabbana
121. Kitson
122. Lisa Kline

123. Taschen
124. Westfield Century City

Where to Stay:
43. Renaissance Hollywood
    Hotel & Spa
44. Hollywood Roosevelt Hotel
45. Magic Castle Hotel
46. Highland Gardens Hotel
47. Orange Drive Hostel
90. Chateau Marmont
91. The Standard
92. Mondrian

93. Andaz West Hollywood
94. Sunset Tower Hotel
95. London West Hollywood
96. Grafton on Sunset
97. Orbit Hotel and Hostel
125. Beverly Hills Hotel and
     Bungalows
126. Luxe Hotel Rodeo Drive
127. Beverly Wilshire
     Beverly Hills
128. Thompson Beverly Hills
129. Beverly Terrace

HOLLYWOOD

• SNAPSHOT •

From Tinseltown star to down-and-out urchin, Hollywood personifies both glamour and grit. Development of this one-time agricultural zone began in the late 1800s; by 1904, the area connected to Downtown by a Hollywood Boulevard trolley. Cecil B. DeMille directed *Squaw Man*, the first feature film here, in 1913, and the industry took off. At its apogee, the area's glitz was reflected by the number of film studios, record companies, and radio businesses. But after its stars moved to more exclusive Beverly Hills, the entertainment industry exited, and the Hollywood 'hood started looking more like New York's seedy Times Square of old rather than the seductive siren the name implies. That story is changing, thanks to a revitalization plan that includes residential and commercial projects centered on Hollywood Boulevard, however. The Hollywood & Highland shopping/entertainment district is home to the Kodak Theatre, site of the Academy Awards. CBS Columbia Square, formerly CBS Studios, is also slated as a mixed-use project, while a W Hotel and condos are planned for the famed intersection of Hollywood and Vine. Hollywood Boulevard is also home to Thai Town and Little Armenia. On the first Sunday in April, Thai Town celebrates Songkran, the Thai New Year, by closing off Hollywood Boulevard.

PLACES TO SEE
Landmarks:

Hooray for Hollywood and its **Hollywood Sign (1)** *(www.hollywoodsign.org)*, with its 45-foot-tall letters spanning 450

feet along the southern slope of Mount Lee. Erected in 1923 to promote real estate development, it originally said "Hollywoodland." Visible for miles, it can be seen from various locations. One of the best routes is to go north up Beachwood Drive. The entertainment world's contributors are acknowledged on the mile-long **TOP PICK!**

★**HOLLYWOOD WALK OF FAME (2)** *(Hollywood Blvd. from Gower St. to LaBrea Ave., Vine St. from Yucca St. to Sunset Blvd.)*, administered by the **Hollywood Chamber of Commerce** *(7918 Hollywood Blvd., 323-469-8311, www.hollywoodchamber.net)*. Contact them for celebrity-star locations and info on future installations. Its terrazzo-and-brass sidewalk stars commemorate notables ranging from Humphrey Bogart to Big Bird. **Tip:** You'll see signs for a self-guided Hollywood history tour starting with #01 at the location of the Garden Court Apartments *(7021 Hollywood Blvd.)*; visit the chamber Web site *(www.hollywoodchamber.net)* for details. **Hollywood and Vine (3)** was the nexus for film and radio in the 1920s. North of the famed intersection is the **Capitol Records Tower (4)** *(1750 N. Vine St.)*, resembling a stack of records. The light on its tower spells out "Hollywood" in Morse code. Luminaries making final curtain calls at **Hollywood Forever Cemetery (5)** *(6000*

Santa Monica Blvd., 323-469-1181, www.hollywood forever.com, summer daily 8AM–6PM, winter daily 8AM–5PM) include **Rudolph Valentino**, **Jayne Mansfield**, and **Peter Lorre**. Mel Blanc's tombstone reads "That's all, folks!" The 'hood's last major film studio, **Paramount Studios (6)** *(5555 Melrose Ave., 323-956-1777, www.paramount.com)* offers two-hour, behind-the-scenes tours; call for reservations. The Hollywood Hills, part of the eastern Santa Monica Mountains dividing L.A. from the San Fernando Valley, is the site of the William Mulholland–designed **Hollywood Reservoir (7)**, or Lake Hollywood, constructed in 1924 to provide the city with water. There are hiking and jogging trails throughout the area.

Arts & Entertainment:

RockWalk (8) at the Guitar Center *(7425 Sunset Blvd., 323-874-1060, www.rockwalk.com, M–Sa 10AM–6PM, Su 11AM–6PM)* features musician handprints and a memorabilia display at the site of this legendary guitar store. The temple-like **Grauman's Chinese Theater (9)** *(6925 Hollywood Blvd., 323-464-8111, www. manntheatres.com)* is a cultural landmark that dates to 1927; its opening feature was Cecil B. DeMille's *King of Kings*. Though it still shows movies, the theater's main claim to fame is its courtyard of celebrity hand and foot imprints. *(VIP tours available, call 323-463-9576)*. Across the street, **El Capitan Theatre (10)** *(6968 Hollywood Blvd., http://disney.go.com/disney pictures/el_capitan)*, now owned by Disney, opened a year before Sid Grauman's. Newly restored, it presents films and live performances. **Egyptian Theater (11)** *(6712 Hollywood Blvd., 323-466-3456, www.egyptiantheatre. com)*, also restored, is the home of American Cinematheque. Visitors enjoy its 55-minute Forever Hollywood documentary; call for schedule and tour info. **Kodak Theatre (12)** *(6801 Hollywood Blvd., 323-308-6300, www.kodaktheatre.com)* began hosting the Academy Awards *(www.oscars.org)* in 2001 and showcases top acts such as Prince and events like *American Idol* finals. Call for information on guided tours. The site of the Oscars from 1949 to 1959, **Pantages Theatre (13)** *(6233 Hollywood Blvd., 323-468-1770, www.pantagestheater.com)* now presents Broadway musicals. One of the best spots to catch a Hollywood blockbuster in Hollywood: **ArcLight Cinemas (14)** *(6360 W. Sunset Blvd., 323-464-4226, www.arclight cinemas.com)*, a state-of-the-art multiscreen complex that also features a refurbished, early-1960s three-projector **Cinerama Dome**. For true Tinseltown, try the **Hollywood Museum (15)** *(1660 N. Highland Ave., 323-464-7776, www.thehollywoodmuseum.com, W–Su 10AM–5PM)*, boasting some 10,000 pieces of memorabilia, such as boxing gloves from *Rocky* and a Rolls Royce used by Cary Grant. It's housed in an Art Deco landmark that was a 1928 Max Factor beauty salon. One of the city's premier entertainment venues since 1922, the **Hollywood Bowl (16)** *(2301 N. Highland Ave., 323-850-2000 www.hollywoodbowl.com)* exudes glamour. Summer home of the Los Angeles Philharmonic, the 18,000-seat amphitheater has hosted the Beatles, Pavarotti, and Baryshnikov. On-site: the small **Hollywood Bowl Museum** *(2301 N. Highland Ave., 323-*

850-2058, Tu–Sa 10AM–showtime, Su 4PM–showtime; off season: Tu–F 10AM–5PM).

PLACES TO EAT & DRINK
Where to Eat:

Providence (17) ($$$) *(5955 Melrose Ave., 323-460-4170, www.providencela.com, M–F 6PM–10PM, F noon–2:30PM, Sa 5:30PM–10PM, Su 5:30PM–9PM)* resides on many a "Best Restaurant" list for seafood delights and presentation. Seafood is also the call of **the hungry cat (18) ($$)** *(1535 N. Vine St., 323-462-2155, www.thehungrycat.com, M–Sa noon–midnight, raw bar noon–1AM, Su 11AM–10PM, raw bar 11AM–11PM)*, where patrons cozy up to a zinc bar for raw oysters, crab cakes, and littleneck clams. Sushi denizens seek out **Yamashiro (19) ($$$)** *(1999 N. Sycamore Ave., 323-466-5125, www.yamashirorestaurant.com, Su–Th 5:30PM–10PM, F–Sa till 11PM, Lounge Su–Th 5PM–midnight, F–Sa till 1AM)* for sashimi and sensational views. Dating to

1919, **Musso & Frank Grill (20) ($$)** *(6667 Hollywood Blvd., 323-467-7788, Tu–Sa 11AM–11PM)* is Hollywood's oldest eatery. Celeb patrons have included Chaplin, Faulkner, Hemingway, Bukowski, and Orson Wells. High-energy **Osteria Mozza (21) ($$-$$$)** *(6602 Melrose Ave., 323-297-0100, www.mozza-la.com, M–F 5:30PM–11PM, Sa 5PM–11PM, Su till 10PM)* is one of L.A.'s hottest tables, showcasing the creativity of chef Mario Batali and mozzarella maven Nancy Silverton. The duo also run local favorite **Pizzeria Mozza (22) ($-$$)**

(641 N. Highland Ave., 323-297-0101, www.mozza-la.com, daily noon– midnight), with its unique take on the pie, such as pizza with wild spinach and olive tapenade.

In search of something healthy? **M Café de Chaya (23) ($)** *(7119 Melrose Ave., 323-525-0588, http://mcafedechaya. com, M–Sa 9AM–10PM, Su 9AM–9PM)* delivers delicious haute macrobiotic cuisine—sans refined sugar, eggs, dairy, red meat, or poultry—for everyone. At the opposite end of the spectrum, **Grub (24) ($)** *(911 N. Seward St., 323-461-3663, www.grub-la.com, M–F 11AM–3PM, Sa–Su 9AM–3PM, Su–Th 5PM–9PM, F–Sa till 10PM)* packs 'em in for French toast and grilled cheese. Legendary **Pink's Hot Dogs (25) ($)** *(709 N. La Brea Ave., 323-931-4223, www.pinkshollywood.com, daily 9:30AM–2AM, F–Sa till 3AM)* is to L.A. what Nathan's is to New York, and then some. Local legend **Roscoe's House of Chicken and Waffles (26) ($)** *(1514 N. Gower St., 323-466-7453, www.roscoeschickenandwaffles.com, Su–Th 8AM–midnight, F–Sa 8AM–4AM)* is a late-night magnet. Rosewater ice cream is a must-try at **Mashti Malone's Ice Cream (27)** *(1525 N. La Brea Ave., 323-874-0144, www.mashtimalone.com, M–Th 11:30AM–11:30PM, F–Sa till midnight)*.

Bars & Nightlife:
Located in the 1926 Henry Fonda Theatre, **The Music Box (28)** *(6126 Hollywood Blvd., 323-464-0808, www. henryfondatheater.com, hours vary)* rocks

with live indie, vintage punk, and alternative acts. **The Knitting Factory (29)** *(7021 Hollywood Blvd., 323-463-0204, www.knittingfactory.com, hours vary)*, the West Coast outlet of the New York institution, hosts alternative, underground, punk, and new talent. Kitschy **La Velvet Margarita Cantina (30)** *(1612 N. Cahuenga Blvd., 323-469-2000, www.velvetmargarita.com, M–F 11:30AM–2AM, Sa–Su 6PM–2AM)* welcomes with salsa and roving mariachis. Powerful drinks, rock music, and no cover keep cool **Three Clubs (31)** *(1123 Vine St., 323-462-6441, www.threeclubs.com, 6PM–2AM)* on the short list of local hangouts. **L'Scorpion (32)** *(6679 Hollywood Blvd., 323-464-3026, www.scorpion hollywood.com, daily 6PM–2AM)* seduces with bordello decor and buzz-inducing tequila. **The Well (33)** *(6255 W. Sunset Blvd., 323-467-9355, M–Su 5PM–2AM)* mixes unpretentious with uber-cool—no cover, no lines, just a chill lounge. Landmark **Pig N' Whistle (34)** *(6714 Hollywood Blvd., 323-463-0000, www.pignwhistle.com, Su–W 11:30AM–1:30AM, Th–Sa, 11:30AM–2AM)* hosted Judy Garland's 15th birthday and the Oscars' first after-party. Rock-'n'-roll crowd haunts include **Burgundy Room (35)** *(1621-½ N. Cahuenga Blvd., 323-465-7530, daily 8PM–2AM)*, **Frolic Room (36)** *(6245 Hollywood Blvd., 323-462-5890, M–Su 11AM–2AM)*, and **Tiny's K.O. (37)** *(6377 Hollywood Blvd., 323-462-9777, www.tinysko.com, daily 4PM–2AM)*.

WHERE TO SHOP

Hollywood & Highland (38) *(6801 Hollywood Blvd., 323-817-0200, www.hollywoodandhighland.com, M–Sa 10AM–10PM, Su 10AM–7PM)* shopping and entertainment complex features names like **Fossil**, **Louis Vuitton**, and **Lucky Brand Jeans**. A **Visitor Information Center** *(323-467-6412)* provides guidance through the maze. Music lovers are attracted to Amoeba (39) *(6400 W. Sunset Blvd., 323-245-6400, M–Sa 10:30AM–11PM, Su 11PM–9PM)* for its vast selection and special events. In business for over 60 years, Larry Edmunds (40) *(6644 Hollywood Blvd., 323-463-3273, www.larryedmunds. com, daily 10AM–5:30PM)* carries over 500,000 movie photos and other memorabilia. Frederick's of Hollywood (41) *(6751 Hollywood Blvd., 323-957-5953, www.fredericks.com, M–Sa 10AM–9PM, Su 11AM–7PM)* flaunts its stuff in a location that's smaller than its original 1947 flagship store, and its bra museum has been minimized, but the merchandise still sets standards in sexy. Halloween central, Hollywood Toys and Costumes (42) *(6600 Hollywood Blvd., 323-464-4444, www.hollywoodtoysandcostumes. com, M–F 9AM–7PM, Sa–Su 10:30AM–7PM)* sells everything from pirate shirts to Shrek ensembles.

WHERE TO STAY

Chic **Renaissance Hollywood Hotel & Spa (43)** ($$-$$$) *(1755 N. Highland Ave., 323-856-1200, www.renais sancehollywood.com)*, part of Hollywood & Highland

Center, is done up with 1950s furnishings and offers fine views. The 1927 **Hollywood Roosevelt Hotel (44)** **($$$)** *(7000 Hollywood Blvd., 323-462-8056, www.holly woodroosevelt.com)* enjoyed a recent restoration with designer Dodd Mitchell at the helm. It's home to the **Dakota ($$$)** steakhouse *(323-769-8888, Su–Th 6PM–10:30PM, F–Sa till 11PM)* and popular **Tropicana** bar *(323-769-7260, 7AM–6PM, 9PM–2AM)*, at the David Hockney pool. Attentive service and spacious rooms are no illusion at **Magic Castle Hotel (45) ($$$)** *(7025 Franklin Ave., 323-851-0800, www.magiccastlehotel. com)*. Cocktails are served and magic shows performed within the adjacent private club, home of the Academy of Magical Arts. Rat Packers and Janis Joplin, among others, stayed at the former Hollywood Landmark, now the **Highland Gardens Hotel (46) ($$)** *(7047 Franklin Ave., 323-850-0536, www.highlandgardenshotel.com)*, providing basic rooms and a pool and garden. A converted Hollywood mansion, **Orange Drive Hostel (47) ($)** *(1764 N. Orange Dr., 323-850-0350, www.orangedrivehostel. com)* offers dorm or private accommodation for those on a shoestring.

WEST HOLLYWOOD

• SNAPSHOT •

Celebrity sightings, A-list bars, haute cuisine, galleries, and boutiques, combined with a progressive counterculture, make up this popular destination. West Hollywood, or "WeHo," buzzes with tourists and locals shopping on Melrose Avenue, clubbing along Sunset Strip, or dining on La Cienega's restaurant row. The area's history lies in its politics. WeHo sprouted as Sherman, California, established by Moses Sherman, who used it as a base for his Los Angeles Pacific Railway. The area had fewer regulations than districts incorporated into Los Angeles County, paving the way for nightclubs and casinos to open on Sunset Boulevard along the stretch now known as the Sunset Strip. The Strip and surrounds attracted stars (and later, a hippie culture) to its fabled clubs, such as Whisky A Go-Go. In the 1970s, gays and lesbians moved here to escape the jurisdiction of the LAPD; today, West Hollywood is world-renowned for its gay bars, clubs, and pride festival. On its eastern Fairfax District border, the community is also home to a concentration of Russian Jews. A coalition of gays, Jews, and seniors helped push to make West Hollywood its own city, succeeding in 1984. Modern WeHo has its own laws, including bans on religious discrimination, harassment based on sexual orientation, and even a law against declawing cats.

PLACES TO SEE
Landmarks:

Sunset Strip (48) *(Sunset Blvd. bet. Hollywood/Beverly Hills, www.thesunsetstrip.com)* was the epicenter of glamour in the 1930s and 1940s at the height of WeHo's flirtation with moviemakers. When the film industry faded, the strip became known for its music scene, and still is today. One prime Strip location: **Sunset Plaza (49)** *(bet. Alta Loma Rd./Horn Ave.)*, filled with boutiques, cafés, and celebrities. West Hollywood's gay and lesbian community centers around **Santa Monica Boulevard (50)** *(bet. La Brea Ave./Doheny Dr.)*, a stretch often referred to as **Boys' Town** *(GoGayWestHollywood.com)*. This area does it up for the Christopher Street West Gay Pride Parade in June, and for October 31, when the West Hollywood Halloween Carnaval takes to the streets.

Arts & Entertainment:

The **Avenues of Art & Design (51)** *(Melrose Ave., Robertson Blvd., and Beverly Blvd., www.avenuesartdesign.com)* are home to over 30 galleries, antique and design stores, coffeehouses, bookshops, and boutiques. The neighborhood's centerpiece: mammoth **Pacific Design Center (52)** *(8687 Melrose Ave., 310-657-0800, www.thepacific designcenter.com, M–F 9AM–5PM)*. Catering to interior  designers with 130 showrooms, it also features two Wolfgang Puck restaurants, a luxury film venue, and the **Museum of Contemporary Art**

(MOCA) *(213-626-6222, T, W, F 11AM–5PM, Th till 8PM, Sa–Su till 6PM)*. Staged in avant Austrian architect Rudolph Schindler's 1922 **Schindler House**, the **MAK Center for Art & Architecture (53)** *(835 N. Kings Rd., 323-651-1510, www.makcenter.org, W–Su 11AM–6PM)* offers tours and exhibitions. West Hollywood is home to a plethora of galleries, many on Melrose, such as the contemporary **Kantor/Feuer Gallery (54)** *(7025 Melrose Ave., 323-933-6976, www.kantorfeuer.com, Tu–Sa 10AM–6PM)*. The **Improv (55)** *(8162 Melrose Ave., 323-651-2583, www.hollywoodimprov.com, get there at 7PM for 7:30PM show, dinner at 6PM)* is a launching pad for up-and-coming comics.

PLACES TO EAT & DRINK
Where to Eat:
Sophisticated setting and award-winning cuisine keep **Sona (56) ($$$)** *(401 N. La Cienega Blvd., 310-659-7708, www.sonarestaurant.com, Tu–Th 6PM–10PM, F–Sa 6PM–11PM)* at the apex of L.A. culinary couture; chef David Myers' French brasserie **comme Ça (57) ($$-$$$)** *(8479 Melrose Ave., 323-782-1178, www.comme carestaurant.com, Su–Th 8AM–11PM, F–Sa 8AM–midnight)* also garners raves. At **The Foundry on Melrose (58) ($$$)** *(7465 Melrose Ave., 323-651-0915, www.thefoundryonmelrose.com, Tu–W 6PM–10PM, Th–Sa 6PM–11PM, Su 5:30PM–10PM, F–Su bar till 2AM)*, chef Eric Greenspan wins accolades; his Sunday "Be Bop Brunch" features live jazz. Suzanne Goin of **Lucques (59) ($$$)** *(8474 Melrose Ave., 323-655-6277, www.lucques. com, M–Tu 6PM–10PM, Tu–Sa noon–2:30PM, W–Sa*

6PM–11PM, Su 5PM–10PM) pleases sophisticated palates, especially with prix fixe Sunday supper. **Koi (60) ($$$)** *(730 N. La Cienega Blvd., www.koirestaurant.com, 310-659-9449, Su–W 6PM–11PM, Th 6PM–11:30PM, F–Sa 6PM–midnight)* presents Japanese fusion in Zen-inspired surrounds. A bit peckish post-club? Venetian-style **All' Angelo (61) ($$$)** *(7166 Melrose Ave., 323-933-9540, www.allangelo.com, M–F noon–2:30PM, M–Sa 6PM–10:30PM)* lifts Melrose to new heights. **Table 8 (62) ($$$)** *(7661 Melrose Ave., www.table8la.com, 323-782-8258, M–Th 6PM–10PM, F–Sa 6PM–10:30PM)* features late-night small plates. **Dan Tana's (63) ($$)** *(9071 Santa Monica Blvd., 310-275-9444, www.dantanasrestaurant. com, daily 5PM–1:30AM)* has been tempting with Old World Italian and behemoth portions for four decades. Nobody does pancakes like **Griddle Café (64) ($)** *(7916 W. Sunset Blvd., 323-874-0377, www.thegriddlecafe.com, M–F 7AM–4PM, Sa–Su 8AM–4PM).* Enjoy L.A.'s "Best Caffé Latte" *(L.A. Times)* on the patio at hip **Urth Caffé (65) ($)** *(8565 Melrose Ave., 310-659-0628, www.urth caffe.com, M–Th, Su 9AM–11PM, F–Sa 9AM–midnight).*

Bars & Nightlife:

Sunset Strip (48) remains a force in live music. Discover indie sensations at **House of Blues Sunset Strip (66)** *(8430 Sunset Blvd., 323-848-5100, www.hob.com, hours vary),* and don't miss its Sunday Gospel Brunch *(10AM and 1PM—call for reservations).* Historic **Troubadour (67)** *(9081 Santa Monica Blvd., 310-276-6168, www.trouba dour.com)* helped further the careers of Tom Waits and Guns N' Roses, among many others. Since 1964,

Whisky A Go-Go (68) *(8901 Sunset Blvd., 310-652-4202, www.whiskyagogo.com)* has played host to everyone from Janis Joplin to the L.A. punk crowd. Hotel bars take center stage in WeHo, with star-studded **Bar Marmont (69)** *(Chateau Marmont, 8171 W. Sunset Blvd., 323-650-0575, www.chateaumarmont.com, daily 6PM–2AM)* topping the list. **Skybar (70)** *(Mondrian, 8440 W. Sunset Blvd., 213-848-6025, www.mondrianhotel.com, daily 6PM–2AM)* still draws a line and the occasional celeb. Paris and peers sometimes imbibe at **Hyde (71)** *(8029 W. Sunset Blvd., 323-525-2444, www.sbeent.com, daily 10PM–2AM)*. The club's owners also run **Area (72)** *(643 N. La Cienega Blvd., 310-652-2012, M–W, F–Su 10PM–2AM)*, where the Botoxed and beautiful take the dance floor. There's more star spotting outside **Villa (73)** *(8623 Melrose Ave., www.villalounge.com, 310-289-8623, daily 9PM–2AM)*, an A-list-only zone. Don't miss West Hollywood's best people-watching patio,

The Abbey (74) *(692 N. Robertson Blvd., 310-855-9977, www.abbeyfoodand bar.com, daily 9AM–2AM)*, popular with gays, straights, locals, and Hollywood heavies. Happy hour at gay fave **O-Bar (75)** *(8279 Santa Monica Blvd., 323-822-3300, www.obarrestaurant.com,* *Su–W 6PM–midnight, Th–Sa 6PM–2AM)* features drinks like The Exorcist and Spring Break. Russian-themed **Bar Lubitsch (76)** *(7702 Santa Monica Blvd., 323-654-1234, M–F 6PM–2AM, Sa–Su 8PM–2AM)* boasts more than 200 vodkas. **Lola's (77)** *(945 N. Fairfax Ave., 323-654-5652, www.lolasla.com, nightly 5:30PM–2AM)* serves up 50 varieties of the martini to a chill, 30-something clientele.

WHERE TO SHOP

Star couturier **Tracey Ross (78)** *(8595 W. Sunset Blvd., 310-854-1996, www.traceyross.com, M–Sa 10AM–7PM, Su noon–5PM)* stocks irresistible fashions. Prepare to spend. Melrose institution **Fred Segal (79)** *(8118 Melrose Ave., 323-655-3734, M–Sa 10AM–7PM, Su noon–6PM)* still packs a punch with trendy labels. Labels like Preen and Isabel Marant lure Cameron Diaz and others to **Curve (80)** *(154 N. Robertson Blvd., 310-360-8008, www.shopcurve.com, M–Sa 11AM–7PM, Su noon–6PM)*. **Maxfield (81)** *(8825 Melrose Ave., 310-274-8800, M–Sa 11AM–7PM)* offers a sophisticated slant on fashion, while **Paul Smith (82)** *(8221 Melrose St., 323-951-4800, www.paulsmith.co.uk, M–Sa 11AM–7PM, Su noon–6PM)* is playful in his sprawling, hot pink boutique. For vintage, shop **Jet Rag (83)** *(825 N. La Brea Ave., 323-939-0528, M–Sa 11AM–7:30PM, Su 9AM–7PM)*, known for its selection of jeans and dresses. **Tip:** Sunday mornings, bargain merch is lugged to the parking lot for a dollar sale; and **Decades (84)** *(8214-½ Melrose Ave., 323-655-0223, www.decadesinc.com, M–Sa, 11:30AM–6PM)* has dressed the likes of Nicole Kidman and J Lo. **Bodhi Tree Bookstore (85)** *(8585 Melrose Ave., 310-659-1733, www.bodhitree.com, M–Su 10AM–11PM)* is devoted to metaphysics and mysticism. **Book Soup (86)** *(8818 W. Sunset Blvd., 310-659-3110, www.booksoup.com, daily 9AM–10PM)* is one of WeHo's last large independent bookstores. **A Different Light Bookstore (87)** *(8853 Santa Monica Blvd., 310-854-*

6601, *www.adlbooks.com, daily 10AM–11PM)* focuses on gay and lesbian lit. Japan LA (88) *(648 N. Fuller Ave., 323-934-5201, www.japanla.com, Su–Th 11AM– 7PM, F–Sa 11AM–8PM)* hawks Japanese pop-culture gifts and T-shirts from Gama-go. Art toys by the likes of Frank Kozik are the focus of Kidrobot (89) *(7972 Melrose Ave., 323-782-1411, www.kidrobot.com, M–Sa 11AM–7PM, Su till 6PM),* as is its own line of funky apparel.

WHERE TO STAY

Modeled after Loire Valley's Château d'Amboise, Chateau Marmont (90) ($$$) *(8221 W. Sunset Blvd., 323-656-1010, www.chateaumarmont.com)* caters to celebrity clientele. This is the place where John Belushi died. Its hotelier, André Balazs, is also responsible for The Standard (91) ($$) *(8300 W. Sunset Blvd., 323-650-9090, www.standardhotels.com),* where shag carpeting, a blue Astroturf sundeck, **Poolside Lounge**, and nightly front-desk DJs up the groovy vibe. Chic, elegant Mondrian (92) ($$$) *(8440 W. Sunset Blvd., 323-650-8999, www.mondrianhotel.com)* is the work of hotelier Ian Schrager and French designer Philippe Starck; expect simple white rooms with city views. Legendary rock lodging spot Andaz West Hollywood (93) ($$) *(8401 W. Sunset Blvd., 323-656-1234, www.westhollywood. hyatt.com)* may not be quite as lively as in its heyday

(when Led Zeppelin rode motorcycles through the hotel, inspiring the nickname "Riot Hyatt"), but Hyatt's new brand

is more upscale, and their motto is "sophistication made simple." Meticulously restored Art Deco **Sunset Tower Hotel (94) ($$-$$$)** *(8358 W. Sunset Blvd., 323-654-7100, www.sunsettowerhotel.com)* has hosted the likes of Marilyn Monroe, Truman Capote, and Howard Hughes. Its popular **Tower Bar** is located in Bugsy Siegel's old apartment. All-suite **London West Hollywood (95) ($$$)** *(1020 N. San Vicente Blvd., 866-282-4560, www.londonwesthollywood.com)* (formerly Bel Age) boasts a rooftop pool and spa. Feng shui and theme suites, such as the "Rat Pack Suite," amp the hip factor at **Grafton on Sunset (96) ($$)** *(8462 W. Sunset Blvd., 323-654-4600, www.graftononsunset.com)*. Mod **Orbit Hotel and Hostel (97) ($)** *(7950 Melrose Ave., 323-655-1510, www.orbithotel.com)* dubs itself "sexiest hostel in the world." Featured: movie nights, barbecues, and special access to select clubs.

BEVERLY HILLS/CENTURY CITY

• SNAPSHOT •

Ostentatious mansions, Rolls Royces, immaculate streets, exclusive shops, and the Hollywood elite are all hallmarks of Beverly Hills. Preened, primed, nipped, tucked, this is the place for stargazing and window shopping. Development of this once-rural area began in 1919, when Douglas Fairbanks and Mary Pickford built their Pickfair home on Summit Drive. Other stars streamed in, attracted to the larger tracts of land. The city of Los Angeles threatened to annex Beverly Hills in 1923, but the effort failed, allowing Beverly to remain independent. Today, retail rules; the main commercial area, dubbed the Golden

Triangle, is bounded by North Canon Drive, Wilshire Boulevard, and Santa Monica Boulevard South; famous Rodeo Drive runs through its center.

PLACES TO SEE
Landmarks:

Fashionistas worth their weight in plastic are roped in by ★RODEO DRIVE (98) *(from Wilshire to Santa Monica Blvds.)*. A "who's who" of haute couture, the thoroughfare is

TOP PICK!

perfect for celebrity spotting and window-shopping. The city's most famous shopping street is only three

blocks long, and probably one of the most expensive shopping areas in the world. The Gothic **Greystone Mansion (99)** *(905 Loma Vista Dr., 310-550-4654, www.greystonemansion.org)*, a filming location for everything from *The Big Lebowski* to *There Will Be Blood*, was a gift from oil baron Edward L. Doheny to his son in 1928; the son lived here only four months before an untimely death. Check Web site for tour and special event information. Built in the early 1960s on 20th Century Studios' back lot, **Century City (100)** *(www.centurycitycc.com)* includes offices, residences, and entertainment businesses. Its main features: **Century City Towers** *(Ave. of the Stars and Constellation Blvd.)*, designed by Minoru Yamasaki, and shopping mall **Westfield Century City (124)** *(10250 Santa Monica Blvd., 310-277-3898, www.westfield. com/centurycity)*.

Arts & Entertainment:

Paley Center for Media (101) *(465 N. Beverly Dr., 310-786-1000, www.paleycenter.org, W–Su noon–5PM)*, the former Museum of Television & Radio, celebrates broadcasting with thousands of programs spanning 100 years of TV and radio history. Larry Gagosian's **Gagosian Gallery (102)** *(456 N. Camden Dr., 310-271-9400, www.gagosian.com, Tu–Sa 10AM–5:30PM)* is an integral part of the local art scene. Another L.A. art staple, **Ace Gallery (103)** *(Institute of Contemporary Art, 9430 Wilshire Blvd., 310-858-9090, www.acegallery.net,*

Tu–Sa 10AM–6PM) exhibits works by Rauschenberg and Warhol. The **Museum of Tolerance (104)** *(9786 W. Pico Blvd., 310-553-8403, www.museumoftolerance.com, M–F 10AM–5PM, Su 11AM–5PM, closes F 3PM Nov–Mar)* combines exhibits about the Holocaust with special events. **Tip:** Call ahead to reserve tickets.

PLACES TO EAT & DRINK
Where to Eat:

Wolfgang Puck's flagship **Spago (105) ($$$)** *(176 N. Canon Dr., 310-385-0880, www.wolfgangpuck.com, M–F 11:30AM–2:15PM, Sa noon–2:30PM, Su–Th 5:30PM–10:30PM, F–Sa 5:30PM–11PM)* still draws an A-list power-lunch crowd. Dining and gawking is de rigueur at Puck's other hotspot, **CUT (106) ($$$)** *(Beverly Wilshire Hotel, 9500 Wilshire Blvd., 310-276-8500, www.wolfgangpuck.com, M–Th 5:30PM–10PM, F–Sa 5:30PM–10:30PM)*. Tom Cruise, Matthew McConaughey, and Avril Lavigne may not require reservations, but the rest of us may find it tough to get one. Yet another celeb hub, **The Ivy (107) ($$$)** *(113 N. Robertson Blvd., 310-274-8303, M–F 11:30AM–10PM, Sa 11AM–11PM, Su 10:30AM–10PM)* serves the likes of Demi Moore, Brad Pitt, executives, tourists, and locals at its outdoor patio. Don't skip dessert. At $275 a head, **Urasawa (108) ($$$$)** *(218 N. Rodeo Dr., 310-247-8939, M–Su 6PM–9PM)* ranks among L.A.'s most extravagant eateries. But Chef Hiroyuki Urasawa's omakase includes

more than 20 decadent courses, some dusted with gold flakes. Restaurateur Nobu Matsuhisa's **Matsuhisa (109) ($$)** *(129 N. La Cienega Blvd., 310-659-9639, www.nobumatsuhisa.com, M–F 11:45AM–2:15PM, Sa–Su 5:30PM–10:15PM)* is another omakase blowout, with over 100 delicacies on the menu. **Mastro's Steakhouse (110) ($$$)** *(246 N. Canon Dr., 310-888-8782, www.mastrossteakhouse.com, Su–Th 5PM–11PM, F–Sa till midnight)* is a favorite for its steaks and Rat Pack–era decor. A mature clientele savors New French delights at **La Cachette (111) ($$$)** *(Century City, 10506 Santa Monica Blvd., 310-470-4992, www.lacachette restaurant.com, M–F noon–2PM, M–Th 6PM–9:30PM, F–Sa 6PM–10:30PM).*

Top chef Tom Colicchio scores with dining sensation **Craft (112) ($$$$)** *(Century City, 10100 Constellation Blvd., 310-279-4180, www.craftrestaurant.com, M–F 11:30AM–2:30PM, M–Th 6PM–10PM, F–Sa till 10:30PM, Su 5PM–9PM)*, renowned for working seasonal ingredients into understated master-pieces.

Jewish deli **Nate 'N Al (113) ($)** *(414 N. Beverly Dr., 310-274-0101, www.natenal.com, M–Su 7AM–9PM)* is just the place if you want a pastrami on rye. Indulge that sweet tooth at **Sprinkles Cupcakes (114) ($)** *(9635 S. Santa Monica Blvd., 310-274-8765, www.sprinkles cupcakes.com, M–Sa 9AM–7PM, Su 10AM–6PM).*

Bars & Nightlife:

Many Hills bars are set in chic hotels. A favorite: relaxed **blue on blue (115)** *(Avalon Hotel, 9400 W. Olympic Blvd., 310-277-5221, www.avalonbeverlyhills.com, daily 7AM–11PM)* restaurant/bar, with pool and cabanas. **Polo Lounge (116)** *(Beverly Hills*

Hotel & Bungalows, 9641 Sunset Blvd., 310-276-2251, www.thebeverlyhillshotel.com, daily 7AM–1:30AM) pours martinis for chic clientele and veteran Hollywood players. **Nic's Beverly Hills (117)** *(453 N. Canon Dr., 310-550-5707, www.nicsbeverlyhills.com, M–Sa 5PM–closing)* is known for its walk-in, drink-in **Vodbox** vodka freezer. Button up.

WHERE TO SHOP

Versace, Prada, Bulgari, Cartier, and more strut their stuff for gold-card holders and window-shoppers alike along **Rodeo Drive (98)** *(www.rodeodrive-bh.com)*. **Two Rodeo (118)** *(2 Rodeo Dr., www.tworodeo.com, M–S 10AM–6PM, Su 11AM–5PM)*, features salons, boutiques (such as Versace and Tiffany), and restaurants. Other standouts: jeweler **Harry Winston (119)** *(310 N. Rodeo Dr., 310-271-8554,*

www.harrywinston.com, M–F 10AM–6PM, Sa 11AM–5PM, Su noon– 5PM) and **Dolce & Gabbana (120)** *(312 N. Rodeo Dr., 310-888-8701, www.dolcegabbana.com, M–Sa 10AM–6PM, Su noon–5PM)*. Upscale boutiques also line **Robertson Boulevard**, including **Kitson (121)** *(115 S. Robertson*

Blvd., 310-859-2652, www.shopkitson.com, M–F 10AM–8PM, Sa 9AM–8PM, Su 11AM–7PM), dressing Nicole Richie, Paris Hilton, and other celebutantes. A "who's who" list of shoppers favor the feminine couture of Lisa Kline (122) *(136 S. Robertson Blvd., 310-246-0907, www.lisakline.com, M–Sa 10AM–7PM, Su noon–7PM)*. Trendy Taschen (123) *(354 N. Beverly Dr., 310-274-4300, www.taschen.com, M–Sa 10AM–7PM, Su noon–5PM)* stocks books on art, architecture, and pop culture. At Westfield Century City (124) *(10250 Santa Monica Blvd., 310-277-3898, www.westfield.com/centurycity, M–Sa 10AM–9PM, Su noon–7PM)*, you'll find Bloomingdale's, Macy's, and dozens of other stores and eateries.

WHERE TO STAY

Splurge on a stay at the 1912 Beverly Hills Hotel and Bungalows (125) ($$$) *(9641 Sunset Blvd., 310-276-2251, www.thebeverlyhillshotel.com)*, as decadent today as when Rudolph Valentino held court here. Boutique Luxe Hotel Rodeo Drive (126) ($$$) *(360 N. Rodeo Dr., 310-273-0300, www.luxehotelrodeodrive.com)* focuses on personal services. Glamorous Beverly Wilshire Beverly Hills (127) ($$$) *(9500 Wilshire Blvd., 310-275-5200, www.fourseasons. com/beverlywilshire)* dates back to 1928. Chic

Thompson Beverly Hills (128) ($$$) *(9360 Wilshire Blvd., 310-273-1400, www.thompsonbeverlyhills.com)* is decked out in late 1970s and early 1980s "cool," thanks to designer Dodd Mitchell. It offers a private rooftop bar/pool lounge and **BondSt ($$$)** *(Su–W 7AM–11PM, Th–Sa till midnight)* sushi restaurant. Asian inspired **Beverly Terrace (129) ($$)** *(469 N. Doheny Dr., 310-274-8141, www.hotelbeverlyterrace.com)* is a bargain for its location, pool, and garden setting. Dine at **Trattoria Amici ($$)** *(310-858-0271, www.tamici.com, M–F noon–2:30PM, daily 6PM–10:30PM)* for traditional Italian.

chapter 5

WESTWOOD

BRENTWOOD/BEL-AIR

WEST L.A.

CULVER CITY

WESTWOOD
BRENTWOOD/BEL-AIR
WEST L.A.
CULVER CITY

Places to See:

1. Los Angeles California Temple
2. Westwood Memorial Park
3. University of California, Los Angeles
4. Armand Hammer Museum of Art and Culture Center
5. Geffen Playhouse
6. Fowler Museum at UCLA
22. GETTY CENTER ★
23. Skirball Cultural Center
24. Leslie Sacks Fine Art
40. Los Angeles National Cemetery
60. Sony Pictures Studio Tour
61. The Jazz Bakery
62. Kirk Douglas Theatre
63. Museum of Jurassic Technology
64. Museum of Design Art & Architecture
65. Blum & Poe
66. Star Eco Station

Places to Eat & Drink:

7. Soleil
8. Napa Valley Grille
9. Gushi
10. Native Foods
11. Lamonica's New York Pizza
12. Diddy Riese Cookies
13. Whiskey Blue
14. Palomino Restaurant Rotisseria Bar
15. Tengu
25. Takao
26. Saketini
27. Sushi Sasabune
28. Katsuya
29. Osteria Latini
30. Toscana
31. Mulholland Grill
32. Vibrato Grill Jazz...etc.
33. Brentwood Restaurant and Lounge
41. The Apple Pan
42. Pinkberry
43. Hide Sushi

★ *Top Pick*

44. Furaibo Restaurant
45. Echigo
46. Nanbankan
47. Wakasan
48. John O'Groats
49. Liquid Kitty
50. Karaoke Bleu
51. Max Karaoke
67. Fraiche
68. Akasha
69. Ford's Filling Station
70. Wilson
71. Café Brasil
72. Tender Greens
73. Hiko Sushi
74. Versailles
75. S&W Country Diner
76. Alibi Room
77. Vinum Populi
78. Backstage Bar & Grill
79. Boardwalk 11
80. Mandrake Bar
81. Cinema Bar
82. Saints & Sinners

Where to Shop:

16. Aahs
17. Skyla
18. Buffalo Exchange
34. Aristeia
35. Dragon Books
36. Grace Home Furnishings
52. Westside Pavilion
53. Giant Robot
54. Tokyo Japanese Outlet
55. Happy Six
56. Children's Book World
57. Out of the Closet
58. Wally's Wines & Spirits
83. Westfield Fox Hills
    Shopping Center
84. HD Buttercup
85. Indie Collective
86. Last Chance Boutique

Where to Stay:

19. W Los Angeles-Westwood
20. Hotel Palomar
    Los Angeles-Westwood
21. Hilgard House Hotel
37. Hotel Bel-Air
38. Hotel Angeleno
39. Luxe Hotel Sunset
    Boulevard
59. Holiday Inn Express West
    Los Angeles
87. Culver Hotel
88. Four Points by Sheraton
    Los Angeles Westside
89. Radisson Hotel
    Los Angeles Westside

WESTWOOD

• SNAPSHOT •

Affluent Westwood is the site of the University of California, Los Angeles (UCLA). Its main shopping district, Westwood Village *(www.westwoodblvd.com)*, is home to galleries, museums, movie theaters, restaurants, and shops. The village, developed in 1928, is an architectural milieu of everything from New Orleans Revival to post-war Modern, and is frequented by students as well as Westside residents of Brentwood, Bel-Air, Holmby Hills, Beverly Hills, and other affluent neighborhoods. Along Westwood Boulevard there is an established Iranian community, dubbed Little Persia.

PLACES TO SEE
Landmarks:

The **Los Angeles California Temple (1)** *(10777 Santa Monica Blvd., 310-474-5569, www.ldschurchtemples. com)*, the second-largest temple operated by The Church of Jesus Christ of Latter-day Saints, sits on land purchased from the Harold Lloyd Motion Picture Company in 1937. The temple's visitors center is open to the public *(daily 9AM–9PM)*. **Westwood Memorial Park (2)** *(1218 Glendon Ave., 310-474-1579, daily 8AM–dusk)* is the resting place of Marilyn Monroe, Dean Martin, and Frank Zappa, among others. The campus of the **University of California, Los Angeles (3)** *(405 Hilgard Ave., 310-825-8764, www.ucla.edu)* is worth exploring for its performance spaces, museums, and the **Franklin D. Murphy Sculpture Garden** *(310-443-7000, www.ham mer.ucla.edu)*, featuring works by Alexander Calder, Auguste Rodin, Henri Matisse, and Henry Moore, among others, and the **Mildred E. Mathias Botanical Garden** *(entrance on Tiverton Ave., 310-825-1260 www.botgard.ucla.edu, M–F 8AM–5PM [4PM in winter], Sa–Su 8AM–4PM)* with more than 5,000 species.

Arts & Entertainment:

 UCLA's **Armand Hammer Museum of Art and Culture Center (4)** *(10899 Wilshire Blvd., 310-443-7000, www.hammer.ucla.edu, Tu–W, F–Sa 11AM–7PM, Th 11AM–9PM, Su 11AM–5PM)* features the collections of its entrepreneurial namesake. Contemporary art mingles with the likes of Monet, van Gogh, and Rembrandt. The museum also houses the **Billy Wilder Theater**, run by the UCLA Film and Television Archive. **Geffen Playhouse (5)** *(10886 Le Conte Ave., 310-208-5454, www.geffenplayhouse.com, M–F 10AM–6PM, Sa–Su 11AM–6PM)* once served as the UCLA Masonic Lodge and the Westwood Playhouse. It was donated to UCLA in the '90s and is named after David Geffen. **Audrey Skirball Kenis Theater** at the Geffen Playhouse was built in 2005 as part of the theater's most recent renovation. The **Fowler Museum at UCLA (6)** *(405 Hilgard Ave., 310-825-4361, www.fowler. ucla.edu, W–Su noon–5PM, Th till 8PM)* focuses on art from Africa, Asia, and the Pacific, as well as the Americas.

UCLA Live *(www.uclalive.org)* presents dance, music, spoken word, and experimental theater at campus venues, including **Royce Hall** *(310-825-4401)*, **Schoenberg Hall**, and the **Freud Playhouse**.

PLACES TO EAT & DRINK
Where to Eat:

Francophiles will delight in beef bourguignon at **Soleil (7) ($$)** *(1386 Westwood Blvd., 310-441-5384, www. soleilwestwood.com, Tu 5PM–9PM, W–F 11:30AM–3PM, 5PM–10PM, Sa 10AM–10PM, Su 10AM–9PM)*; pumpkin ravioli and other pastas balance the menu. **Napa Valley Grille (8) ($$-$$$)** *(1100 Glendon Ave., 310-824-3322, www.napavalleygrille.com, M–F 11:30AM–3PM, Sa–Su 11AM–3PM, M–Th 5:30PM–10PM, F 5:30PM–11PM, Sa 5PM–11PM, Su 5PM–9:30PM)* focuses on organic and sustainable ingredients in its seasonal California menu. Heaps of inexpensive Korean fare at **Gushi (9) ($)** *(978 Gayley Ave., 310-208-4038, M–Sa 11AM–11PM)* satisfies the UCLA college crowd. Vegans flock to **Native Foods (10) ($)** *(1110-½ Gayley Ave., 310-209-1055, www. nativefoods.com, daily 11AM–10PM)* for creative fare like soy tacos and faux pepper steak. The cheese is piled high and the crust done just right at **Lamonica's New York Pizza (11) ($)** *(1066 Gayley Ave., 310-208-8671, M–Th, Su 10:30AM–midnight, F–Sa 11AM–2AM)*, appeasing East Coast transplants. Local legend **Diddy Riese Cookies (12) ($)** *(926 Broxton Ave., 310-208-0448, www.diddyriese.com, M–Th 10AM–*

midnight, F 10AM–1AM, Sa noon–1AM, Su noon–midnight) features all-natural cookies, from chocolate chip to cinnamon sugar. They also offer delicious make-your-own ice-cream sandwiches.

Bars & Nightlife:

A beautiful bar for beautiful people, **Whiskey Blue (13)** *(W Los Angeles-Westwood, 930 Hilgard Ave., 310-443-8232, www.starwoodhotels.com, daily 5PM–2AM)* lures hipsters and a smattering of celebs with seductive, private lounges and artsy decor. At **Palomino Restaurant Rotisseria Bar (14)** *(10877 Wilshire Blvd., 310-208-1960, www.palomino.com, bar hours: M–Th 11:30AM–midnight, F till 1AM, Sa 4PM–1AM, Su 4PM–10PM)*, happy hour buzzes with strong drinks and addictive finger foods. Skip the sushi and come to **Tengu (15)** *(10853 Lindbrook Dr., 310-209-0071, www.tengu. com, nightly 5:30PM–11PM)* for happy hour or sake cocktails.

WHERE TO SHOP

Gag gifts, costumes, and kitsch make Westwood Village's **Aahs (16)** *(1090 Westwood Blvd., 310-824-1688, www.aahs.com, daily 9:30AM–10PM, Sa till 10:30PM, Su till 9PM)* an irresistible stop. For casual frocks and tees, check out spacious **Skyla (17)** *(1073 Broxton Ave., 310-208-2120, www.shopskyla.com, M–Sa 11AM–8PM, Su till 6PM)*, which features a plethora of accessories and good sales. Secondhand buffs will find treasures galore at Buffalo Exchange (18) *(10914 Kinross Ave., 310-208-7403, www.buffaloexchange.com, M–Sa 11AM–7PM, Su noon–6PM).*

WHERE TO STAY

Modern decor, an inviting pool, and Bliss Spa are the attractions at W Los Angeles-Westwood (19) ($$$) *(930 Hilgard Ave., 310-208-8765, www.starwoodhotels.com),* also home to dining option **NineThirty**. Eco- and pet-friendly Hotel Palomar Los Angeles-Westwood (20) ($$$) *(10740 Wilshire Blvd., 310-475-8711, www.hotelpalo mar-lawestwood.com)* marks the 2008 makeover of an old Doubletree, bringing the Kimpton Hotels brand name to the Westside with a state-of-the-art fitness center, outdoor pool, and 268 rooms. European-style Hilgard House Hotel (21) ($$) *(927 Hilgard Ave., 310-208-3945, www.hilgardhouse.com)* is a stylish, affordable option in a prime location.

• SNAPSHOT •

Fabulous homes and fabulous people set the scene for Brentwood and Bel-Air. Brentwood was developed circa 1915 by real estate agent Bundy, while Bel-Air was the early 1920s brainchild of Alphonzo E. Bell. Each took

advantage of hillside locales, fashioning upper-class residential communities drawing celebrities and wealthy business folk. Brentwood residents have included Clark Gable, Marilyn Monroe, Joan Crawford, Henry Fonda, and O.J. Simpson and Nicole Brown

Simpson. (The famous televised freeway chase ending at Simpson's Brentwood home took place here.) Hundreds of homes, including many owned by stars, were destroyed in a 1961 brush fire. Today, both Bel-Air and Brentwood remain largely residential, though the Getty Center brings an influx of tourists.

PLACES TO SEE
Arts & Entertainment:

TOP PICK!

A spectacular blend of art, architecture, and landscaping, the ★GETTY CENTER (22) *(1200 Getty Center Dr., 310-440-7300, www.getty. edu, Tu–F, Su 10AM–5:30PM, F–Sa till 9PM)*, designed by architect Richard Meier, beckons with exquisite gardens and hilltop views. Its showpiece is the **J. Paul Getty Museum**, five pavilions that house the billionaire Getty's collection of European paintings, drawings, sculptures, illuminated manuscripts, decorative arts, and European and American photographs. The Getty also offers concerts, lectures, films, and other programming. **Skirball Cultural Center (23)** *(2701 N. Sepulveda Blvd., 310-440-4500, www.skirball.org, Tu–F noon–5PM, Th till 9PM, Sa–Su 10AM–5PM)*, an affiliate of Hebrew Union College, spotlights the experiences of the Jewish people over 4,000 years with artifacts, photos, art and multimedia exhibitions, and interactive family displays. **Leslie Sacks Fine Art (24)** *(11640 San Vicente Blvd., 310-820-9448, www.lesliesacks.com, M–Sa 10AM–6PM)* specializes in fine prints and works on paper, though the gallery also showcases paintings, ceramics, illustrated books, and African tribal art.

PLACES TO EAT & DRINK
Where to Eat:
Takao (25) ($$) *(11656 San Vicente Blvd., 310-207-8636, M–Sa 11AM–2:30PM, 5:30PM–10:30PM, Su 5PM–10PM)* excels at the basics, including an emphasis on its nigiri and sashimi. Can't decide? Let the chef with his omakase menu. **Saketini (26) ($$)** *(150 S. Barrington Ave., 310-440-5553, www.saketini.com, M–Sa 11:30AM–2:30PM, daily 5PM–10:30PM)* blends Japanese and Korean ingredients, everything from *Saketini kalbi* (short ribs) to a spicy tuna roll. A hot spot for sushi purists, **Sushi Sasabune (27) ($$$)** *(12400 Wilshire Blvd., 310-820-3596, M–F noon–2PM, 5:30PM–9:30PM)* limits its offer-

ings to sushi and sashimi. **Katsuya (28) ($$-$$$)** *(11777 San Vicente Blvd., 310-207-8744, www.sbe.com/katsuya, M–Th, Su 11:30AM–11PM, F–Sa 11:30AM–midnight)* is a Brentwood glamour queen, with au moderne Philippe Starck design and trendy sushi and robata grill. **Osteria Latini (29) ($$)** *(11712 San Vicente Blvd., 310-826-9222, www.osterialatini.com, M–F 11:30AM–2:30PM, M–Sa 5:30PM–10:30PM, Su 5PM–10PM)* chef and owner Paolo Pasio dubs his creations "Italian fusion," with specials like osso buco and calamari stuffed with crabmeat. Top it with homemade peanut butter gelato. Offering authentic Italian risotto or seafood, **Toscana (30) ($$$-$$$$)** *(11633 San Vicente Blvd., 310-820-2448, www.ristorantelatoscana.com, M–Sa 11:30AM–3PM, 5:30PM–11PM, Su 5PM–10PM)* serves sophisticated yet unstuffy clientele. Hiding in a Bel-Air strip mall, **Mulholland Grill (31) ($$-$$$)** *(2932 N. Beverly Glen Cir., 310-470-6223, www.mulhollandgrill.com, M–F 11:30AM–2:30PM, 5:30PM–10PM, F till 10:30PM, Sa 5:30PM–10:30PM, Su 5:30PM–9PM)* remains a local secret. Pastas and mains are accented by over 200 wines.

Bars & Nightlife:

An older crowd frequents **Vibrato Grill Jazz…etc. (32)** *(2930 Beverly Glen Circle, 310-474-9400, www. vibratogrilljazz.com, Tu–Su 5:30PM–11PM)*, a swanky jazz club/steakhouse co-owned by Herb Alpert. Come for the comfort food or just a comfort drink at the **Brentwood Restaurant and Lounge (33)** *(148 S. Barrington Ave., 310-476-3511, www.brentwoodrestaurant.com, daily 5PM–10PM, Tu–Sa 10PM–midnight).*

WHERE TO SHOP

Needlepoint your thing? Stop at **Aristeia (34)** *(141 S. Barrington Pl., 310-476-6977, www.aristeianeedle point.com, M–Tu 10AM–8PM, W–Th 10AM–5PM, F–Sa 10AM–4PM)*, which showcases finished works and hosts workshops and classes. **Dragon Books (35)** *(2954 Beverly Glen Circle, 310-441-8545, www.dragonbooks.com, Tu–Sa 11AM–9PM, Su till 8PM)* specializes in rare and antiquarian books, including first editions.

Grace Home Furnishings (36) *(11632 Barrington Ct., 310-476-7176, www.grace homefurnishings.com, M–Sa 10AM–6PM)*, named after the owner's dog, combines retro design with sleek accents and stocks everything from handblown glass vases to Chinese ceramic jars.

WHERE TO STAY

Lush **Hotel Bel-Air (37)** **($$$$)** *(701 Stone Canyon Rd., 310-472-1211, www.hotelbelair)*, set in 12 landscaped acres, features European-designed rooms with private terraces, as well as exotic gardens and a spa. Dine at its acclaimed **The Restaurant**. Boutique-style **Hotel Angeleno (38)** **($$)** *(170 N. Church Ln., 310-476-6411, www.jdv hotels.com/angeleno)* offers a sophisticated setting, private balconies, and plasma televisions. Guests can dine at the **West Restaurant and Lounge**. **Luxe Hotel Sunset Boulevard (39)** **($$$)** *(11461 Sunset Blvd., 310-476-6571, www.luxehotelsunsetblvd.com)* is set on a private seven-acre estate complete with lush greenery, tennis courts, fitness facilities, and spa.

WEST L.A.

• SNAPSHOT •

Bustling West Los Angeles is a melting pot of Japanese and Mexican flavors, as well as hip eateries and a burgeoning arts scene. Once part of the Rancho San Vicente y Santa Monica, the area became farmland, which attracted Japanese immigrants who established orchards and nurseries. The central nerve of West L.A. was and continues to be Sawtelle, a less-than-two-square-mile district that was briefly an independent municipality. Today, Sawtelle Boulevard is home to some of the city's best sushi and Japanese cuisine.

PLACES TO SEE
Landmarks:

The Los Angeles National Cemetery (40) *(950 S. Sepulveda Blvd., 310-268-4675)*, dedicated in 1889, is the final resting place of some 85,000 veterans (including Spanish-American War veterans) and their families.

PLACES TO EAT & DRINK
Where to Eat:

Sample a slice of Americana at **The Apple Pan (41) ($)** *(10801 W. Pico Blvd., 310-475-3585, Tu–Th, Su 11AM–midnight, F–Sa till 1AM)*, dishing out burgers and crowd-pleasing apple pie. Legendary **Pinkberry (42) ($)**

(11301 W. Olympic Blvd., 310-231-0172, www.pink berry.com, daily 11AM–11PM, F–Sa till midnight) has one of many locations here. Though celebs stick to the Beverly Hills outlet, this frozen yogurt shop boasts all the trimmings. Sawtelle Boulevard is a hub for Japanese cuisine. Join the line for sushi at **Hide Sushi (43) ($$)** *(2040 Sawtelle Blvd., 310-477-7242, Tu–Sa 11:30AM– 9PM, Su 11:30AM–8PM)*. The fried chicken wings at **Furaibo Restaurant (44) ($$)** *(2068 Sawtelle Blvd., 310- 444-1432, www.furaibou.com, lunch M–F 11:30AM– 2PM, dinner daily 5:30PM–11PM)* keep locals coming back. Despite its mall setting, **Echigo (45) ($-$$)** *(12217 Santa Monica Blvd., 310-820-9787, M–Sa noon–2PM, 5:30PM–9:30PM)* serves some of the freshest sushi around. No tempura or California rolls, this is for serious fish lovers only. **Nanbankan (46) ($$)** *(11330 Santa Monica Blvd., 310-478-1591, daily 5PM–11PM)* skewers its yakitori and izakaya in a sleek yet unpretentious set- ting. Dabble in 12 delectable courses on the omakase menu at **Wakasan (47) ($$)** *(1929 Westwood Blvd., 310- 446-5241, M–Th 6PM–midnight, F–Sa till 1AM, Su 6PM–11PM)*. Bulk up at **John O'Groats (48) ($)** *(10516 W. Pico Blvd., 310-204-0692, www.ogroatsrestaurant.com, daily 7AM–3PM)*, on everything from lemon pancakes to huevos O'Groats.

Bars & Nightlife:

Arguably one of the best martinis in town is found at **Liquid Kitty (49)** *(11780 W. Pico Blvd., 310-473-3707, www.thekitty.com, M–F 5PM–2AM, Sa–Su 8PM–2AM)*. DJs spin soul, funky jazz, and old hip-hop, among other genres. Kitty-oke Monday nights. Crave more karaoke? Check out **Karaoke Bleu (50)** *(2064 Sawtelle Blvd., 310-477-4794, daily 8PM–2AM)* or **Max Karaoke (51)** *(2130 Sawtelle Blvd., 310-479-1477, www.maxkaraokestudio. com, daily 1PM–3AM, F–Sa till 4AM)*.

WHERE TO SHOP

Westside Pavilion (52) *(10800 W. Pico Blvd., 310-470-8752, www.westside pavilion.com, M–F 10AM–9PM, Sa 10AM–8PM, Su 11AM–6PM)* is home to over 100 restaurants and shops, from Macy's to indie **Power Anime**, featuring Super Mario Bros., Pokémon, and more. As its name implies, **Giant Robot (53)** *(2015 Sawtelle Blvd., 310-478-1819, www.giantrobot.com, M–Sa 11:30AM–8PM, Su noon–6PM)* is all about toys and T-shirts of the Japanese variety. Shop Hello Kitty paraphernalia at **Tokyo Japanese Outlet (54)** *(2109 Sawtelle Blvd., 310-914-5320)*. **Happy Six (55)** *(2115 Sawtelle Blvd., 310-479-5363, www.happysix.com, daily 11AM–11PM)* is cute central with Tokidoki bags and Angry Girl gear. Stock up on Harry Potter and Nancy Drew at **Children's Book World (56)** *(10580-½ W. Pico Blvd., 310-559-2665, M–F 10AM–5:30PM, Sa 10AM–5PM, www.childrensbookworld.com)*. **Out of the Closet (57)** *(10749 W. Pico Blvd., 310-481-0013, www.out ofthecloset.org, M–Sa 10AM–7PM, Su 10AM–6PM)* sells vintage sec-ondhand goods to benefit AIDS

Healthcare Foundation. Wine connoisseurs can uncork heaven at Wally's Wines & Spirits (58) *(2107 Westwood Blvd., 310-475-0606, www.wallywine.com, M–Sa 10AM–7:30PM, Su 10AM–6PM)*.

WHERE TO STAY
Holiday Inn Express West Los Angeles (59) ($$) *(11250 Santa Monica Blvd., 310-478-1400, www.hiewestla. com)* offers reasonable accommodations, including a fitness center and a complimentary deluxe continental breakfast, in a central location.

CULVER CITY

• SNAPSHOT •

Formerly heralded as the Heart of Screenland, Culver City has been a nexus for the film industry since the 1920s, when silent film producer Hal Roach and Metro Goldwyn Mayer (MGM) built studios here. Hundreds of movies were filmed in Culver City, including *The Wizard of Oz*, *Gone With the Wind*, *Citizen Kane*, and the original *King Kong*; its television shows have included *Jeopardy!* and *Lassie*. After years of decline, Culver City is seeing a rebirth, with star chef restaurants, boutiques, theaters, and a proliferation of galleries that has been likened to New York City's Chelsea district.

PLACES TO SEE
Landmarks:
Sony Pictures Studio Tour (60) *(10202 W. Washington Blvd., 310-244-8687, www.sonypicturesstudiotours.com, tours M–F 9:30AM, 10:30AM, 1:30PM, 2:30PM)* gives visitors a glimpse of old Hollywood and new, with walking tours of former sets for such films as *Spider Man*, *Men in Black*, and *The Wizard of Oz*.

Arts & Entertainment:
L.A.'s premiere jazz venue, **The Jazz Bakery (61)** *(3233*

Helms Ave., 310-271-9039, www.jazzbakery.com, shows daily 8PM, 9:30PM, Su also 4PM), is located in part of the old Helms Bakery, part of the 11-acre Furniture District. It also houses the Antique Guild (where Helms memorabilia, including a restored coach, are displayed), the **Gascon Theatre**, and **La Dijonaise** restaurant. Opened in 2004, the **Kirk Douglas Theatre (62)** *(9820 Washington Blvd., 213-628-2772, www.centertheatregroup.org)* is one outlet for the Center Theatre Group, which presents world premieres as well as theatrical classics. The **Museum of Jurassic Technology (63)** *(9341 Venice Blvd., 310-836-6131, www.mjt.org, Th 2PM–8PM, F–Su noon–6PM)* has nothing to do with dinosaurs or Steven Spielberg. Instead it houses a collection of curiosities like decaying dice, a bat that can fly through walls, and other twisted oddities, some fact, some fiction. It's up to you to distinguish which is which. An upstairs tea room serves complimentary refreshments. Free movie screenings hourly. The **Museum of Design Art & Architecture (64)** *(8609 Washington Blvd., 310-558-0902, www.modaagallery.com, M–F 9AM–6PM)* presents works on the relationship between art and architecture. Culver City's concentration of contemporary and alternative art galleries dates to 2003, when **Blum & Poe (65)** *(2754 S. La Cienega Blvd., 310-836-2062, www.blumandpoe.com, Tu–Sa 10AM–6PM)* moved from Santa Monica. Since then, more than 30 galleries have mushroomed into the Culver City Arts District.

Kids:

Wildlife rescue **Star Eco Station (66)** *(10101 W. Jefferson Blvd., 310-842-8060, www.ecostation.org)* features tropical birds, alligators, mammals, and other beasts. Hands-on tours are available every half hour from 10AM–4PM on weekends and seven days a week from 1PM to 5PM in the summer.

PLACES TO EAT & DRINK
Where to Eat:

At Mediterranean-influenced **Fraiche (67) ($$-$$$)** *(9411 Culver Blvd., 310-839-6800, www.fraicherestau rantla.com, M–F 11:30AM–2:30PM, daily 5:30PM–10:30PM)*, dine on a platter of fruits de mer or duck leg confit. **Akasha (68) ($$)** *(9543 Culver Blvd., 310-845-1700, www.akasharestaurant.com, M–F 11:30AM–2:30PM, M–Sa 5:30PM–11PM)*, located in the historic Hull Building, is Culver City's new hip celeb haunt, serving sustainable seafood and meats and a hearty selection of veggie dishes. Gastropub **Ford's Filling Station (69) ($$-$$$)** *(9531 Culver Blvd., 310-202-1470, www.fordsfillingstation.net, M–Sa 11AM–11PM, Su 10AM–10PM)*, brainchild of Ben Ford, son of Harrison, emphasizes organic and sustainable ingredients. **Wilson (70) ($$-$$$)** *(8631 Washington Blvd., 310-287-2093, www.wilsonfoodandwine.com, S–Th 5:30PM–10PM, F–Sa 5:30PM–11PM)*, located in the Museum of Design Art and Architecture, is a high-end wine bar and café. Spunky **Café Brasil (71) ($)** *(11736 W. Washington Blvd., 310-391-1216, www.cafe-brasil.com, daily 11AM–10PM)* sticks to the traditional fare of South America, including Brazilian churrasco and empanadas. Organic **Tender Greens (72) ($)** *(9523 Culver Blvd., 310-842-8300, www.tendergreensfood.com, S–Th 11:30AM–9PM, F–Sa till 10PM)* is the place for salads, range-raised chicken, and line-caught fish. **Hiko Sushi (73) ($$$)** *(11275 National Blvd., 310-473-7688, M–F noon–1:45PM, 6PM–9:30PM)* scores with fresh fish. No fancy rolls, and it's omakase only at the bar. Garlic chicken with plantains, rice, and beans is the mainstay at Cuban eatery **Versailles (74) ($)** *(10319 Venice Blvd., 310-558-3168, Su–Th 11AM–10PM, F–Sa till 11PM)*, with five L.A. locations. The best Culver City breakfast spot is **S&W Country Diner (75) ($)** *(9748 Washington Blvd., 310-204-5136, M–F 7AM–3PM, Sa–Su 8AM–3PM)*. Locals line up for buckwheat pancakes and eggs Benedict.

Bars & Nightlife:

Chic, minimalist **Alibi Room (76)** *(12236 W. Washington Blvd., 310-390-9300, www.alibiroomla.com, M–Sa 6PM–2AM)* pours a wide variety of beer to wash down the grub. Best spot is the patio out back. Pay for a debit card and self-serve wine samples at **Vinum Populi (77)** *(3865 Cardiff Ave., 310-204-5645, www.vinumpopuli.com, daily 5:30PM–12:30AM, F–Sa till 1:30AM)*. European boutique wines dominate the menu. Dive **Backstage Bar & Grill (78)** *(10400 Culver Blvd., 310-839-3892, www. backstageculvercity.com, daily 11AM–2AM)*, across from Sony Studios, has

historically been an escape for those filming. Beware: The karaoke machine comes out on weekends. Brush up before that *American Idol* audition at **Boardwalk 11 (79)** *(10433 National Blvd., 310-837-5245, www.boardwalk11.com, daily 5PM–2AM)*, where karaoke is always in full swing. Art meets alcohol at **Mandrake Bar (80)** *(2692 S. La Cienega Blvd., 310-837-3297, www.mandrakebar.com, M 6PM–midnight, Tu–Th 5PM–midnight, F–Sa 5PM–1AM, Su 6PM–midnight)*, featuring strong cocktails, alterna-rock, occasional DJs, and a gallery toward the back. Drink to history at Culver City's oldest watering hole, **Cinema Bar (81)** *(3967 Sepulveda Blvd., 310-390-1328, daily 2PM–2AM)*, the size of a thumbprint, but filled with stiff drinks, an older crowd, and occasional live bands. Whichever side you choose, **Saints & Sinners (82)** *(10899 Venice Blvd., 310-842-8066, www.saintsn sinnersbar.com, daily 5PM–2AM)* tempts with '70s-style decor, potent drinks like Angel Dust and Hell Fire, and weekend DJs.

WHERE TO SHOP

Mega mall **Westfield Fox Hills Shopping Center (83)** *(294 Fox Hills Mall, 310-390-5073, www.westfield.com/ foxhills, M–F 10AM–9PM, Sa 10AM–8PM, Su 11AM–6PM)* has over 100 stores. **HD Buttercup (84)** *(3225 Helms Ave., 310-558-8900, www.hdbuttercup.com, M–Sa 10AM–7PM, Su 11AM–6PM)* gathers more than 50 furniture manufacturers under one massive emporium roof. Named after the owner's clothing line, tiny Indie

Collective (85) *(6039-A Washington Blvd., 310-837-7714, Tu–Sa noon–7PM, www.indiecollective.com)* squeezes in an eclectic array of one-of-a-kind designs. Dress for less with designer discount stock from Last Chance Boutique (86) *(8712 Washington Blvd., 310-287-2333, M–F 10AM–6PM, Sa till 5PM)*.

WHERE TO STAY

The 1924 landmark Culver Hotel (87) ($$) *(9400 Culver Blvd., 310-838-7963, www.culverhotel.com)*, formerly owned by John Wayne, has lodged everyone from Greta Garbo, Buster Keaton, Clark Gable, Ronald Reagan, to cast members from the original *Wizard of Oz*. Big name hotels include Four Points by Sheraton Los Angeles Westside (88) ($$) *(5990 Green Valley Circle, 310-641-7740, www.starwoodhotels.com)*, which features a complimentary fitness center, pool, and outdoor fireplace; and Radisson Hotel Los Angeles Westside (89) ($$) *(6161 W. Centinela Ave., 310-649-1776, www.radisson.com/culvercityca)*, with a state-of-the-art exercise facility and outdoor heated pool and Jacuzzi.

chapter 6

MALIBU/PACIFIC PALISADES

SANTA MONICA

VENICE

MARINA DEL REY

MALIBU/PACIFIC PALISADES
SANTA MONICA
VENICE
MARINA DEL REY

Places to See:

1. Zuma Beach
2. Malibu Lagoon State Beach
3. Malibu Pier
4. Point Dume State Beach
5. Leo Carrillo State Beach
6. Robert H. Meyer Memorial State Beach
7. Topanga State Park
8. Malibu Creek State Park
9. Will Rogers State Historic Park
10. Point Mugu State Park
11. Temescal Canyon Gateway Park
12. Malibu Ocean Sports
13. Getty Villa Malibu
14. Montgomery Arts House for Music and Architecture
31. SANTA MONICA PIER ★
32. Santa Monica State Beach
33. Palisades Park
34. Bergamot Station
35. Santa Monica Historical Society Museum
36. California Heritage Museum
37. Santa Monica Playhouse
38. Aero Theater
39. Pacific Park
40. Santa Monica Pier Aquarium
41. Santa Monica Puppetry Center
66. Muscle Beach
67. Venice Canals
68. Norton House
69. LA Louver Gallery
70. Sponto Gallery
71. Ten Women Venice
72. Ballerina Clown
73. Chiat-Day Building
94. Fisherman's Village
95. Mother's Beach
96. Dockweiler State Beach
97. Ballona Wetlands
98. Burton W. Chace Park

Places to Eat & Drink:

15. Nobu Malibu
16. Gladstone's Malibu

★ *Top Pick*

17. Geoffrey's Malibu
18. Malibu Seafood Fresh
    Fish Market and Patio Café
19. Moonshadows
20. Inn of the Seventh Ray
21. Duke's Malibu
22. Cholada Thai Cuisine
23. Malibu Inn
24. Paradise Cove Beach Café
42. Melisse
43. Drago
44. The Hump
45. The Lobster
46. Valentino
47. The Counter
48. Library Alehouse
49. Cameo at the Viceroy
50. Father's Office
51. Temple Bar
52. Zanzibar
53. Harvelle's Blues Club
74. Piccolo Ristorante
75. Primitivo Wine Bistro
76. Joe's Restaurant
77. Axe
78. Hama Sushi
79. Hal's Bar & Grill
80. The Otheroom
81. On the Waterfront Café
82. Beechwood
83. Roosterfish
99. Sapori Restaurant
100. Café Del Rey
101. Jer-ne Restaurant and Bar

102. Organic Panificio
103. Aunt Kizzy's Back Porch
104. Irori Japanese Restaurant
105. The Shack
106. Glow
107. Tony P's Dockside Grill

Where to Shop:

25. Malibu Country Mart
26. Village Books
54. Third Street Promenade
55. Aura
56. Hey Kookla
57. Blonde
58. Dolce Vita
59. Black & Blue
84. Heist
85. Brick Lane
86. Anonymous Clothing
    Company
87. Pamela Barish
88. Strange Invisible Perfumes
89. Equator Books
90. Small World Books
108. Waterside Marina del Rey
109. Villa Marina Marketplace

Where to Stay:

27. Casa Malibu
28. Malibu Beach Inn,
    Carbon Beach
29. Malibu Bella Vista
30. Surfrider Beach Club
60. Shutters on the Beach

61. Viceroy Santa Monica
62. Fairmont Miramar Hotel
63. Casa del Mar
64. Georgian Hotel
65. Ambrose
91. Venice Beach House
92. The Cadillac Hotel

93. Inn at Venice Beach
110. Ritz-Carlton Marina del Rey
111. Marina del Rey Marriott
112. Marina International
     Hotel and Bungalows
113. Inn at Playa del Rey

Los Angeles has of course been
called every name in the book,
from "19 suburbs in search of a
metropolis" to a "circus without
a tent" to "less a city than a
perpetual convention."

—*Inside U.S.A.*, JOHN GUNTHER

151

MALIBU/PACIFIC PALISADES

• SNAPSHOT •

Fires, floods, mudslides, Santa Ana winds—Malibu makes headline news. Despite the natural disasters, movie stars and entertainment bigwigs—from David Geffen to Barbra Streisand—call this 21-mile stretch of coastline home. There is good reason. Malibu boasts many of L.A.'s most spectacular beaches and state parks, and its canyons run straight up to the Santa Monica Mountains. The Pacific Coast Highway **(PCH)** meanders along the coastline, affording postcard views from bluffs, and glimpses of celebrity homes and gated communities. Pepperdine University is found here, as are landmark restaurants and trendy shops. The adjacent community of Pacific Palisades melds private upscale residences with alluring public parks.

PLACES TO SEE
Landmarks:

Malibu marks the northern tip of the **South Bay Bicycle Trail**, the longest beach path of its kind in the world, stretching 22 miles south to Torrance, passing through beach towns such as Santa Monica and Venice along the way. The trail is open to bicycles, rollerblades, and anything else on wheels (sans motor). One of Malibu's most popular ocean venues is **Zuma Beach (1)** *(30050 PCH,*

818-880-0350) known for long, wide sands and top-tier surf conditions. **Malibu Lagoon State Beach (2)** *(23200 PCH, 818-880-0350)* has 22 acres of wetlands, gardens, and beachfront, plus a bird sanctuary, the Adamson House, and the Malibu Lagoon Museum. The **Adamson House** *(23200 PCH, 310-456-8432, www.adamson house.org)* was built in 1930 for the last owners of the Malibu Spanish Land Grant. The highlight is the tile work inside. The **Malibu Lagoon Museum** depicts the area's history through photos and memorabilia *(house/museum hours W–Sa 11AM–3PM)*. Close by: **Malibu Surfrider Beach**, world-renowned surfing mecca, and home of the 1905 **Malibu Pier (3)** *(23000 PCH, 310-456-8031)*. Scan the sea for California gray whales along **Point Dume State Beach (4)** *(Westward Beach Rd., 805-488-1827)* from December through March, during migration. **Leo Carrillo State Beach (5)** *(35000 PCH, 818-880-0350)* features nature walks, a beach, tide pools, coastal caves, and reefs, as well as back-country hiking access. **Robert H. Meyer Memorial State Beach (6)** *(33000 PCH, 818-880-0350)* is made up of several coves, or pocket beaches, named *El Pescador, La Piedra,* and *El Matador.* The **Santa Monica Mountains National Recreation Area** is the largest urban national park in the United States. For hiking, biking, and horseback riding, **Topanga State Park (7)** *(20829 Entrada Rd., 310-455-2465, www.parks.ca.gov)* offers 36 miles of trails. The 7,000-acre **Malibu Creek State Park (8)** *(1925 Las Virgenes Rd., 818-880-0367, www.parks.*

ca.gov) sits on land once owned by 20th Century Fox and was a filming site for *Planet of the Apes* and *M*A*S*H*. It also offers hiking trails and camping, is home to mountain lions, bobcats, and golden eagles, and includes several nature preserves. The remains of Reagan Ranch, once owned by the former president, are part of the park. **Will Rogers State Historic Park (9)** *(1501 Will Rogers Park Rd., 310-454-8212, www.parks.ca.gov)* dates back to the 1920s, when the humorist bought land to develop a ranch. Park staff and docents offer tours of the Ranch House *(Tu–Su 11AM, 1PM, and 2PM)*. **Point Mugu State Park (10)** *(9000 W. PCH, 818-880-0350)* combines five miles of ocean shoreline with rocky bluffs, sand dunes, beaches, two river canyons, and open valleys. There are more than 70 miles of trails. Get lost in the views from **Temescal Canyon Gateway Park (11)** *(15601 Sunset Blvd., 310-589-3200)*, spanning 141 acres. **Malibu Ocean Sports (12)** *(29500 PCH, 310-456-6302)* offers kayak rentals, kayak tours, and surfing lessons.

Arts & Entertainment:

Worship the goddess at **Getty Villa Malibu (13)** *(17985 PCH, 310-440-7300, www.getty.edu, Th–M 10AM–5PM)* where Greek, Roman, and Etruscan artifacts are organized by theme, such as the Trojan War. Dedicated to the late Martha Montgomery, wife of Alfred Newman, the **Montgomery Arts House for Music and Architecture (14)** *(6307 Busch Dr., 310-589-0295, www.montgomeryartshouse.org)* was designed by architect Eric Lloyd Wright. It presents classical concerts, dances, and speakers.

PLACES TO EAT & DRINK
Where to Eat:

Sushi master Nobu Matsuhisa has set up camp in the Malibu Country Mart with **Nobu Malibu (15) ($$$)** *(3835 Cross Creek Rd., 310-317-9140, www.nobu matsuhisa.com, Su–Th 5:45PM–10PM, F–Sa till 11PM)*, a celebrity haunt known for signature dish *tiradito*—red snapper with fresh cilantro and a dash of hot sauce. Seafood is only part of the story at **Gladstone's Malibu (16) ($$)** *(17300 PCH, 310-454-3474, www.gladstones. com, Su–Th 8AM–10PM, F–Sa till 11PM)*, where picture windows and patio lend stunning views of the Pacific. **Geoffrey's Malibu (17) ($$$)** *(27400 PCH, 310-457-1519, www.geoffreysmalibu.com, M–F 10:30AM–10PM, Sa–Su 10:30AM–11PM)* personifies perfection with flawless California cuisine, impeccable service, and jaw-dropping ocean-bluff views. Denizens of the deep can skip all the fanfare and fill up on invitingly priced grilled dishes, hearty seafood soups, and fish and chips at

Malibu Seafood Fresh Fish Market and Patio Café (18) ($) *(25653 PCH, 310-456-3430, www.malibuseafood.com, daily 11AM–close)*. Asian-inspired **Moonshadows (19) ($$$)** *(20356 PCH, 310-456-3010, www.moonshadows malibu.com, M–F 11:30AM–3:30PM, Sa–Su opens 11AM, M–Th 4:30PM–10:30PM, F–Sa till 11PM, Su till 10PM)* entices with selections like tamarind-marinated free-range chicken. Start with a seaside drink in its **Blue Lounge** *(Su–Th till midnight, F–Sa till 1:30AM)*. Romantic **Inn of the Seventh Ray (20) ($$$)** *(128 Old Topanga Canyon Rd., 310-455-1311, www.innofthe seventhray.com, daily 11:30AM–3PM, 5:30PM–10PM, Sa opens 10:30AM, Su opens 9:30AM)*, overlooking Topanga Canyon, goes green with a largely vegan menu. It's a picture-perfect brunch at **Duke's Malibu (21) ($$)** *(21150 PCH, 310-317-0777, www.dukesmalibu.com, M–Th 11:30PM–10PM, F 11:30AM–10:30PM, Sa 11:30AM–11PM, Su 10AM–10PM)*, with made-to-order omelets, Hawaiian-style ceviche, and a Pacific panorama. Or come to Duke's outdoor **Barefoot Bar** for a Beach Boy daiquiri. An unexpected treasure, **Cholada Thai Cuisine (22) ($)** *(18763 PCH, 310-317-0025, www.choladathaicuisine. com, M 4:30PM–9:30PM, Tu–F 11:30AM–9:30PM, Sa–Su noon–10PM)* simmers up Thai curries and soups.

Bars & Nightlife:

Popular beach spot **Malibu Inn (23)** *(22969 PCH, 310-456-6060, www.malibu-inn.com, daily 8AM–2AM)* first opened in 1923 across the street from the Malibu Pier. Though it seems an unlikely locale, the bar presents indie and punk rock as well as reggae and other genres.

Bob Morris's **Paradise Cove Beach Café (24)** *(28128 PCH, 310-457-2503, www.paradisecovemalibu.com, daily 8AM–11PM, Sa–Su opens 7AM)* has been a film location for everything from *Charlie's Angels* to a Paris Hilton music video. Enjoy the view with a guava mojito.

WHERE TO SHOP

Six-acre Malibu Country Mart (25) *(3835 Cross Creek Rd., www.malibucountrymart.com)* encompasses over 60 eclectic shops, restaurants, and galleries, plus a picnic area and playground. In Pacific Palisades, avid readers will find words everywhere at Village Books (26) *(1049 Swarthmore Ave., 310-454-4063, www.palivillagebooks. com, M–F 10AM–8PM, Sa–Su 10AM–6PM)*, from the stocked shelves to the floor, decorated with quotes from Thoreau, Einstein, and even Mae West.

WHERE TO STAY

Cozy Casa Malibu (27) **($$)** *(22752 PCH, 310-456-2219)* entices with 21 beachfront and garden-view rooms and suites, many with private decks and fireplaces. It's surprisingly affordable. Private and quiet Malibu Beach Inn, Carbon Beach (28) **($$$-$$$$)** *(22878 PCH, 310-456-6444, www.malibubeachinn.com)* sits on what is dubbed "Billionaire's Beach." Many rooms feature private balconies and ocean views. B&B style Malibu Bella Vista (29) **($-$$)** *(25786 Piuma Rd., 818-591-9255, www.malibubellavista.com)* is a hideaway in Malibu Canyon with hiking trails nearby. Surfrider Beach Club (30) **($)** *(23033 PCH, 310-456-6559)*, across from Surfrider Beach, offers basic rooms and a prime location.

SANTA MONICA

• SNAPSHOT •

One of L.A.'s most pedestrian-friendly communities, Santa Monica bursts at the seams with museums, galleries, and public art. Santa Monica first blossomed as a seaside resort in the late 1800s and became its own incorporated city in 1887. Its tranquil appeal changed forever in 1966 with the building of the Santa Monica Freeway, sparking an influx of young, well-to-do home buyers. Since then, Santa Monica has become one of L.A.'s crown jewels, retaining its history with the Santa Monica Pier and Pacific Park while forging new ground with top art galleries, restaurants, and bars.

PLACES TO SEE
Landmarks:

TOP PICK!

Historic ★**SANTA MONICA PIER (31)** *(www. santamonicapier.org)*, at the foot of Colorado Avenue, marks the finish line of Route 66. Built in 1909, the pier's early popularity attracted Coney Island carousel builder Charles Looff to construct his own Looff Pleasure Pier adjacent to the municipal pier. Looff Pier's Moorish-style Hippodrome

building has housed a number of vintage merry-go-rounds and Wurlitzer organs. Locals united to save the pier when demolition threatened in the '70s; in the '80s it underwent an overhaul. Now it attracts tourists, especially to its Twilight Dance Series summer concerts. Popular Santa Monica State Beach (32) spans 3.5 miles of coastline. Santa Monica has more than 420 acres of public open space, including a number of city parks *(www.santamonica.com)*.

Palisades Park (33) runs along Ocean Avenue overlooking the beach. The park features public art and **Camera Obscura**, a life-size, walk-through pinhole camera. Take in views of the beach, pier, and some days even Catalina Island from the park, also home to the **Santa Monica Visitor Information Kiosk** *(310-393-7593, daily 9AM–5PM in summer, 10AM–4PM in winter)*.

Arts & Entertainment:

Bergamot Station (34) *(2525 Michigan Ave., 310-829-5854, www.bergamotstation.com, Tu–F 10AM–6PM, Sa 11AM–5:30PM)*, a former Red Line trolley train depot, encompasses some 30 eclectic art galleries. The **Santa Monica Museum of Art** *(2525 Michigan Ave., 310-586-6488, www.smmoa.org, Tu–F 11AM–6PM, Sa till 8PM)*, in a corner of the station, features exhibits of leading international contemporary artists. The new Santa Monica Historical Society Museum (35) *(1539 Euclid St., 310-395-2290, www.santamonicahistory.org, Tu–F 10AM–4:30PM, 2nd and 4th Su 1PM–4PM)* chronicles the history and culture of Santa Monica and Westside with maps, photos, and artifacts. Built in 1894 by renowned architect Sumner P. Hunt for the son of Santa Monica's founder, Roy Jones, the **California Heritage Museum (36)** *(2612 Main St., www.californiaheritagemuseum.org, 310-392-8537, W–Su 11AM–4PM)* building features period furnishings. The **Santa Monica Playhouse (37)** *(1211 Fourth St., 310-394-9779, www.santamonica playhouse.com)*, presents live theater as well as theater workshops. **Aero Theater (38)** *(1328 Montana Ave., 310-260-1528, www.americancinematheque.com)*, a 1940s-restored movie house, showcases classics, rare films, film festivals, and musical performances.

Kids:

The **Santa Monica Pier** and **Pacific Park (39)** *(380 Santa Monica Blvd., 310-260-8744, www.pacpark.com, Su–Th 11AM–11PM, F–Sa till 12:30AM)* is home to the 1922 **Looff Hippodrome Carousel**, a National Historic Landmark; this is where Paul Newman's character worked in *The Sting*. Under the carousel, the **Santa Monica Pier Aquarium (40)** *(www.healthebay.org/smpa,*

Tu–F 2PM–6PM, Sa–Su 12:30PM–6PM) offers hands-on presentations and interactive exhibits of creatures from the bay, plus story hours and films. **Pacific Park** provides bumper cars, a motion-simulator theater, a live circus show, arcade games, and other attractions. The pier's **Pacific Wheel** is the only giant Ferris wheel over water in California, and is the world's first solar-powered Ferris wheel. **Santa Monica Puppetry Center (41)** *(1014 Broadway, 310-656-0483, www.puppetmagic. com)* presents **Puppetolio!**, the city's longest-running puppet show.

PLACES TO EAT & DRINK
Where to Eat:

Melisse (42) ($$$$) *(1104 Wilshire Blvd., 310-395-0881, www.melisse.com, Tu–Th 6PM–9:30PM, F–Sa till 10PM)* perfects French cuisine with an American twist. Chef Josiah Citrin presides over this, one of the city's finest restaurants. Can't decide between California squab roulade or truffle-crusted lamb loin? Try the tasting menu. Older foodies frequent **Drago (43) ($$)** *(2628 Wilshire Blvd., 310-828-1585, www.celestinodrago.com, M–F 11:30AM–3PM, M–Sa 5:30PM–11PM, Su till 10PM)*. Chef Celestino Drago dishes out fine Northern Italian cuisine, including seafood risotto with black squid ink and pumpkin tortellini. Airport dining enters another dimension at **The Hump (44) ($$$$)** *(3221 Donald Douglas Loop S., 310-313-0977, www.thehump.biz, Tu–F noon–2PM, Su–Th 6PM–10PM, F–Sa till 10:30PM)*. Gorge on succulent sashimi, and be prepared for the bill if you choose the omakase. Crustacean connoisseurs can't get enough of **The Lobster (45) ($$- $$$)** *(1602 Ocean Ave., 310-458-9294, www.thelobster.com, Su–Th 11:30AM– 10PM, F–Sa till 11PM)*, a landmark since 1923, with a menu of more than 60 fresh seafood items. The tasting menu showcases fresh pastas and seasonal entrées at local favorite **Valentino (46) ($$$)** *(3115 Pico Blvd., 310-829-4313, www.valentinorestaurant.com, F 11AM–2PM, M–Sa 5PM–10:30PM)*. The wine list offers over 2,500 selections. California takes on the burger at **The Counter (47) ($)** *(2901 Ocean Park Blvd., 310-399-*

8383, *www.thecounterburger.com, M–Th 11AM–10PM, F–Sa till 11PM, Su 11:30AM–9PM)*, where toppings for build-your-own include herb goat cheese spread or guacamole. **Library Alehouse (48) ($$)** *(2911 Main St., 310-314-4855, www.libraryalehouse.com, daily 11:30AM–midnight)* fulfills mainstream burger, ribs, and beer cravings.

Bars & Nightlife:

Swank **Cameo at the Viceroy (49)** *(1819 Ocean Ave., 310-260-7505, www.viceroysantamonica.com, Su–W 11AM–midnight, Th–Sa till 1AM)* pours cocktails by the poolside, attracting industry moguls in film and fashion. The line starts early at **Father's Office (50)** *(1018 Montana*

Ave., 310-393-2337, www.fathers office.com, M–Th 5PM–1AM, F 4PM–2AM, Sa noon–2AM, Su noon–midnight), an upscale pub known for blue-cheese-stuffed burgers and beers on tap. Underground musicians catch a break at **Temple Bar (51)** *(1026 Wilshire Blvd., 310-393-6611, www.templebar live.com, nightly 8PM–2AM)*, which also features progressive hip-hop and funk DJs. An eclectic mix of DJs spices up the dance floor at African-themed **Zanzibar (52)** *(1301 5th St., 310-451-2221, www.zanzibarlive.com, M–Su 9PM–2AM)*. Established in 1931, **Harvelle's Blues Club (53)** *(1432 4th St., 310-395-1676, www.harvelles. com, nightly 8PM–2AM)* is the oldest live music venue on the Westside. It also showcases some of the city's best jazz and blues performances.

WHERE TO SHOP

Third Street Promenade (54) *(Third St. bet. Broadway/Wilshire Blvd., 310-393-8355, www.thirdstreetpromenade.org)* boasts 150 stores and 70 restaurants and coffeehouses. The strip, lined with chain stores, was converted from a street to a pedestrian mall in 1965, one of the first

of its kind. More upscale shopping can be found on **Montana Avenue**. One of the city's best bargain events occurs on the third weekend in May, when stores along Montana set up shop on the sidewalk and slash prices. Unique boutiques include **Aura (55)** *(1528 Montana Ave., 310-451-0181, www.aura-boutique.com, M–Sa 10AM–6PM, Su 11AM–5PM)*, an exquisite shop by Kristin Tutor Eberts, former set and costume designer. **Hey Kookla (56)** *(1329 Montana Ave., 310-899-9499, www.heykookla.com, M–Sa 10AM–7PM, Su 11AM–6PM)* offers limited edition atelier pieces, handmade jewelry, and other accessories. **Main Street** *(www.mainstreetsm.com)* from Pico Blvd. to Navy St., is another chic shopping enclave. Highlights include **Blonde (57)** *(2430 Main St., 310-396-9113, www.blondela.com, daily 11AM–7PM)* where clothing reps, designers, and stylists come to do business. **Dolce Vita (58)** *(2710 Main St., 310-314-5460, www.shopdolcevita.com, M–Sa 11AM–7PM, Su till 6PM)* marks the perfect balance between sass and chic. Men get their chance at stylish **Black & Blue (59)** *(2711 Main St., 310-664-9400, www.blackandblueus.com, M–Sa 11AM–7PM, Su till 6PM)*.

WHERE TO STAY

Dressed up as a Cape Cod hideaway, **Shutters on the Beach (60) ($$$$)** *(1 Pico Blvd., 310-458-0030, www.shuttersonthebeach.com)* seems more like a homey beach cottage than upscale resort. Guest room perks include balconies, whirlpool tubs, and white shutters. Dine at popular **One Pico**. Luxe seaside **Viceroy Santa Monica (61) ($$$$)** *(1819 Ocean Ave., 310-260-7500, www.viceroysantamonica.com)* is home to popular restaurant **Whist**, known for its Sunday brunch. Elegant, sophisticated **Fairmont Miramar Hotel (62) ($$$-$$$$)** *(101 Wilshire Blvd., 310-576-7777, www.fairmont.com)*, Santa Monica's oldest hotel, has hosted the likes of Greta Garbo, Humphrey Bogart, Clark Gable, and Presidents Kennedy and Clinton. Splurge for a bungalow. The storied past of **Casa del Mar (63) ($$$$)** *(1910 Ocean Way, 310-581-5533, www.hotelcasadelmar.com)* began in 1926 when it was a posh retreat for Hollywood bigwigs. Over the years it served as a WWII military hotel and rehab center before being returned to grandeur following a 1999 makeover. Hollywood heavies have returned. Art Deco **Georgian Hotel (64) ($$-$$$)** *(1415 Ocean Ave., 310-395-9945, www.georgianhotel.com)* and its speakeasy served as a Prohibition-era hideaway for Fatty Arbuckle and Bugsy Siegel; Clark Gable also retreated to this spot. The speakeasy now serves as a breakfast room. Touting green initiatives, boutique-style **Ambrose (65) ($$)** *(1255 20th St., 310-315-1555, www.ambrosehotel.com)* appeals to eco-conscious travelers. Asian accents and feng shui design shape the vibe at this secluded spot on the residential edge of town.

VENICE

• SNAPSHOT •

One part Coney Island, one part East Village, and a dash of San Francisco's Haight Street, Venice is a sideshow, underground cultural haven, and neo-hippie retreat all in one. Developed by Abbot Kinney in 1904, Venice arose when Kinney organized thousands of men to dredge canals in an area of marshland he'd purchased. The project was dubbed by locals as "Kinney's Folly."

Kinney's dream was for his Venice to become a cultural center. He created canals, a boardwalk, a pier, a lagoon, and Venetian-style architecture, some of which still exist. Venice went through a downturn following the 1960s, overtaken by drug gangs and panhandlers. But today the area bustles with art galleries, bistros, and funky boutiques. Abbot Kinney Boulevard is its commercial heart.

PLACES TO SEE
Landmarks:

Chain-saw jugglers, guitar-playing roller skaters, fortune-tellers, bronzed bikini-clad locals, and vendors hawking everything from incense to handmade jewelry crowd Venice's **Ocean Front Walk**. More a sidewalk than a true boardwalk, this five-block stretch draws tourists and gawkers for its daily freak show. It's also home to a bike trail, volleyball courts, handball courts, and paddle tennis courts. Famed **Muscle Beach (66)**, an outdoor weight room, has been the stomping grounds of Arnold Schwarzenegger and other famous body-builders. Since the '30s, Muscle Beach has shaped celebrities like Kirk Douglas, Clark Gable, Jayne Mansfield, and Joe Gold—founder of Gold's Gym and World Gym. Day passes are available. Emulating its namesake in Italy, Venice had its own version of the **Venice Canals (67)** *(Washington Blvd. at Pacific Ave.)*, 16 miles of man-made waterways. The automobile prompted most of the canals to be filled in 1929. Real estate along the remaining canals drew Jim Morrison and other rock stars; later, affluent home buyers. One notable property, the Frank Gehry-designed **Norton House (68)** *(12541 Beatrice St.)*, faces the waterfront path just north of the Venice Pier; it's worth a detour for its outrageous use of concrete, tile, and stucco.

Arts & Entertainment:

Hallmark **LA Louver Gallery (69)** *(45 N. Venice Blvd., 310-822-4955, www.lalouver.com, Tu–Sa, 10AM–6PM)* showcases contemporary masters, including glass artist Dale Chihuly and David Hockney, as well as up-and-coming artists. **Sponto Gallery (70)** *(7 Dudley Ave., 310-399-2078)* was the home of the Venice West Café from the late '50s to the early '60s—birthplace of the Beat movement. Today it hosts local artists and the **7 Dudley Cinema**, presenting screenings and live events. **Ten Women Venice (71)** *(1237 Abbot Kinney, 310-452-2256, www.tenwomen.org, daily 11AM–6PM)* is actually home to 22 artists who churn out paintings, prints, photographs, decorative objects, and more. Jonathan Borofsky's 1989-constructed **Ballerina Clown (72)** *(255 Main St.)*, a 30-foot tall hobo clown with tutu, juts out of the Renaissance Building. Claes Oldenburg's **Giant Binoculars**, plus a boat-shaped wing, are part of the Frank Gehry–designed **Chiat-Day Building (73)** *(340 Main St.)*, constructed in 1991.

PLACES TO EAT & DRINK
Where to Eat:

Appropriately, the decor and flawless Northern Italian cuisine at **Piccolo Ristorante (74) ($$-$$$)** *(5 Dudley Ave., 310-314-3222, www.piccolovenice.com, M–Th 5:30PM–10PM, F–Sa 5PM–11PM, Su 5PM–10PM)* reflect the original Venice more than its L.A. namesake. Authentic flavors include risotto with homemade quail sausage. Dine al fresco at Mediterranean-style **Primitivo Wine Bistro (75) ($$)** *(1025 Abbot Kinney Blvd., 310-396-5353, www. primitivowinebistro.com, M–F noon–2:30PM, Su–Th 5:30PM–10:30PM, F–Sa 5:30PM–midnight)*, serving cold and hot tapas, potent sangria, and a full-bodied selection of wines. Unassuming **Joe's Restaurant (76) ($$-$$$)** *(1023 Abbot Kinney Blvd., 310-399-5811, www.joes restaurant.com, Tu–F noon–2:30PM, Su, Tu–Th 6PM–10PM, F–Sa 6PM–11PM, Sa, Su brunch 11AM–2:30PM)* raises Venice dining to haute levels with Cal-French flair. Find a table near the open kitchen or out on the patio. Artsy types fill the minimalist surrounds at **Axe (77) ($$)**

(1009 Abbot Kinney Blvd., 310-664-9787, www.axe restaurant.com, Tu–F 11:30AM–3PM, Sa–Su 9AM–3PM, Tu–Th 6PM–10PM, F–Sa till 10:30PM, Su 5:30PM–9:30PM)—pronounced *a-shay*. Axe mixes Mediterranean accents with its California-style menu, focusing on organic. It's not gourmet, but casual **Hama Sushi (78) ($$)** *(213 Windward Ave., 310-396-8783, www.hama sushi.com, M–Th 6PM–11PM, F–Sa till 11:30PM, Su 5PM–10:30PM)* serves California-ized rolls, such as the Venice roll with a jalapeño twist. Hama was one of the country's first sushi restaurants, opening in 1979. The seasonal menu at **Hal's Bar & Grill (79) ($$$)** *(1349 Abbot Kinney Blvd., 310-396-3105, www.halsbarandgrill.com, M–F 11:30AM–2AM, Sa–Su 10AM–2AM)* includes everything from sweet potato ravioli to pan-roasted duck. Live jazz Sundays and Mondays.

Bars & Nightlife:

Perpetually packed, **The Otheroom (80)** *(1201 Abbot Kinney Blvd., 310-396-6230, www.theotheroom.com, nightly 5PM–2AM)* is stocked with beers and wines. The dark lounge appeals with a laid-back vibe. The place to people watch, **On the Waterfront Café (81)** *(205 Ocean Front Walk, 310-392-0322, www.waterfrontcafe.com, M noon–midnight, Tu–F 11AM–midnight, Sa–Su 9AM–midnight)*, serving German beers on tap plus build-your-own burgers. Locals hit **Beechwood (82)** *(822 Washington Blvd., 310-448-8884, www.beechwood restaurant.com, Tu–Th 6PM–close, F 5PM–1:30AM, Sa 6PM–1:30AM, Su–M*

6PM–11PM) for the lounge, blending upscale trimmings with a low-key attitude. An upbeat spot is old-time gay bar **Roosterfish (83)** (1302 Abbot Kinney Blvd., 310-392-2123, www.roosterfishbar.com, daily 11AM–2AM), is known for strong drinks and welcoming clientele.

WHERE TO SHOP

Heist (84) (1104 Abbot Kinney Blvd., www.shopheist.com, M–Sa 11AM–7PM, Su noon–6PM) describes its wares as elusive, edgy, and eclectic. Brick Lane (85) (1132 Abbot Kinney Blvd., 310-392-2525, www.bricklaneuk.com, Tu–Sa 11AM–7PM, Su–M noon–6PM) is filled with high-end Eurocentric men's and women's clothing and accessories. Anonymous Clothing Company (86) (517 Ocean Front Walk, 310-392-7121, www.anonymousvenice.com, daily 10AM–6PM) makes a name for itself with custom-made pop culture T-shirts and cutting-edge fashions. Former stylist for the rock world, Pamela Barish (87) (1327-½ Abbot Kinney Blvd., 310-314-4490, www.pamelabarish.com) showcases her own couture here, emphasizing elegant classics with a twist. Like fine wine, the distillation of organic flowers, plants, and resins makes all the difference when creating custom scents at Strange Invisible Perfumes (88) (1138 Abbot Kinney Blvd., 310-314-1505, www.siperfumes.com, Tu–Sa 11AM–7PM, Su noon–6PM). Equator Books (89) (1103 Abbott Kinney Blvd., 310-399-5544, *www.equatorbooks.com, Tu–Th 11AM–10PM, F–Sa 11AM–11PM, Su 11AM–5PM)* spans a converted garage, with out-of-print and first editions. It's also home to **Equator Vinyl**, embracing old-school records. Independent bookseller Small World Books (90) *(1407 Ocean Front Walk, 310-399-2360, www.smallworld books.com, daily 10AM–8PM)* houses fiction, nonfiction, poetry, and science fiction.

WHERE TO STAY

Craftsman-style **Venice Beach House (91) ($$)** *(15 30th Ave., 310-823-1966, www.venicebeachhouse.com)* dates from 1911. Rooms at this welcoming B&B are named after Venice notables who've stayed there. **The Cadillac Hotel (92) ($-$$)** *(8 Dudley Ave., 310-399-8876, www.thecadillachotel.com)*, built in 1914, was once the summer residence of Charlie Chaplin. Done up in pink and turquoise Art Deco trimmings, the hotel is a bargain for the location. Spacious rooms and proximity to the beach add to the appeal of the **Inn at Venice Beach (93) ($$)** *(327 Washington Blvd., 310-821-2557, www.innatvenicebeach.com)*.

MARINA DEL REY

• SNAPSHOT •

For all its history as a manufactured community, Marina del Rey has much to offer with its natural setting. The largest man-made boat harbor in the world, the marina is a yachting and sailing haven, with moorings for more than 5,300 small boats. Lining the waterfront are high-rise condos, hotels, restaurants, and shops, as well as part of the 22-mile South Bay Bicycle Trail, stretching from Malibu to Torrance. Dating from the late 1950s, development is seated on wetlands between Venice and the LAX Airport, and is the fulfillment of the dream of M.C. Wicks, who proposed the idea more than 70 years earlier. The community became Marina del Rey, Spanish for "Harbor of the King."

PLACES TO SEE
Landmarks:

Fisherman's Village (94) *(13755 Fiji Way)*, designed to resemble a New England seaport, offers souvenir shops, waterfront dining, boat rentals, and cruises. **Marina Boat Rentals** *(13719 Fiji Way, 310-574-2822, www.boats 4rent.com)* lets you explore the calm harbor waters in kayaks, wave runners, and pedal boats. On Thursday and Saturday evenings free concerts in the Lighthouse Plaza feature

everything from local jazz to salsa. **Marina del Rey Sportfishing** *(13759 Fiji Way, 310-822-3625, www. marinadelreysportfishing.com)* provides fishing as well as whale-watching and dolphin tours from January through March. **Hornblower Cruises and Events** *(13755 Fiji Way, 310-301-6000, www.hornblower.com)* offers weekend sunset cruises, Friday night blues cruises, and Sunday champagne brunch cruises. For local transport, take the **Marina del Rey Water Bus**, operating summer weekends, holidays, and concert nights; it stops at six spots at the Marina, including Burton W. Chace Park, Fisherman's Village, Mother's Beach and Waterfront Walk. **Mother's Beach (95)** *(14000 Palawan Way, 310-305-9546, daily 8AM–9PM)* is a safe lagoon with lifeguards and no surf (it faces away from the ocean). Playa del Rey is a residential spot that also has a lagoon, a number of bird species, and **Dockweiler State Beach (96)** *(12000 Vista del Mar, 310-305-9546)*. This beach is not the most relaxing spot, with planes flying overhead, but provides firepits and opportunity for volleyball. One of the area's highlights, **Ballona Wetlands (97)** *(Friends of Ballona Wetlands: 7740 W. Manchester Ave., 310-306-5994, www.ballonafriends.org)*, once spanned over 2,000 acres through what is today Marina del Rey, Venice, and parts of West Los Angeles. But the development of Marina del Rey and channeling of Ballona Creek in the '30s reduced the habitat to today's 190 acres. Restoration plans are in the works to increase the habitat to 340 acres. On the second and fourth

Saturday of the month *(10AM–11AM)*, Friends of Ballona Wetlands offers nature tours of the salt marsh and dunes. **Burton W. Chace Park (98)** *(13650 Mindanao Way, 310-305-9595, www.chacepark.com)* has some of the best viewpoints of the area. During July and August the park is the site of free evening pop and classical music concerts on alternating Thursdays and Saturdays.

PLACES TO EAT & DRINK
Where to Eat:

Locals indulge in four-cheese gnocchi at **Sapori Restaurant (99) ($$)** *(13723 Fiji Way, 310-821-1740, www.sapori-mdr.com, daily 11:30AM–10PM)*, an intimate spot tucked away in Fisherman's Village. Come for romantic views at **Café Del Rey (100) ($$$-$$$$)** *(4451 Admiralty Way, 310-823-6395, www.cafedelreymarina. com, M–Sa 11:30AM–3PM, 5:30PM–9:30PM, Sa till 10:30PM, Su 10:30AM–2:30PM, 5PM–9:30PM)*, and try the truffle pizza. Posh waterfront **Jer-ne Restaurant and Bar (101) ($$$-$$$$)** *(4375 Admiralty Way, 310-574-4333, www.ritzcarlton.com, M–Su 6:30AM–10PM)* at the Ritz-Carlton melds French flavors with California fresh, serving delicacies like grilled filet mignon with mushroom risotto. Italian **Organic Panificio (102) ($$)** *(4211 Admiralty Way, 310-448-8900, www.organicpanificio. com, M–F 11AM–10PM, Sa–Su 8:30AM–10PM)* dishes out handmade pizza and gelato. Southern belle **Aunt Kizzy's Back Porch (103) ($)** *(4325 Glencoe Ave., 310-578-1005, www.auntkizzys.com, daily 11AM–9PM, F–Sa till 10PM)* serves down-home soul food like cornbread muffins and chicken-fried steak. Fresh sashimi takes center stage at **Irori Japanese Restaurant (104) ($$)** *(4371 Glencoe Ave., 310-822-3700, M–F 11:30AM–2PM, M–Th 5:30PM–10PM, F till 10:30PM Sa–Su 5PM–10:30PM, Su till 9:30PM)*, Marina del Rey's top sushi spot (despite strip mall surrounds). Burger fanciers head to **The Shack (105) ($)** *(185 Culver Blvd., 310-823-6222, daily 11AM–1:30AM)* to fill up for cheap.

Bars & Nightlife:

Swank outdoor lounge **Glow (106)** *(4100 Admiralty Way, 310-578-4152, www.glow-bar.com, daily 5PM–1AM)*, at the Marriott, sets the mood with candles, torches, and fireplaces, as well as bottle service at private cabanas. Start the night with an espresso martini. Sports fans get their game on at **Tony P's Dockside Grill (107)** *(4445 Admiralty Way, 310-823-4534, www.tonyps. com, M–F 11:30AM–10PM, F till 11PM, Sa–Su 9AM–10PM, Sa till 11PM)* with big-screen TVs and a vast choice of beers.

WHERE TO SHOP

Shopping haven Waterside Marina del Rey (108) *(4700 Admiralty Way, 323-900-8080, www.shopwaterside.com, M–Th 10AM–7PM, F–Sa 10AM–8PM, Su 11AM–6PM)* features local boutiques and specialty shops, as well as restaurants and cafés. Popular clothing purveyors include **M. Fredric Women** *(310-305-1272)* and **M. Fred Man** *(310-305-8749)*, and **Jill Roberts** *(310-821-2300)*. Villa Marina Marketplace (109) *(13450 Maxella Ave.,*

310-827-1740, www.villamarinamarketplace.com, M–F 10AM–9PM, Sa 10AM–8PM, Su 11AM–6PM) has more than 70 stores and restaurants, plus movie theaters.

WHERE TO STAY

Elegantly welcoming **Ritz-Carlton Marina del Rey (110) ($$$-$$$$)** *(4375 Admiralty Way, 310-823-1700, www.ritzcarlton.com)* dares its guests to drag themselves out of exquisitely comfortable beds. For those who do, a spa, destination restaurant **Jer-ne**, and the waterfront await. **Marina del Rey Marriott (111) ($$$)** *(4100 Admiralty Way, 310-301-3000, www.marriott.com)* delivers all the comforts, including popular bar **Glow** *(see page 174)*. **Marina International Hotel and Bungalows (112) ($-$$)** *(4200 Admiralty Way, 310-301-2000, www.marinaintlhotel.com)* features guest rooms and bungalows with patios and balconies and includes a pool and spa. For a touch of romance and luxury, boutique-style **Inn at Playa del Rey (113) ($$)** *(435 Culver Blvd., 310-574-1920, www.innatplayadelrey.com)* overlooks sailboats in Marina del Rey and 200 acres of natural marshes.

chapter 7

SOUTH BAY—MANHATTAN BEACH,
HERMOSA BEACH, REDONDO BEACH

SAN PEDRO/PALOS VERDES

LONG BEACH

CATALINA ISLAND

DISNEYLAND

SOUTH LOS ANGELES/LEIMERT PARK

SOUTH BAY—MANHATTAN BEACH,
HERMOSA BEACH, REDONDO BEACH
SAN PEDRO/PALOS VERDES
LONG BEACH
CATALINA ISLAND
DISNEYLAND
SOUTH LOS ANGELES/
LEIMERT PARK

Places to See:

1. Manhattan Beach Pier
2. Hermosa Beach
3. Redondo Beach
4. Seaside Lagoon
5. Redondo Beach
   Pier/Fisherman's Wharf
6. Madrona Marsh Preserve &
   Nature Center
7. Redondo Beach Performing
   Arts Center
8. Hermosa Beach Playhouse
37. Point Vicente Lighthouse
38. Wayfarer's Chapel
39. South Coast Botanic
   Garden
40. Angels Gate Park
41. Point Fermin Park
42. Ports O'Call Marketplace
43. Los Angeles Maritime
   Museum
44. Warner Grand Theatre
45. Angels Gate Cultural Center
46. Cabrillo Marine Aquarium
61. RMS *QUEEN MARY* ★
62. Russian Foxtrot Submarine
63. Long Beach Museum of Art
64. Museum of Latin
   American Art
65. Long Beach Convention &
   Entertainment Center
66. Carpenter Performing Arts
   Center
67. Long Beach Playhouse
68. Aquarium of the Pacific
69. The Pike at Rainbow
   Harbor
90. Watts Towers
91. Kenneth Hahn State
   Recreation Area
92. Hollywood Park Racetrack

★ *Top Pick*

93. Museum of African American Art
94. William Grant Still Arts Center
95. Vision Theatre

Places to Eat & Drink:
9. Café Pierre
10. Rock'N Fish
11. Mama D's Italian
12. Petros Greek Cuisine and Lounge
13. North End Caffé
14. Uncle Bill's Pancake House
15. La Sosta Enoteca
16. Chez Mélange
17. The Lighthouse Café
18. Mermaid
19. Poop Deck
20. The Shellback Tavern
21. Side Door
22. Tony's on the Pier
23. Café Boogaloo
47. Papadakis Taverna
48. J Trani's Ristorante
49. Rex's Café
50. 22nd Street Landing Seafood Grill and Bar
51. San Pedro Brewing Company
52. The Whale and Ale
53. The Copper Room
70. La Parolaccia Osteria Italiana

71. Alegria Cocina Latina
72. Frenchy's Bistro
73. Open Sesame
74. Parker's Lighthouse
75. Coffee Cup Café
76. Observation Bar
77. Puka Bar
78. CasaVino
79. V Room
80. Alex's Bar
96. Harold & Belle's
97. R & R Soul Food Restaurant
98. M&M Soul Food
99. Pann's Restaurant
100. Phillips Bar-B-Que
101. Woody's Bar-B-Que
102. Ackee Bamboo
103. Babe's and Ricky's Inn
104. The World Stage
105. Café-Club Fais Do-Do

Where to Shop:
24. Riviera Village
25. South Bay Galleria
26. Fernandos
27. Re: Style
28. Third Gallery
29. Dollyrocker
30. Stars Antique Market
54. Williams Book Store
55. Joanne's Closet
56. Behind the Scenes Costumes

178

81. Blue Windows
82. BeMe
83. Fern's Garden
84. Iguana Import Gallery
85. The Vintage Collective
106. Zambezi Bazaar
107. Gallery Plus
108. Eso Won Books

Where to Stay:
31. Shade Hotel
32. The Belamar Hotel
33. Sea View Inn at the Beach
34. Beach House at Hermosa

35. Portofino Hotel & Yacht Club
36. Palos Verdes Inn
57. Crowne Plaza Harbor Hotel
58. Doubletree Hotel San Pedro
59. Hostelling International—Los Angeles South Bay
60. Terranea Resort
86. Queen Mary Hotel
87. Renaissance Long Beach Hotel
88. Coast Long Beach Hotel
89. The Turret House

• SNAPSHOT •

South Bay includes the business hotel zone of the LAX airport area, through El Segundo and onward to Hermosa Beach, Redondo Beach, and Manhattan Beach, each with its own character and clientele. For those in search of the Beach Boys' version of California, this is it—sun, sand, surfers, volleyball—the works.

PLACES TO SEE
Landmarks:

Sculpted bodies pour out of upscale condos in **Manhattan Beach**, known for its surf, sand, and beach volleyball. Celebrities and sports stars also inhabit the

neighborhood's four square miles; the average home price is well over $1 million. Centerpiece **Manhattan Beach Pier (1)**, features a 1920s roundhouse containing the

Roundhouse Marine Lab & Aquarium *(310-379-8117, www.roundhouseaquarium.org, M–F 3PM–sunset, Sa–Su 10AM–sunset)*, bursting with colorful marine fish and invertebrates, as well as a restaurant and vistas of beaches and surfers. Funky **Hermosa Beach (2)** is ideal for sunbathing, volleyball, surfing and paddleboarding. Along

Hermosa's promenade are boutiques, restaurants, and bars, while the Hermosa Valley Greenbelt, a trail through the city from south to north, is well-trodden with joggers. Family-friendly **Redondo Beach (3)** accommodates visitors with beaches,
a pier and marina, and revitalized Riviera Village, with boutiques, eateries, and wine-tasting galleries. Activities include sailing, kayaking, and whale watching in January. Spend an afternoon at **Seaside Lagoon (4)** *(200 Portofino Way, 310-318-0681, daily throughout the summer 10AM–5:45PM)* at Redondo Beach, a saltwater lagoon with man-made beaches and beach volleyball courts. The **Redondo Beach Pier / Fisherman's Wharf (5)** *(100 Fisherman's Wharf, 310-318-0631, www.redondopier.com)* features boardwalk/arcade—**Fun Factory** *(123 International Boardwalk, 310-379-8510)*. **King's Harbor** offers cruises on the *Voyager* *(310-372-2461)*. **Madrona Marsh Preserve & Nature Center (6)** *(3201 Plaza del Amo, Torrance, 310-782-3989, Tu–Su, 10AM–5PM)* acquaints visitors with one of the last remaining vernal marshes in Southern California. You can bike between the beach cities along part of South Bay Bicycle Trail (aka the Strand); bike rentals are available from **Marina Bike Rentals** *(505 N. Harbor Dr., 310-318-2453)* in **Redondo Beach** and **Hermosa Cyclery** *(20 13th St., 310-374-7816, www.hermosacyclery.com)*. Catch a wave with a private surfing lesson from **Surf Academy** *(302 19th St., 310-372-2790, www.surf academy.com)* in Hermosa Beach.

Arts & Entertainment:

Civic Light Opera of South Bay Cities *(2226 Artesia Blvd., 310-372-4477, www.civiclightopera.com)* performs at

the **Redondo Beach Performing Arts Center (7)** *(1935 Manhattan Beach Blvd., 310-937-6607, www.redondo.org)*. The center also presents Los Angeles Ballet performances and a star-studded speaker series. **Hermosa Beach Playhouse (8)** *(Pier Ave. at PCH, 310-372-4477, www. hermosabeachplayhouse.com)*, also a division of the Civic Light Opera, presents plays and musicals.

PLACES TO EAT & DRINK
Where to Eat:

In Manhattan Beach, Francophiles find their calling at **Café Pierre (9) ($$-$$$)** *(317 Manhattan Beach Blvd., 310-545-5252, www.cafepierre.com, Tu–F 11:30AM– 2:30PM, Su–W 5:30PM–10PM, Th–Sa till 11PM)*; Dungeness crab fritters and beef cheeks mingle with other Mediterranean fare. **Rock'N Fish (10) ($$$)** *(120 Manhattan Beach Blvd., 310-379-9900, www.rockn fishmb.com, Su–W 11:30PM–10PM, Th till 10:30PM, F–Sa till11PM)* lives up to its name with fresh seafood. Low-key **Mama D's Italian (11) ($$)** *(1125 Manhattan Ave., 310-546-1492, M–F 11:30AM–9PM, Sa–Su 12:30PM–10PM)* serves pasta in a homey setting. Greek taverna goes upscale at **Petros Greek Cuisine and Lounge (12) ($$$)** *(451 Manhattan Beach Blvd., 310-545-4100, www.petrosrestaurant.com, Su–Th 11AM–11PM, F–S till* *midnight*), serving everything from feta-crusted rack of lamb to Greek sea bass. Breakfast is king in Manhattan Beach. Local spots include **North End Caffé (13) ($)** *(3421 Highland Ave., 310-546-4782, daily 8:30AM–7PM)*, with 13 different egg sandwiches, and **Uncle Bill's Pancake House (14) ($)** *(1305 Highland Ave., 310-545-5177, M–F 6AM–3PM, Sa–Su 7AM–3PM)*, with banana buckwheat pancakes and peanut butter muffins. In Hermosa Beach, **La Sosta Enoteca (15) ($$$)** *(2700 Manhattan Ave., 310-318-1556, Tu–Th 6PM–11:30PM, F–Su till midnight)* seduces with Northern Italian fare. Try the gnocchi. **Chez Mélange (16) ($$$)** *(1611 S. Catalina Ave., 310-540-1222, www.chezmelange.com, M–F 11:30AM–2:30PM, M–Th 5:30PM–9:30PM, F–Sa till 10PM, Su till 9PM, Sa–Su brunch 9:30AM–2:30PM)* features two dining options—a gastropub up front, and an upscale bistro serving natural organic foods from local farmers.

Bars & Nightlife:

The Lighthouse Café (17) *(30 Pier Ave., 310-372-6911, www.thelighthousecafe.net, M–F 6PM–2AM, Sa–Su 11AM–2AM)* is a haven for jazz musicians, including house band the **Lighthouse All-Stars**. Greats like Miles Davis and Chet Baker have stopped by for Sunday afternoon jazz brunch, still a tradition. **Mermaid (18)** *(11 Pier Ave., 310-374-9344, M–F 10AM–10:30PM, Sa–Su 9AM–10:30PM)* is better for drinks than eats. Cheap beers and seaside locale are the main attractions at the **Poop Deck (19)** *(1272 The Strand, 310-376-3223, M–Th 11AM–10PM, F–Sa 10AM–1AM, Su till 10PM)*, another institution. On Manhattan Beach, **The Shellback Tavern (20)**

(116 Manhattan Beach Blvd., 310-376-7857, www.shellbacktavern.com, M–F 11AM–2AM, Sa–Su 9AM–2AM), is a mainstay with dive appeal, including video games and cheap grub. Tiny **Side Door (21)** *(900 Manhattan Ave., 310-372-5759, daily 5:30PM–1AM)* is a pleasant martini stop, if you can squeeze in. Redondo Beach is home to **Tony's on the Pier (22)** *(210 Fisherman's Wharf, 310-374-1442, www.oldtonys.com, M–Th 11:30PM–midnight, F till 1:30AM, Sa 11:30AM–1:30AM, Su 11:30AM–midnight)*, known as Old Tony's, which opened in 1952. **Café Boogaloo (23)** *(1238 Hermosa Ave., 310-318-2324, www.boogaloo.com, Tu–F 5PM–2AM, Sa 3PM–2AM, Su 10AM–2AM)* serves up live blues and microbrews.

WHERE TO SHOP

Riviera Village (24) *(Catalina Ave., www.rivieravillage. org)* in Redondo Beach is a six-block enclave of independent retailers, including boutiques, gift shops, galleries, restaurants, and cafés. South Bay Galleria (25) *(1815 Hawthorne Blvd., 310-371-7546, www.southbay galleria.com, daily 10AM–8PM)* is the place for mainstream and retail therapy. Popular Fernandos (26) *(1242 Hermosa Ave., 310-372-7906 www.fernandoshermosa. com, M–Sa 10:30AM–6PM, Su noon–5PM)* stocks eclectic clothes and accoutrements. Re: Style (27) *(138 Pier Ave., 310-798-1534, www.restyle.org, M–Sa 11AM–8PM, Su 11AM–7PM)* has been a purveyor of punk clothes and accessories since 1981. Manhattan Beach fixture boutiques include Third Gallery (28) *(208 Manhattan Beach Blvd., 310-376-4735)* and trendy Dollyrocker (29) *(212*

Manhattan Beach Blvd., 310-374-3396, both stores M–F 11AM–7PM, Sa 10AM–6PM, Su 11AM–6PM). Treasure hunters haunt Stars Antique Market (30) *(526 Pier Ave., 310-318-2800, M–Sa 11AM–6PM, Su till 5PM)* an old barn stuffed with vintage furniture and collectibles.

WHERE TO STAY

Get pampered at Manhattan Beach's posh Shade Hotel (31) ($$$-$$$$) *(1221 N. Valley Dr., 310-546-4995, www.shadehotel.com).* Guest rooms include spa tubs, private balconies, cocktail shakers, and espresso makers. Partake of wine at Zinc Bar or mojitos at the Skydeck. Chic boutique The Belamar Hotel (32) ($$-$$$) *(3501 N. Sepulveda Blvd., 310-750-0300, www.the belamar.com)* offers five-star touches such as in-room spa service, marble bathrooms, and rooms with private balconies overlooking Belamar gardens. Though on a busy street, Sea View Inn at the Beach (33) ($$) *(3400 Highland Ave., 310-545-1504, www.seaview-inn.com)* is Manhattan Beach's closest hotel to the beach itself. In Hermosa Beach, Beach House at Hermosa (34) ($$$) *(1300 The Strand, 310-374-3001, www.beach-house. com)* is a romantic cottage hideaway bordering The Strand. Splurge for ocean-views. Redondo Beach offers waterfront luxury at the Portofino Hotel & Yacht Club (35) ($$$) *(260 Portofino Way, 310-379-8481, www.hotelportofino.com),* on a private peninsula on King Harbor close to the Redondo Beach Pier. The loudest noise comes from local sea lions. Oldest hotel in the South Bay, Palos Verdes Inn (36) ($) *(1700 PCH, 310-316-4211, www.palosverdesinn.com)* is a budget option conveniently located, plus a heated pool.

SAN PEDRO/PALOS VERDES

• SNAPSHOT •

Traditionally a fishing village and seaport town, San

Pedro retains working-class roots and Mediterranean flavor. It also serves as the busiest port in the country. Historic Old San Pedro, bordered by Pacific Avenue, 6th and 7th Streets, and Harbor Boulevard, spills with Greek and Italian restaurants, al fresco dining, bars, and coffee-houses. Palos Verdes Peninsula, just north of town, is largely residential, yet the gorgeous vistas from its cliff-lined shores are enjoyed by all.

PLACES TO SEE
Landmarks:

Lush green **Palos Verdes Peninsula** overlooks the South Bay, best viewed by car along Palos Verdes Drive. Sites to the south include **Point Vicente Lighthouse (37)** *(31550 Palos Verdes Dr. W., 310-541-0334)*, atop cliffs that face Catalina Island. The grounds and lighthouse are normally closed to the public, but the tower and a small museum are open the second Saturday of the month between 10AM and 3PM. Also en route: **Wayfarer's Chapel (38)** *(5755 Palos Verdes Dr. S., 310-377-1650, www.wayfarerschapel.org, daily 8AM–5PM)*, a memorial to philosopher and religious reformer Emanuel Swedenborg. The chapel, constructed of redwood, glass, and local stone, was designed by Lloyd Wright (son of Frank Lloyd Wright) and is surrounded by gardens. The **South Coast Botanic Garden (39)** *(26300 Crenshaw Blvd., 310-544-1948, www.southcoastbotanic garden.org, daily 9AM–5PM)* features an 87-acre garden and culture center with over 2,500 species of plants and trees. Within San Pedro's **Angels Gate Park (40)** *(3601 S. Gaffey St., 310-548-7705, daily 10AM–5PM, cultural center galleries Tu–Su 11AM–4PM)* is Fort MacArthur, a U.S. Army post. Tour the old bunkers and peruse photos and memorabilia at **Fort MacArthur Museum** *(www.ftmac.org, Tu, Th, Sa–Su noon–5PM)*. Also see the 17-ton **Korean Friendship Bell**, a 1976 gift from the South Korean government. The bell is rung four times each year: July 4th, August 15th (Korean Independence Day), New Year's Eve, and every September to coincide with bell ringings around the country to celebrate Constitution week. Angels Gate is also home to the **Marine Mammal Care Center** *(310-548-5677, daily 10AM–4PM)*, which rehabilitates sick and injured seals and sea lions, and presents exhibits and educational information on marine mammals. **Point Fermin Park (41)** *(807 Paseo Del Mar, 310-548-7705)* marks the southernmost point in Los Angeles. The park features 37 acres of lawns, gardens, and a promenade. From the bluffs, Catalina Island is visible, as are seals and dolphins in season. **Point Fermin Lighthouse** *(310-241-0684, www.pointferminlighthouse. org, tours Tu–Su 1PM–4PM)*, built in 1874, is one of the oldest lighthouses on the West Coast. It was used for safe

passage between the Channel Islands and into the harbor for nearly 100 years. The new **San Pedro Waterfront Promenade**, a pedestrian-oriented waterfront parkway dotted with trees and gardens, features a band of granite that relates the history of San Pedro. **Ports O' Call Marketplace (42)** *(1100 Nagoya Way, 310-548-8076)* is the departure point for narrated harbor cruises, fishing excursions, sunset cruises, Catalina Island sailing cruises, and whale-watching cruises (January through March). The village is also home to 15 acres of shops, restaurants, and attractions.

Arts & Entertainment:

Sprawling **Los Angeles Maritime Museum (43)** *(Berth 84 at the foot of 6th St., 310-548-7618, www.lamaritime museum.org, Tu–Sa 10AM–5PM, Su noon–5PM)* showcases more than 700 ship and boat models, has an operating amateur radio station, and offers exhibits on everything from whaling industry history to seaworthy arts and crafts. Art Deco classic **Warner Grand Theatre (44)** *(478 W. 6th St., 310-833-4813, www.warnergrand.org)* features foreign and American classic films as well as live performances. The **Angels Gate Cultural Center (45)** *(3601 S. Gaffey St., 310-519-0936, www.angelsgateart. org, Tu–Su 10AM–5PM)* presents exhibitions in buildings that housed soldiers over the years and provides studio space for 52 artists.

Kids:

Introducing local marine life and the history of California's gray whales, the **Cabrillo Marine Aquarium (46)** *(3720 Stephen White Dr., 310-548-7562, www. cabrilloaq.org)* engages visitors with 35 aquariums, touch tanks, and other facilities, including a hands-on **Exploration Center**.

PLACES TO EAT & DRINK
Where to Eat:

More spectacle than dining experience, a meal at **Papadakis Taverna (47) ($$-$$$)** *(301 W. 6th St., 310-548-1186, www.papadakistaverna.com, daily 5PM–10:30PM)* includes waitstaff who break into Greek song and dance. The more sedate, family-owned **J Trani's Ristorante (48) ($$)** *(584 W. 9th St., 310-832-1220, Tu–F 11:30AM–2:30PM, Tu–Th 5:30PM–9PM, F–Sa 5PM–9:30PM, Su–M 5PM–9PM)*, a San Pedro institution, serves authentic Italian fare to a loyal following. Locals start the day at breakfast spot **Rex's Café (49) ($)** *(2136 S. Pacific Ave., 310-519-7190, 7AM–2PM)*, which serves healthy morning fare like Eggs Benny and fresh baked muffins. At **22nd Street Landing Seafood Grill and Bar (50) ($$$)** *(141 W. 22nd St., 310-548-4400, www.22ndstreet.com, Tu–F 11:30AM–9PM, Sa noon–10PM, Su 11AM–10PM)*, take in sunset views of the San Pedro Marina while dining.

Bars & Nightlife:

San Pedro Brewing Company (51) *(331 W. 6th St., 310-831-5663, www.sanpedrobrewing.com, M–Th, Su*

10:30AM–midnight, F–Sa till 2AM), part brew house, part club, brews its own ales and lagers on a Czech-made system. The brew house, next to the stage in the main dining room, is the backdrop for local rock and punk bands on Fridays and Saturdays. British pub **The Whale and Ale (52)** *(327 W. 7th St., 310-832-0363, www.whaleandale.com, M–Th 11:30AM–9:30PM, Sa till 10PM, Su till 9PM, bar daily 11:30AM–late)* features a selection of imported draught beers, as well as its own label, and live entertainment most Saturdays. An older crowd comes Fridays for the piano bar. If West Hollywood headed south, it would lounge at **The Copper Room (53)** *(589 W. 9th St., 310-831-6200, www.thecopperroom.com, restaurant Tu–Sa 5PM–10PM, bar M–Sa 4PM–2AM)*, a cocktail bar and tapas hot spot in one. Indulge in a black chocolate martini. Nibble on crab cakes or Spanish cheeses.

WHERE TO SHOP

Grand dame Williams Book Store (54) *(443 W. 6th St., 310-832-3631, www.williamsbookstore.com, M–Th 10AM–6PM, F till 8PM, Sa till 6PM, Su 11AM–4PM)* has the distinction of being the oldest bookstore in L.A. Founded in 1909, the shop has outlived its chain store competitors. Joanne's Closet (55) *(389 W. 6th St., 310-514-3219, www.shopjoannescloset.com, Tu–Sa 10AM–6PM, Su 11AM–3PM)* is a sleek boutique offering contemporary clothes from True Religion, Michael Stars, and Juicy Couture, among other trendy labels. Return to Versailles at Behind the Scenes Costumes (56)

(285 W. 6th St., 310-521-9000, www.behindthescenes costumes.com, M–Sa 11AM–6PM), specializing in hand-crafted costumes hearkening the era of Marie Antoinette. Designs use embroidered silks, Italian brocades, and French lace.

WHERE TO STAY

For tried-and-true brand names, San Pedro and surrounds offer the **Crowne Plaza Harbor Hotel (57) ($$)** *(601 S. Palos Verdes St., 310-519-8200, www.ichotelsgroup. com)* and **Doubletree Hotel San Pedro (58) ($$)** *(2800 Via Cabrillo Marina, 310-514-3344, www.doubletree1. hilton.com).* Lodgings at **Hostelling International—Los Angeles South Bay (59) ($)** *(3601 S. Gaffey St. Building 613, 310-831-8109, www.hihostels.com)* provide panoramic views of the Pacific Ocean and Catalina Island. New oceanfront **Terranea Resort (60)** *(6610 Palos Verdes Dr. S., 866-366-7474, www.terranea.com),* with 582 rooms, which includes suites, bungalows, casitas, and villas, has something for guests on every level. Also features a spa, pools with a 140-foot waterslide, and golf.

LONG BEACH

• SNAPSHOT •

If any part of L.A. has had an extreme makeover in the past century, Long Beach is it. First settled as part of a sprawling Spanish land grant to soldier Manuel Nieto, the area encompassed the 28,000-acre Ranch Los Alamitos and its sister rancho, 27,000-acre Rancho Los Cerritos. Development began in the 1800s, and with the introduction in 1902 of the Pacific Electric trolley, Long Beach became the fastest growing city in the country. During that era, it was also home to Balboa Studios, a silent movie business that drew the likes of Fatty Arbuckle, who decided to reside here. Then, in 1921, oil was discovered on Signal Hill and Long Beach flourished. About a decade later, the settled area was leveled by an earthquake. Tourism got a boost with the mooring of the *Queen Mary* in Long Beach Harbor in 1967. In 1975 the city embarked on an ongoing multibillion dollar redevelopment program, which resulted in entertain-

ment and shopping venues like the Long Beach Town Centre, CityPlace, and Shoreline Village, among other attractions. The Port of Long Beach is the second busiest in the country next to the Port of Los Angeles in San Pedro. Today, Long Beach has several lively areas, including former factory district Pine Avenue, a dining/shopping haven. Second Street in the upscale Belmont Shore district has trendy retailers, ethnic restaurants, and Mexican cantinas. A burgeoning East Village Arts District lends space to art galleries and funky shops.

PLACES TO SEE
Landmarks:

Get a glimpse of Old World decadence on the ★ **RMS *QUEEN MARY* (61)** *(1126 Queens Hwy., 562-435-3511, www.queenmary.com, daily 10AM–6PM)*, which sailed the North Atlantic seas from 1936 to 1967. Anchored at Long Beach Harbor since its last voyage, the ship is now a tourist attraction and hotel. Marvel at this 81,237-ton Art Deco liner as you walk the teakwood decks and hold onto Bakelite handrails. Mingle with the undead on the ship's **Ghosts and Legends Tour**. Though the Cold War may be over, the *Scorpion*, the **Russian Foxtrot Submarine (62)** *(1126 Queens Hwy., 562-432-0424, www.russiansublongbeach. com, daily 10AM–6PM)*, is a reminder of the Soviet era.

TOP PICK!

Arts & Entertainment:

Long Beach Museum of Art (63) *(2300 E. Ocean Blvd., 562-439-2119, www.lbma.org, Tu–Su 11AM–5PM)* rivals big city counterparts with approximately 3,000 paintings, drawings, sculptures, works on paper, and decorative arts. Take in 300 years of ceramics, early-20th-century European art, and California Modernism works and contemporary California art. The museum is housed in a Craftsman mansion built by heiress Elizabeth Milbank

Anderson. The newly expanded **Museum of Latin American Art (64)** *(628 Alamitos Ave., 562-437-1689, www.molaa.org, Tu–F 11:30AM–7PM, Sa 11AM–7PM, Su till 6PM)* spotlights contemporary fine art from established masters as well as emerging artists in a variety of media. The museum is located in the developing **East Village Arts District** of Long Beach, home to the **Second Saturday Art Walk** every month and the **Tour des Artistes**, an annual June street festival focused on visual and performing arts. The well-respected **Long Beach Symphony** *(562-436-3203, www.lbso.org)* performs at **Long Beach Performing Arts Center**, part of the **Long Beach Convention & Entertainment Center (65)** *(300 Ocean Blvd., 562-436-3636)*. Special productions take place at Terrace Theater, also part of the entertainment center; the award-winning, nonprofit **International City Theatre** *(562-436-4610, www.ictlongbeach.org)*, founded in 1985, presents innovative, thought-provoking productions. The **Long Beach Opera** *(507 Pacific Ave., 562-439-2580, www.longbeachopera.org)*, the oldest established professional opera company in the L.A. area, performs at **Carpenter Performing Arts Center (66)** *(6200 E. Atherton St., 562-985-7000, www.carpenterarts.org)*, which hosts music, dance, comedy, and cabaret events. **Long Beach Playhouse (67)** *(5021 E. Anaheim St., 562-494-1014, www.lbph.com)* presents 16 shows annually with a new play or musical every three weeks.

Kids:

Aquarium of the Pacific (68) *(100 Aquarium Way, 562-590-3100, www.aquariumofpacific.org, daily 9AM–6PM)*, as its name implies, focuses on marine life, spanning some 500 species. Kids can also find diversions at **The Pike at Rainbow Harbor (69)** *(95 S. Pine Ave., 562-432-8325, www.thepikeatlongbeach.com, daily 11AM–close)*, a waterfront entertainment district with a carousel, a Ferris wheel, restaurants, and entertainment venues.

PLACES TO EAT & DRINK
Where to Eat:

Waits of an hour are not unheard of for the authentic fare at **La Parolaccia Osteria Italiana (70) ($$)** *(2945 E. Broadway, 562-438-1235, www.laparolacciausa.com, M–F 5:30PM–10PM, Sa–Su 11:30AM–10PM)*. Service can be slow, but once you're seated, the lively spot compensates with homemade pastas and affordable fresh mains. **Alegria Cocina Latina (71) ($$)** *(115 Pine Ave., 562-436-3388, www.alegriacocinalatina.com, M–Th 11:30AM–11PM, F 11:30AM–midnight, Sa noon–midnight, Su 4PM–10PM)* tempts with Spanish flair—sangria, tapas, and flamenco performances. On the east side of Long Beach, **Frenchy's Bistro (72) ($$$)** *(4137 E. Anaheim St., 562-494-8787, www.frenchysbistro.com, Tu–F 11:30AM–2:30PM, Tu–Su 5:30PM–9:30PM)* surprises with haute classics, like duck à l'orange, escargots, and soufflés. **Open Sesame (73) ($)** *(5215 E. 2nd St., 562-621-1698, www.opensesamegrill.com, Su–Th 11AM–10:30PM, F–Sa till 11PM)* adds Middle Eastern spice to the downtown area. Romantic **Parker's Lighthouse (74) ($$$)** *(435 Shoreline Village Dr., 562-432-6500, M–F 11AM–3PM, Sa–Su till 3:30PM, M–Th 5PM–10PM, F till 11PM, Sa 4PM–11PM, Su till 10PM)* impresses with waterside views and fresh seafood. Wake up to banana wheat pancakes or vegetarian chorizo at breakfast spot **Coffee Cup Café (75) ($)** *(3734 E. 4th St., 562-433-3292, M–F 7AM–2PM, Sa–Su till 3PM)*.

Bars & Nightlife:

Swanky **Observation Bar (76)** *(1126 Queens Hwy., 562-435-3511, www.queenmary.com, M–Th noon–11PM, F–Sa 10AM–1AM, Su till 11PM)* makes for the best excuse to board the *Queen Mary*. This Art Deco masterpiece is a prime setting for a martini, happy hour hors d'oeuvres, and live entertainment. Tiki-style **Puka Bar (77)** *(710 W. Willow St., 562-997-6896, M–F 4PM–2AM, Sa–Su 2PM–2AM)* plays up the Polynesian with its decor and fruity cocktails. **CasaVino (78)** *(51 S. Pine Ave., 562-216-1590, www.casavinowinebar.com, W–Sa 5PM–close)* treats wine like art, coupling flights and tastings with a visual arts backdrop. Local DJs and a chill vibe make this a local favorite. Long Beach has its share of dives, including **V Room (79)** *(918 E. 4th St., 562-437-4396, daily 6AM–1:30AM)*, with cheap drinks and a rockin' jukebox. Punk rock lives at **Alex's Bar (80)** *(2913 E. Anaheim St., 562-434-8292, www.alexsbar.com, M–Th 3PM–2AM, F–Su noon–2AM)* with bands and DJs.

WHERE TO SHOP

Funky Blue Windows (81) *(5276 E. 2nd St., 562-434-7195, M–Th 10AM–9PM, F–Sa till 10PM, Su till 8PM)* is gift central, with handmade bags, jewelry, even crazy pajamas. Out-trend the trendies at BeMe (82) *(3500 E. Anaheim St., 562-961-8468, Tu–Sa 11AM–8PM)*. The owner is helpful and outspoken while outfitting her patrons. **Fern's Garden (83)** *(5308 E. 2nd St., 562-434-6425, www.fernsgarden.com, M–Sa 10AM–9PM, Su 11AM–8PM)*, which started 25 years ago with wind chimes, has morphed into an eclectic venue for the vanishing American artisan. Unique items, from a pocket pewter labyrinth to good-luck Chilean pigs, can be found here. **Iguana Import Gallery (84)** *(3440 E. Broadway, 562-433-1713, www.culturalgiftshop.com, M–Sa 10:30AM–8:30PM, Su till 6PM)* features artisan furnishings and accessories, including locally designed jewelry, Mexican folk art, and imported handicrafts. **The Vintage Collective (85)** *(2122 E. 4th St., www.thevintagecollective.com, M–W 11AM–6PM, Th–Sa till 7PM, Su noon—6PM)*, a 4,000-square-foot consignment mall with 25 dealers, also acts as a showroom for furnishings, ranging from Art Deco through Mid-Century Modern.

WHERE TO STAY

Sleep like royalty at the **Queen Mary Hotel (86) ($$)** *(1126 Queens Hwy., 562-435-3511, www.queenmary.com)*, with 307 original staterooms on three decks. Enjoy top-level service at **Renaissance Long Beach Hotel (87) ($$-$$$)** *(111 E. Ocean Blvd., 562-437-5900, www.marriott.com)*, providing full business amenities and popular chophouse **Tracht's**. The **Coast Long Beach Hotel (88) ($$)** *(700 Queensway Dr., 562-435-7676, www.coasthotels.com)* is a good value considering its waterside locale. **The Turret House (89) ($$)** *(556 Chestnut Ave., 562-624-1991, www.turrethouse.com)* was built in 1906 by a Kansas carpenter and features fireplaces in each of the five cozy Victorian rooms.

CATALINA ISLAND

See Catalina Island Chamber of Commerce (www.catalina.com), Santa Catalina Island Conservancy (125 Claressa Ave., Avalon, 310-510-2595, www.catalinaconservancy.org). Catalina Express (310-519-1212, www.catalinaexpress.com) operates year-round boat service to Catalina Island with up to 30 round-trip daily departures from Long Beach, San Pedro, and Dana Point to Avalon and Two Harbors. The Catalina-Marina del Rey Flyer (310-305-7250, www.catalinaferries.com) runs from Marina del Rey to Avalon in an hour and a half and also stops at Two Harbors. For an even quicker trip, try Island Express Helicopters (310-510-2525, www.islandexpress.com) from San Pedro or Long Beach.

Santa Catalina Island, 22 miles offshore from Long Beach, is a tranquil escape from L.A's freeway congestion, though weekends can get crowded. Touted for its Mediterranean vibe, the island offers numerous outdoor options, including swimming, snorkeling, scuba diving, parasailing, fishing, and kayaking, or land-based excursions like horseback riding, bicycling, sightseeing, or golfing. Chewing gum magnate William Wrigley Jr. purchased shares in the company that was developing the island in 1919. He built a replica of Wrigley Field that was used until 1951 for the Chicago Cubs spring training. In 1975, his son

Philip Wrigley deeded the Wrigley shares in the Santa Catalina Island Company to the Catalina Island Conservancy, which is now in charge of nearly 90 percent of the island.

Island highlights include a walk down **Green Pleasure Pier** along main drag Crescent Avenue, and the 1929-era **Casino**, a former Art Deco dance hall that still hosts big-band dances on occasion. On the Casino bottom floor is the **Catalina Island Museum** *(1 Casino Way, 310-510-2414, daily 10AM–4PM)* and **Casino Art Gallery** *(310-510-0808)*. At night, dine at one of several popular restaurants, such as **Avalon Seafood ($$)** *(Green Pleasure Pier, 310-510-0197, 11AM–close)*, or **Catalina Country Club ($$$)** *(1 Country Club Dr., 310-510-7404, 11AM–close)* in the old Chicago Cubs clubhouse, or have a quick bite at **Eric's on the Pier ($)** *(Green Pier No. 2, Avalon, 310-510-0894, M–F 8AM–4:30PM, Sa–Su till 5PM)* and see a movie at the historic **Avalon Theatre** *(310-510-0179)*, also in the Casino. **Wrigley Memorial and Botanical Gardens** *(Avalon Canyon Rd., 310-510-2897, daily 8AM–5PM)* features native plants, and **Casino Point Underwater Park** is a marine preserve for snorkelers and divers.

The town's original **Hotel Metropole ($$)** *(205 Crescent Ave., 310-510-1884, www.hotel-metropole.com)*, built in the late 1800s, was Avalon's first hotel. Other hotel options include the **Catalina Canyon Resort & Spa ($$)** *(888 Country Club Dr., 310-510-0325, www.catalina-canyon-resort.pacifica.host.com)*. Or stay in the former William Wrigley Jr. mansion at **Inn on Mt. Ada ($$$)** *(398 Wrigley Rd., 310-510-2030)*.

DISNEYLAND

1313 S. Disneyland Dr., Anaheim, 714-781-4565, disneyland.disney.go.com, (hours change depending on the season). Anaheim Resort Transit (ART) System provides shuttle service from area hotels to the Disneyland Resort, and all L.A. area airports provide shuttle services to the Disneyland Resort.

No family can escape SoCal without a journey to the Magic Kingdom. For all its overcrowding and extreme pricing, this 1955-era Walt Disney landmark still casts enough of a spell to make the visit well worth it.

The park is divided into seven areas, or "lands," including the centerpiece, Main Street USA, harkening early 1900s America. New Orleans Square replicates the French Quarter and includes the popular *Pirates of the Caribbean* ride, now updated to reflect the Johnny Depp phenom. Jeep ride Indiana Jones Adventure is a top draw in Adventureland, while two of the park's best thrill rides are Space Mountain in Tomorrowland and the Matterhorn bobsled ride in Fantasyland.

Aside from Disneyland itself, other highlights of the Resort complex include **Disney's California Adventure Park** and the **Downtown Disney** shopping, dining, and entertainment district.

Disney Resort hotels *(714-956-6425)* include **Disney's Grand Californian Hotel & Spa ($$$$)** *(1600 S. Disneyland Dr.)*, **Disneyland Hotel ($$$)** *(1150 W. Magic Way)*, and **Disney's Paradise Pier Hotel ($$$)** *(1717 S. Disneyland Dr.)*, while onsite dining options include **Steakhouse 55 ($$$)** *(1150 W. Cerritos Ave., 714-781-3463, daily 5:30PM–10PM)*. There are nearly 40 off-site hotels, many of which are more economical than the resort hotels.

Disneyland will never be
completed. It will continue
to grow as long as there is
imagination left in the world.

—WALT DISNEY

SOUTH LOS ANGELES/ LEIMERT PARK

• SNAPSHOT •

South Los Angeles, or South Central, loosely defines the stretch south of Downtown L.A. This historically African-American area has seen its share of racial tension, including the Watts Riots of 1965 and the Los Angeles riots of 1992, also known as the Rodney King riots. The hub of activity from the '20s to the '50s ran along Central Avenue, where jazz clubs, churches, and theaters lined the street. The negative connotations of the rioting around South Central sparked the name change in 2003 to "South L.A." An increasingly Latin American population has taken root here. The rejuvenated Leimert Park, former home to stars like Ray Charles and Ella Fitzgerald, draws visitors. Today it's the cultural heart of South L.A., with art galleries, jazz and blues clubs, and soul food restaurants.

PLACES TO SEE
Landmarks:

It took 33 years for the 1954 folk art **Watts Towers (90)** *(1761–1765 E. 107th St., 213-847-4646, www.wattstowers.net)* to be erected. They're actually a group of 17 intertwined structures built by Italian immigrant Simon Rodia, using found materials, including some 25,000 seashells. The **Watts Towers Arts Center** *(Tu–Sa 10:30AM–4PM, Su noon–4PM)* operates public tours of the towers and hosts concerts, exhibitions, and festivals. **Kenneth Hahn State Recreation Area (91)** *(4100 S. La Cienega Blvd., 323-298-3660, 8AM–5PM)* was the 1932 site of the first Olympic Village. Today, the park offers walking trails and scenic vistas of Los Angeles. It's off to the races at **Hollywood Park Racetrack (92)** *(1050 S. Prairie Ave., 310-419-1500, www.hollywoodpark.com)*, with horse racing and live music.

Arts & Entertainment:
Museum of African American Art (93) *(4005 Crenshaw Blvd., www.maaa-la.org, Th–Sa 11AM–6PM, Su noon–5PM)*, or the MAAA, is a nonprofit space (on the third floor of Macy's at the Baldwin Hills Crenshaw Plaza), dedicated to established and up-and-coming African-American artists. The **William Grant Still Arts Center (94)** *(2520 W. View St., 213-847-1540, daily noon–5PM)*, named after the famed symphony composer, presents African-American exhibits and workshops. The **Vision Theatre (95)** *(3341 W. 43rd Pl., 323-291-7321)*, originally built in the 1930s, is considered one of the last two Art Deco theatres remaining in L.A. Undergoing a major redo, it will host performing arts events, films, and community lectures and exhibits.

PLACES TO EAT & DRINK
Where to Eat:
For a taste of the South "N'awlins-style," **Harold & Belle's (96) ($$-$$$)** *(2920 W. Jefferson Blvd., 323-735-*

9023, Su–Th 11:30AM–10PM, F–Sa till 11PM) channels the Big Easy with jambalaya, fried catfish, and crawfish étouffée. **R & R Soul Food Restaurant (97) ($)** *(18427 Avalon Blvd., 310-715-6716, M–F 8AM–9PM, Sa–Su till 10PM)* piles on heaping portions of stick-to-your-ribs Southern comfort foods like mac & cheese, candied yams, and fried chicken drowned in gravy. **M&M Soul Food (98) ($)** *(3300 W. Manchester Blvd., 310-673-5031, www.mandmsoulfoodonline.com, Tu–Su 8AM–8:30PM)* takes its flavors straight from the Mississippi delta. The original **M&M ($)** *(5496 W. Centinela Ave., 310-215-8186, daily 9AM–9PM)* features home-style soul food like meat loaf and smothered chicken. Greek family-owned **Pann's Restaurant (99) ($-$$)** *(6710 La Tijera Blvd., 323-776-3770, www.panns.com, M–Sa 7AM–11PM, Su till 10PM)* is known more for its angular architecture than its diner fare. Pann's has been featured in top flicks like *Pulp Fiction* and *Bewitched*. Barbecue lovers can choose between **Phillips Bar-B-Que (100) ($)** *(4307 Leimert Blvd., 323-292-7613, M 11AM–8PM, Tu–Th 11AM–10PM, F–Sa till 11PM)* and **Woody's Bar-B-Que (101) ($)** *(3446 W. Slauson Ave., 323-294-9443, M–Sa 11AM–11PM, Su noon–10PM)* for their fix. **Ackee Bamboo (102) ($)** *(4305 Degnan Blvd., 323-295-7275, M–Th 11AM–9PM, F–Sa till 10PM, Su 11:30AM–6PM)* serves up Jamaican jerk chicken.

Bars & Nightlife:

The oldest blues club in Los Angeles, **Babe's and Ricky's Inn (103)** *(4339 Leimert Blvd., 323-295-9112, www.bluesbar.com, Th–M*

4PM–2AM) has attracted B.B. King, Cab Calloway, Duke Ellington, Count Basie, Eric Clapton, and John Lee Hooker. A soul food buffet is served late, 11PM. **The World Stage (104)** *(4344 Degnan Blvd., 323-293-2451, www.theworldstage.org)*, founded by late jazz drummer Billy Higgins and poet Kamau Daáood, is the hub of jazz and literary activity in Leimert Park. The club hosts the Anansi Writers Workshop and has featured jam sessions or classes from jazz greats like Max Roach. **Café-Club Fais Do-Do (105)** *(5257 W. Adams Blvd., 323-954-8080, www.faisdodo. com)* spotlights local blues, jazz, funk, soul, and even Brazilian salsa. The club, in a former 1930s Art Deco bank, has featured such luminaries as Sam Cooke, Billy Preston, and John Coltrane.

WHERE TO SHOP

Zambezi Bazaar (106) *(4334 Degnan Blvd., 323-299-6383, M–Sa 11AM–6PM, Su 11AM–3PM)* sells rare books and magazines, vintage records, greeting cards, and hard-to-find prints, plus jewelry, tunics, soaps, and candles. Gallery Plus (107) *(4333 Degnan Blvd., 323-296-2398, M–Sa 11AM–6PM, Su till 5PM)* spotlights the works of African-American artists, as well as cards, stationery, and literature. Eso Won Books (108) *(4331 Degnan Blvd., 323-290-1048, www.esowon.booksense.com, M–Sa 10AM–7PM, Su noon–5PM)*, co-owned by James Fugate and Tom Hamilton, carries ethnic literature; its book signings have included Bill Clinton and Barack Obama.

chapter 8

STUDIO CITY/WESTERN VALLEY

NORTH HOLLYWOOD/UNIVERSAL CITY

BURBANK/GLENDALE

STUDIO CITY/WESTERN VALLEY
NORTH HOLLYWOOD/
UNIVERSAL CITY
BURBANK/GLENDALE

Places to See:

1. Ronald Reagan Library & Museum
2. Sepulveda Basin Recreation Area
3. Santa Monica Mountains National Recreation Area
4. Paramount Ranch
5. Left Coast Galleries
6. Two Roads Theatre
7. Storyopolis
29. NoHo Arts Center
30. Actors Forum Theatre
31. Lankershim Arts Center
32. Cella Gallery
33. Judith Kaufman Gallery
34. Academy of Television Arts and Science Plaza
35. HaHa Comedy Club
36. Universal Studios Hollywood
56. Forest Lawn Memorial Park
57. Warner Bros. Studios
58. NBC Television Studios
59. Alex Theatre
60. Falcon Theatre

Places to Eat & Drink:

8. Katsu-Ya
9. Sushi Nozawa
10. Asanebo
11. Firefly
12. Hugo's
13. Art's Delicatessen
14. Carney's Restaurant
15. Max
16. Saddle Peak Lodge
17. La Ve Lee
18. Starlite Room
37. Ca del Sole
38. Skaf's Grill
39. Little Toni's
40. Sanam Luang Café
41. Jack's Classic Hamburgers
42. Eat
43. The Baked Potato
44. Bar One
45. The Good Nite
46. Tonga Hut Tiki Lounge
47. California Institute of Abnormal Arts (CIA)
61. Bashan
62. Bistro Provence

63. La Cabanita
64. Corner Cottage
65. Yummy Cupcakes
66. Blue Room
67. Burbank Bar & Grille

Where to Shop

19. Playclothes Vintage
    Fashions
20. Stacey Todd
21. Bedfellows
22. Dari
23. Faire Frou Frou
24. Lemon Rags
25. Taylrz Joynt Boutique
26. Portrait of a Bookstore
48. Iliad Book Shop
49. Age of Innocence
50. Marie et Cie
51. Lucky You

52. Universal CityWalk
68. It's a Wrap
69. Brand Bookshop
70. Atomic Records
71. The Train Shack
72. 8 Ball

Where to Stay

27. Sportsmen Lodge Hotel
28. Nite Inn
53. Beverly Garland's Holiday
    Inn at Universal Studios
54. Hilton Los Angeles
55. Sheraton Universal
73. Hotel Amarano Burbank
74. Safari Inn
75. Coast Anabelle Hotel
76. Hilton Los Angeles
    North/Glendale & Executive
    Meeting Center

STUDIO CITY/WESTERN VALLEY

• SNAPSHOT •

Studio City's moniker dates to the 1920s silent film era, when Mack Sennett moved Mack Sennett Studios from the Echo Park area to Colfax Avenue and Ventura Boulevard. Five years later, Sennett was forced to file bankruptcy, and the studio lot was sold to another film company, Mascot Pictures, which became MTM Enterprises, where the *Mary Tyler Moore Show* was filmed. Other shows filmed over the years here include everything from *Gilligan's Island* to *American Gladiators*; today CBS Studio Center is based here. Studio City's main attractions run along palm-studded Ventura Boulevard, namely a standout culinary scene and a destination shopping locale. One small area, Tujunga Village, offers cafés and boutiques. A number of other neighborhoods sprawl west, including Encino, Simi Valley, Sherman Oaks, Van Nuys, and Calabasas.

PLACES TO SEE
Landmarks:

West of Studio City, in Simi Valley, the **Ronald Reagan Library & Museum (1)** *(40 Presidential Dr., 805-522-8444, www.reaganlibrary.net, daily 10AM–5PM)* is an ode to the Gipper with memorabilia and a faux Oval Office.

The 2,031-acre **Sepulveda Basin Recreation Area (2)** *(17017 Burbank Blvd., 818-756-8060, daily dawn to dusk)* in Encino encompasses parks, Balboa Lake, three golf courses, bike paths, a cricket field, a model airplane field, an archery range, and a wildlife preserve that is home to ducks, geese, herons, and egrets. The **Santa Monica Mountains National Recreation Area (3)** *(401 Hillcrest Ave., 805-370-2301, www.nps.gov/samo, daily 9AM–5PM)* extends into the Valley and includes popular hiking areas like **Coldwater Canyon Park. Mulholland Drive** of the David Lynch movie of the same name, divides L.A. and the Valley, running along the ridgeline of the Santa Monica Mountains and the Hollywood Hills, with views of both the Los Angeles basin and the San Fernando Valley. In this area you'll find the **Paramount Ranch (4)** *(2813 Cornell Rd., 818-735-0876, www.nps.gov/samo, daily 8AM–7PM)*, where you can tour a re-creation of an Old West town that has been used as a backdrop in films and TV.

Arts & Entertainment:

Left Coast Galleries (5) *(12324 Ventura Blvd., 818-760-7010, www.leftcoastgalleries.com, M–Sa 11AM–6PM, Su noon–6PM)*, which bills itself as the "artist/collector connection," showcases contemporary artists and 21st-century impressionism. **A Studio Gallery** *(4260 Lankershim Blvd., 818-980-9100, www.astudio*

gallery.com, M–Th 9AM–4PM, F till noon) devotes itself to black-and-white film photo exhibits and is home to the **Black & White Photographers Guild** *(www.4260 photo.com)*. **Two Roads Theatre (6)** *(4348 Tujunga Ave., 818-762-2272)*, located in Tujunga Village, hosts theater companies and comedy troupes.

Kids:

Storyopolis (7) *(12348 Ventura Blvd., 818-990-7600, www.storyopolis.com, M–Sa 11AM–6PM, Su till 5PM)* splits its allegiance between being an art gallery and a bookstore, with an emphasis on storybook illustration. The shop hosts family-style activities and events on weekends, along with story-time readings.

PLACES TO EAT & DRINK
Where to Eat:

Katsu-Ya (8) ($$) *(11680 Ventura Blvd., 818-985-6976, www.sushikatsu-ya.com, M–Sa 11:30AM–2PM, 5:30PM–10PM, F–Sa till 10:30PM, Su 5:30PM–9:30PM)* is one of the hottest tables in town, notable for succulent sashimi and nigiri sushi. Topping many lists for L.A.'s best sushi, **Sushi Nozawa (9) ($$$)** *(11288 Ventura Blvd., 818-508-7017, www.sushinozawa.com, M–F noon–2PM, 5:30PM–10PM)* transcends its dingy location with some of the city's freshest fish. Yet another L.A. strip mall gem, **Asanebo (10) ($$–$$$)** *(11941 Ventura Blvd., 818-760-3348, Tu–F noon–2PM, 6PM–10:30PM, F–Sa till 11:30PM, Su 6PM–10PM)* goes beyond the usual sushi and sashimi to include creations like the seared toro with

a dash of garlic cream. The front room of **Firefly (11) ($$-$$$)** *(11720 Ventura Blvd., 818-762-1833, M–Sa 6PM–2AM, Su till 1AM)* resembles a cozy library with couches and bookshelves; the dining area is in a covered patio around a fireplace. Temptations include cast-iron skillet mussels and baked Alaska. **Hugo's (12) ($-$$)** *(12851 Riverside Dr., 818-284-4256, www.hugosrestaurant.com, M–F 7:30AM–10PM, Sa–Su 8AM–10PM)* sticks to an organic, sustainable credo with healthy comfort foods. Breakfast options include strawberry chai spice pancakes. **Art's Delicatessen (13) ($)** *(12224 Ventura Blvd., 818-762-1221, www.artsdeli.com, daily 7AM–9PM)* is one of L.A.'s best delis. Slip into a retro booth and dig into corned beef on rye. Located in an old yellow train car, **Carney's Restaurant (14) ($)** *(12601 Ventura Blvd., 818-761-8300, www.carney train.com, M–Th, Su 11AM–10PM, F–Sa till midnight)* vies for top dog position in L.A.'s hot dog contest. Try the double chili cheese. West of Studio City, **Max (15)** *(13355 Ventura Blvd., 818-784-2915, www.maxrestau rant.com, M–F 11:30AM–2:30PM, Su–Th 5:30PM–10PM, F–Sa till 11PM)* is a lesson in Cal-Asian fusion, from miso marinated black cod to coconut shrimp stew. Further out, in the Santa Monica Mountains, **Calabasas** is a small culinary haven. **Saddle Peak Lodge (16) ($$$-$$$$)** *(419 Cold Canyon Rd., 818-222-3888, www.saddlepeaklodge.com, W–Su 5PM–10PM)* sets a romantic tone in a hunting lodge with mountain views. Wash down game meats with a variety of wines.

Bars & Nightlife:

Musicians from Tito Puente to Sheila E. have graced the stage of longtime jazz club **La Ve Lee (17)** *(12514 Ventura Blvd., 818-980-8158, Tu–Su 7PM–1AM)*. The Valley has its own dive spot, the **Starlite Room (18)** *(11411 Moorpark St., 818-766-5807, daily 10AM–2AM)*.

WHERE TO SHOP

Set aside a day to treasure hunt at Playclothes Vintage Fashions (19) *(11422 Moorpark St., 818-755-9559, www.vintageplayclothes.com, M–Sa 11AM–6PM, Su noon–5PM)*. Stacey Todd (20) *(13025-9 Ventura Blvd., 818-981-7567, M–Sa 10AM–6PM, Su noon–5PM)* takes over nearly a whole block with three outlets, one for chic, muted women's wear, a second filled with denim for men and women, and a third for home decor. Bedfellows (21) *(12250 Ventura Blvd., 818-985-0500, M–F 10AM–7PM, Sa 10AM–6PM, Su 11AM–5PM)* is the place for retro-inspired furniture from Sweden, as well as vintage, plus Art Deco mirrors, Tiki masks, and celadon vases. Stars come out to shop at Dari (22) *(12184 Ventura Blvd., 818-762-3274, www.shopdari.com, M–Sa 11AM–6PM, Su noon–5PM)*, owned by *Star Trek* star William Shatner's daughter Melanie. Turn up the sex appeal at Faire Frou Frou (23) *(13017A Ventura Blvd., 818-783-4970, www.fairefroufrou.com, M–F 10AM–6PM, Sa 11AM–5:30PM, Su noon–4PM)*, spilling with lace, silk, and all the seductive trimmings. Lemon Rags (24) *(11950*

Ventura Blvd., 818-760-0101, www.lemonrags.com, M–F noon–8PM, Sa 11AM–6PM) run by husband-wife team, Raul and Resa Rossell, touts itself as a rock 'n' roll, eco-friendly, mom-and-pop T-shirt shop. Find vintage wares and designer duds and jewelry at **Taylrz Joynt Boutique (25)** *(13549 Ventura Blvd., 818-907-7818, www.taylrzjoynt.com, Tu–Sa 11AM–7:30PM, Su 1PM–4PM).* **Portrait of a Bookstore (26)** *(4360 Tujunga Ave., 818-769-3853, www.portraitofabookstore.com, M–Sa 9:30AM–10PM, Su 10AM–10PM)* lines its shelves with an eclectic selection of hand-picked books.

WHERE TO STAY

Sportsmen Lodge Hotel (27) ($$) *(12825 Ventura Blvd., 818-769-4700, www.slhotel.com)* opened in 1962 on the Trout Lakes. It's popular with music stars and crews and Hollywood filmmakers. The hotel's café walls are lined with posters signed by celeb patrons. **Nite Inn (28) ($)** *(10612 Ventura Blvd., 818-508-8022, www.niteinn universal.com)* is within walking distance of Universal Studios.

NORTH HOLLYWOOD/
UNIVERSAL CITY

• SNAPSHOT •

Jammed into one square mile, North Hollywood's cultural center, NoHo Arts District *(www.nohoartsdistrict. com)*, brims with more than 20 theaters and galleries, and the largest concentration of music recording venues west of the Mississippi. Created in 1992 by the City of Los Angeles as a shot of steroids to the formerly run-down area, the NoHo is gaining in popularity as a true arts and culture district. Events include a theater and arts festival in May.

PLACES TO SEE
Arts & Entertainment:

NoHo Arts Center (29) *(11136 Magnolia Blvd., 818-508-7101, www.thenohoartscenter.com)* is North Hollywood's primary theater space and home to the **Open At The Top Theatre Company**, which presents plays and musicals. Since 1975, Actors Forum Theatre (30) *(10655 Magnolia Blvd., 818-506-0600, www.actorsforumtheatre.org)* has produced award-winning plays and has hosted work-shops. The Lankershim Arts Center (31) *(5108 Lankershim Blvd., 818-761-8838, www.roadtheatre.org)* is home to the **NoHo Gallery LA** *(818-761-7784, www.nohogalleryla.com, Th–Sa 2PM–8PM, Su 1PM–6PM)*, as well as **Road Theatre Company**, producing thought-provoking plays. **Cella Gallery (32)** *(5229 Lankershim Blvd., 213-291-7908, www.cellagallery.com, Tu–Th noon–5PM, F–Sa till 8PM)* represents established and up-and-coming contemporary fine artists. Special events include music nights and artists' salons. **Judith Kaufman Gallery (33)** *(5269 Lankershim Blvd., 818-508-0281, www.elportaltheatre.com; hours vary)*, housed in a transformed movie palace, the **El Portal Theatre**, shares space with the 42-seat Studio Theatre, home of **Stuart Roger's Theatre Tribe**, the 95-seat Forum, and the 360-seat MainStage. NoHo public art includes the **Chandler Outdoor Gallery**, a row of murals on Chandler Boulevard, an Emmy statue, and nearly life-size statues of Lucille Ball and Johnny Carson, among others, at the **Academy of Television Arts and Science Plaza (34)** *(5220 Lankershim Blvd., 818-754-2800)*. Comedy and karaoke mix at the **HaHa Comedy Club (35)** *(5010 Lankershim Blvd., 818-508-4995, www.hahacafe.com)*, which also features a restaurant and bar.

Kids:

A bit more dated than some amusement park counterparts, **Universal Studios Hollywood (36)** *(100 Universal City*

Plaza, 818-622-3801, www.universalstudios.hollywood.com; call for hours) still draws the masses for its *Shrek* 4-D animation theater, *Simpsons*-themed ride, and *Revenge of the Mummy* coaster. Newbies can hop on the tram tour.

Northwest of Universal Studios, **Six Flags Magic Mountain** (*26101 Magic Mountain Pkwy., 661-255-4100, www.sixflags.com; call for hours*) is home to rides such as **Riddler's Revenge**, the world's tallest, fastest stand-up coaster at 65 mph, and **Scream**, with a 150-foot drop and 128-foot vertical loop.

PLACES TO EAT & DRINK
Where to Eat:
Designed to mimic a Venetian trattoria, **Ca del Sole (37) ($$)** (*4100 Cahuenga Blvd., 818-985-4669, www.cadel sole.com, M–F 11:30AM–3PM, 5PM–10:30PM, Sa 5:30PM–11:30PM, Su 11AM–9PM*) delivers on all counts, including outstanding Northern Italian fare. Try the Mezzelune—half-moon-shaped pasta stuffed with pumpkin. An affordable culinary "tour" of the Mediterranean, **Skaf's Grill (38) ($)** (*6008 Laurel Canyon Blvd., 818-985-5701, M–Sa 11AM–9PM*) features everything from falafel to shwarma. **Little Toni's (39) ($)** (*4745 Lankershim Blvd., 818-763-0131, M–Sa 5PM–2AM, Su 4PM–2AM*) conjures a New York state of mind with thin-crust pizza and simple pastas. Craving spice? Head to **Sanam Luang Café (40) ($)** (*12980 Sherman Way, 818-764-1180, daily 10AM–4AM*) for authentic Thai. **Jack's Classic Hamburgers (41) ($)** (*11375 Riverside Dr., 818-761-4599, daily 9AM–10PM*) is famed for chili cheese and onion fries. NoHo breakfast joint **Eat (42) ($)** (*11108 Magnolia Blvd., 818-760-4787, M–F 8AM–2:30PM, Sa–Su till 3PM*) satisfies with killer omelets.

Bars & Nightlife:

The Valley's top jazz and blues club, **The Baked Potato (43)** *(3787 Cahuenga Blvd., 818-980-1615, www.the bakedpotato.com, nightly 7PM–2AM)* also serves its namesake stuffed with everything from steak to maple ham-and-cheese. Oenophiles sip nectar of the gods at welcoming **Bar One (44)** *(12518 Burbank Blvd., 818-509-1938)* wine bar. NoHo gets interactive at **The Good Nite (45)** *(10721 Burbank Blvd., 818-286-3929, www.thegoodnite.com, daily 7:30PM–2AM)*, known for "Karaoke Sundays" (and $3 kamikazes to coax you into shameless crooning) and bring-your-own iPod Tuesdays.

Go tropical at **Tonga Hut Tiki Lounge (46)** *(12808 Victory Blvd., 818-769-0708, www.tongahut.com, nightly 4PM–2AM)*, a 1958 Tiki lounge. Original decor includes a kidney-shaped drop ceiling, fountains, and giant "gods." David Lynch meets Coney Island sideshow at **California Institute of Abnormal Arts (CIA) (47)** *(11334 Burbank Blvd., 818-506-6353, www.ciabnormalarts.com, F–Sa 9PM–2AM)*, presenting talent too odd to get booked elsewhere. Freak show artifacts such as the severed arm of a French nobleman and the body of a mummified clown, still in costume and makeup, complement the quirky performances.

WHERE TO SHOP

Locals wax poetic about the used tomes at Iliad Book Shop (48) *(5400 Cahuenga Blvd., 818-509-2665, www.iliadbooks.com, M–Sa 10AM–10PM, Su noon–6PM)*, specializing in pulp fiction, among other genres. Age of Innocence (49) *(11054 Magnolia Blvd., 818-980-0462, M–Sa noon–6PM, Su noon–3PM)* stocks new, retro-looking clothes plus vintage finds, with an accommodating staff. Marie et Cie (50) *(11704 Riverside Dr., 818-508-5049, daily 11AM–6PM)* is part café, part shop, with a hodgepodge of gift items and furniture. Lucky You (51) *(12441 Magnolia Blvd., 818-985-1115, www.lucky youresale.com, M–Sa 10AM–6PM, Su noon–4PM)* offers gently used designer clothes and accessories at great prices. Universal CityWalk (52) *(100 Universal City Plaza, Su–Th 11AM–10PM, F–Sa 11AM–11PM)* boasts a 19-screen cinema, restaurants, and over 30 shops, including **Sparky's** *(818-622-2925)*, with the largest collection of Pez dispensers in the world, and **The Wound & Wound Toy Company** *(818-509-8129)*, appealing to young and old with vintage wind-up toys.

WHERE TO STAY

Beverly Garland's Holiday Inn at Universal Studios (53) ($$) *(4222 Vineland Ave., 818-980-8000, www.beverly garland.com)* boasts a convenient locale for Universal Studios visits, plus a state-of-the-art fitness center after its $2 million update. **Hilton Los Angeles (54) ($$-$$$)** *(555 Universal Hollywood Dr., 818-506-2500, www1.hilton.com)* caters to families, with complimentary transport to Universal Studios and Universal CityWalk. **Sheraton Universal (55) ($$-$$$)** *(333 Universal Hollywood Dr., 818-980-1212, www.sheraton.com)* envelops guests in high-style amenities.

BURBANK/GLENDALE

• SNAPSHOT •

Burbank and Glendale are two of the largest incorporated cities in the Valley. Burbank, "Media Capital of the World," welcomed the motion picture industry as far back as the 1920s. First National Pictures spread across nearly 80 acres, including the David Burbank house. (He was an entrepreneur for whom the city is named.) Warner Bros. took over a few years later; Columbia and Disney soon followed. By the 1960s and 1970s, NBC, home of the *Tonight Show*, moved in. Glendale, which is a largely residential area, lies at the eastern end of the San Fernando Valley. Once known for helping foster the age of aviation with the now defunct Grand Central Airport, it's now famous for the Forest Lawn Cemetery, the resting place of many celebrities.

PLACES TO SEE
Landmarks:

The most star-studded spot in the valley is by far the **Forest Lawn Memorial Park (56)** *(1712 S. Glendale Ave., 800-204-3131, www.forestlawn.com, daily 8AM–5PM)*, final resting place for Nat King Cole, Clark Gable, Walt Disney, and Spencer Tracy, among others. Sculpture and paintings are also on display over the 300 acres.

Arts & Entertainment:

Warner Bros. Studios (57) *(3400 W. Riverside Dr., 818-*

972-8687, *www2.warnerbros.com, M–F 7:30AM–7PM*) offers two-hour tours of sets and soundstages. If a big-name production is being filmed, star sightings are possible. Tours include a visit to the studio's museum, showcasing costumes and scripts from Warner productions, including Harry Potter flicks.

Watch a live television taping at **NBC Television Studios (58)** (*3000 W. Alameda Ave., 818-840-3537, www.nbc.com, M–F 9AM–3PM*), home of the *Tonight Show*. Free tickets to shows are available, or sign up for an hour-long weekday tour that gets you behind the scenes of *Days of Our Lives* and other shows. **Alex Theatre (59)** (*216 N. Brand Blvd., 818-243-2539, www.alextheatre.org*) is an L.A. landmark. From the 1920s through the 1950s, it previewed major Hollywood releases and hosted community events. Today the Alex is used for professional and community performing arts groups, such as the **Los Angeles Ballet** and **Los Angeles Chamber Orchestra**. **Falcon Theatre (60)** (*4252 Riverside Dr., 818-955-8101, www.falcontheatre.com*), built by director/writer Garry Marshall in 1997, presents plays for adults and kids.

PLACES TO EAT & DRINK
Where to Eat:
Bashan (61) ($$$) (*3459 N. Verdugo Rd., 818-541-1532, www.bashanrestaurant.com, Tu–Sa 5:30PM–10PM, Su 5PM–9PM*) excels at its seafood, including roasted Atlantic monkfish. French **Bistro Provence (62) ($$)** (*345 N. Pass Ave., 818-840-9050, www.bistroprovence.net, M–F noon–2PM, M–Sa 5:30PM–9:30PM*) pleases palates

with reasonably priced risotto, beef bourguignon, and special tasting menus. Heading south of the border, **La Cabanita (63) ($$)** *(3447 N. Verdugo Rd., 818-957-2711, M–Th 10AM–10PM, F till 11PM, Sa 8AM–11PM, Su till 10PM)* serves authentic Mexican cuisine, including carne

asada and pork with green mole. Chase it with a frothy margarita. Everyone likes **Corner Cottage (64) ($)** *(310 S. Victory Blvd., 818-843-2567, M–F 6AM–4PM, Sa 7AM–2PM)* for its zesty breakfast burritos. Valley folk are devoted to **Yummy Cupcakes (65) ($)** *(2918 W. Magnolia Blvd., 818-558-1080, www.yummycupcakes.com, M–Sa 10AM–7PM, Su till 5PM)*, with over 130 choices, including multiple versions of the coveted red velvet cupcake.

Bars & Nightlife:

Retro '50s-era decor and stiff drinks add to the charm of **Blue Room (66)** *(916 S. San Fernando Blvd., 323-849-2779, daily 10AM–2AM)*. Sip a gimlet to the Rolling Stones or Curtis Mayfield blaring from the jukebox. Specialty cocktails and local live music converge at **Burbank Bar & Grille (67)** *(112 N. San Fernando Blvd., 818-848-9611, www.bbgrocks.com, M 4PM–midnight, Tu–Th till 1AM, F–Su till 2AM)*, also serving a full menu.

WHERE TO SHOP

Dress like a star at It's a Wrap (68) *(3315 W. Magnolia Blvd., 818-567-7366, itsawraphollywood.com, M–F 10AM–8PM, Sa–Su 11AM–6PM)*, selling props and wardrobe items from movies and TV. Sift through stacks of used titles at Brand Bookshop (69) *(231 N. Brand Blvd., 818-507-5943, M–Th 10AM–9PM, F–Sa till 10PM, Su 11AM–8PM)*, which entices readers with its relaxed atmosphere. As record store chains fall by the wayside, Atomic Records (70) *(3812 W. Magnolia Blvd., 818-848-7090, M–Sa 11AM–7PM, Su noon–5PM)* forges on with used CDs, vinyl, and obscure titles. The Train Shack (71) *(1030 N. Hollywood Way, 818-842-3330, www.trainshack.com, M–F 10AM–6:30PM, Sa till 6PM, Su 11AM–5PM)* specializes in new, used, and collectible toy and model trains. They also stock railroad-centric books, videos, and magazines. Hepcats consult 8 Ball (72) *(3806 W. Magnolia Blvd., 818-845-1155, www.8ballwebstore.com, M–F 11AM–7PM, Sa till 6PM, Su noon–5PM)* for rockabilly fashions and kitsch.

WHERE TO STAY

Boutique-style Hotel Amarano Burbank (73) ($$-$$$) *(322 N. Pass Ave., 818-842-8887, www.hotelamarano.com)* woos sophisticated travelers with comfortable touches, including a rooftop sundeck with views of the Valley. Budget travelers head to Safari Inn (74) ($$) *(1911 W. Olive Ave., 818-845-8586, www.safariburbank.com)*, with basic retro-style rooms. Or, for a slightly more upscale option, sister hotel Coast Anabelle Hotel (75) ($$) *(2011 W. Olive Ave., 818-845-7800, www.coasthotels. com)* fits the bill. The Hilton Los Angeles North/Glendale & Executive Meeting Center (76) ($$-$$$) *(100 W. Glenoaks Blvd., 818-956-5466, www1.hilton.com)* caters to the business crowd. Other amenities include a fitness center and outdoor pool.

chapter 9

PASADENA/
SAN GABRIEL VALLEY

PASADENA/SAN GABRIEL VALLEY

Places to See:

1. Rose Bowl Stadium
2. Tournament House
3. Gamble House
4. Old Pasadena
5. Mount Wilson Observatory
6. Los Angeles County Arboretum & Botanical Gardens
7. Descanso Gardens
8. Jet Propulsion Laboratory
9. NORTON SIMON MUSEUM ★
10. HUNTINGTON LIBRARY AND GARDENS ★
11. Pasadena Museum of California Art
12. Pacific Asia Museum
13. Pasadena Museum of History
14. Pasadena Playhouse
15. Fremont Centre Theatre
16. Kidspace Children's Museum

Places to Eat & Drink:

17. The Dining Room at the Langham
18. Parkway Grill
19. Mi Piace
20. Gale's
21. Maison Akira
22. The CrepeVine Bistro & Wine Bar
23. Azeen's Afghani Restaurant
24. Zankou Chicken
25. Old Towne Pub
26. Pasadena Jazz Institute
27. Vertical Wine Bistro
28. NeoMeze
29. Colorado Bar

Where to Shop:

30. Vroman's Bookstore
31. Distant Lands
32. Lula Mae
33. The Folk Tree
34. Ten Thousand Villages
35. Alternative Outfitters

Where to Stay:

36. The Langham, Huntington Hotel & Spa
37. Artists' Inn
38. The Bissell House

★ *Top Pick*

PASADENA/ SAN GABRIEL VALLEY

• SNAPSHOT •

San Gabriel Valley was once devoted to agriculture. Over the years it's succumbed to suburban sprawl, though the city of Pasadena emerged as its cultural vortex. The world watches Pasadena every New Year's for its Tournament of Roses extravaganza, but the visual outlets don't stop there. Artists find space at the heralded Norton Simon Museum and Pasadena Museum of California Art, while literary devotees take up residence at the Huntington Library. Central areas include Old Pasadena and South Lake Avenue, home to upscale boutiques, designer stores, and restaurants.

PLACES TO SEE
Landmarks:

Of all its cultural riches, Pasadena is best known for its New Year's Day **Rose Bowl**, first played in 1902. The game is played at **Rose Bowl Stadium (1)** *(1001 Rose Bowl Dr., 626-577-3101, www.rosebowl stadium.com)*, built in 1922. Prior to the big game, Pasadena hosts the **Tournament of Roses Parade**, with intricate floral floats gliding down Colorado Boulevard in Old Pasadena. The tournament association's executive offices are located at **Tournament House (2)** *(391 S. Orange Grove Blvd., 626-*

449-4100, *www.tournamentofroses.com*), also known as Wrigley Mansion, an Italian Renaissance-style mansion once owned by chewing-gum pioneer William Wrigley Jr. It's surrounded by the famous centennial rose garden. House highlights include a Waterford rose bowl commissioned for the Tournament of Roses centennial. Free tours are offered *(Th from Feb–Aug, 2PM–4PM)*. **Gamble House (3)** *(4 Westmoreland Pl., 626-793-3334, www. gamblehouse.org, guided one-hour tours Th–Su noon– 3PM)*, built by Charles and Henry Green in 1908 in Arts and Crafts style, was designed for David and Mary Gamble of Procter and Gamble fame. Take a trip back in time in **Old Pasadena (4)** *(bordered by Arroyo Pky./ Pasadena Ave./Walnut St./Del Mar Blvd., 626-666-4156, www.oldpasadena,org)*, where more than 200 buildings date to the 1880s and 1890s. Today, this 22-block neighborhood is packed with restaurants, clubs, stores, boutiques, theaters, galleries, and live music venues. The **San Gabriel Mountains** divide the Greater Los Angeles Area from the Mojave Desert. The highest peak is Mount San Antonio, aka Mt. Baldy. In winter the Mount Waterman and Kratka Ridge resorts offer skiing; in summer, the mountains are a playground for hikers, backpackers, and extreme sports. Atop Mount Wilson is **Mount Wilson Observatory (5)** with a small museum and a 60-inch telescope *(open to visitors Apr–Nov 10AM– 4PM)*. **Los Angeles County Arboretum & Botanical Gardens (6)** *(301 N. Baldwin Ave., 626-821-3222, www.arboretum. org, daily 9AM–5PM)* spans 127 acres.

A tram shuttles visitors to view its 18,000 plants. During the summer, the arboretum hosts the California Philharmonic Concerts on the Green. **Descanso Gardens (7)** *(1418 Descanso Dr., 818-949-4200, www.descanso gardens.com, daily 9AM–5PM)* is camellia heaven, with more than 700 varieties in bloom from Feb–May. Five acres of roses and a number of California native plants are on display. The gardens were also the home of E. Manchester Boddy, publisher and owner of the former *Los Angeles Daily News*. His house is open to the public *(Tu–Su 10AM–4PM)*. **Jet Propulsion Laboratory (8)** *(4800 Oak Grove Dr., 818-354-4321, www.jpl.nasa.gov)* was established by the California Institute of Technology in the 1930s and built the country's first satellite, *Explorer 1*. Day tours *(call in advance, 818-354-9314)* of the spacecraft and facilities run once per week *(M or W at 1PM)* on an alternating basis.

Arts & Entertainment:

TOP PICK!

Showcasing one of the best private collections of 2,000 years of Western and Asian art is the ★**NORTON SIMON MUSEUM (9)** *(411 W. Colorado Blvd., 626-449-6840, www.norton simon.org, Sa–M, W–Th noon–6PM, F till 9PM)*. On display are rare etchings by Goya and Rembrandt, a collection of Picasso's graphics, works by French Impressionists Monet and Renoir, and over 100 works of art by Degas, including his complete set of bronzes. There is also art from

India and Southeast Asia. Stroll the 7-acre sculpture garden to see works by Rodin, and a pond inspired by Monet's garden at Giverny. A must on any visit to L.A., the ★HUNTINGTON LIBRARY AND GARDENS (10) *(1151 Oxford Rd., 626-405-2100, www.huntington.org, M, W, Th–F noon–4:30PM, Sa–Su 10:30AM–4:30PM)*

TOP PICK!

is the legacy of Henry and Arabella Huntington who turned their San Marino Ranch into a world famous cultural landmark. This is one of the largest and most complete research libraries in the country, though the general public can view some of its collection, including rare books and manuscripts, such as the earliest known edition of Chaucer's *Canterbury Tales*. The Huntington Art Collections are spread out among three different buildings, with emphasis on British and French art of the 18th and 19th centuries, as well as a representative collection of American art. The grounds are also worth a visit. Henry Huntington began developing the Botanical Gardens in 1903 and today they span nearly 120 acres with approximately 15,000 kinds of plants, including a 12-acre Desert Garden, a Zen rock garden, rose garden, and Chinese garden. The **Pasadena Museum of California Art (11)** *(490 E. Union St., 626-568-3665, www.pmcaonline.org, W–Su noon–5PM)* displays California art, architecture, and design from 1850 to the present. You'll also be impressed by the view of the San Gabriel Mountains and 1927 City Hall dome from the museum's terrace. Housed in the historic Grace Nicholson Building, the **Pacific Asia Museum (12)** *(46 N. Los Robles Ave., 626-*

449-2742, www.pacificasia museum.org, W–Su 10AM–6PM) houses over 14,000 works of art, including paintings, sculptures, ceramics, and textiles from all over Asia and the Pacific Rim.

Pasadena Museum of History (13) *(470 W. Walnut St., 626-577-1660, www.pasadenahistory.org, W–Su noon–5PM)* is currently the only museum and research library devoted to preserving the history of Pasadena and the west San Gabriel Valley. Tours include a visit to the 1906 Beaux Art Fenyes Mansion and Finnish Folk Art Museum. There are changing exhibits in the History Center Galleries. The **Pasadena Playhouse District** *(Colorado Blvd./El Molino Ave., 626-744-0340, www.playhousedistrict.org)* is anchored by the landmark **Pasadena Playhouse (14)** *(39 S. El Molino Ave., 626-356-7529, www.pasadenaplayhouse.org)*. Its College of Theatre Arts, once Hollywood's star factory, launched the careers of such luminaries as Gene Hackman and Dustin Hoffman. The theater presents more than 300 performances annually, while the district offers a mix of bookstores, antique and specialty shops, restaurants, historic architecture, and art walks. **Fremont Centre Theatre (15)** *(1000 Fremont Ave., 626-441-5977, www.fremont centretheatre.com)*, a small professional theater, is home of the Pasadena Shakespeare Company.

Kids:

Kidspace Children's Museum (16) *(480 N. Arroyo Blvd., 626-449-9144, www.kidspacemuseum.org, Tu–Su 9:30AM–*

5PM, June–Aug daily 9:30AM–5PM) offers an interactive learning environment. Feeding giant bugs and climbing raindrops 40 feet into the air are all part of the fun.

PLACES TO EAT & DRINK
Where to Eat:

Since Chef Craig Strong took the reins, **The Dining Room at the Langham (17) ($$$-$$$$)** *(1401 S. Oak Knoll Ave., 626-577-2867, Tu–Sa 6:30PM–9PM)* has received nothing but praise for upscale modern American cuisine. **Parkway Grill (18) ($$$)** *(510 S. Arroyo Pkwy., 626-795-1001, www.theparkwaygrill.com, M–F 11:30AM–2:30PM, 5:30PM–10PM, Sa 5PM–11PM, Su 5PM–10PM)* garners accolades for handcrafted pizzas, pasta, and oakwood fire-baked fish. The restaurant's organic garden provides fresh herbs and specialty produce. Waits can be long for hot spot **Mi Piace (19) ($$)** *(25 E. Colorado Blvd., 626-795-3131, www.mipiace.com, M–Th 7:30AM–11:30PM, F till 12:30AM, Sa 8AM–12:30AM, Su till 11:30PM)*, known for hearty, New York–style pasta and martinis. More authentic is cozy **Gale's (20) ($$)** *(452 S. Fair Oaks Ave., 626-432-6705, www.gales restaurant.com, Tu–Th 11:30AM–9PM, F–S till 10PM, Su 5PM–9PM)*. Elegant **Maison Akira (21) ($$$)** *(713 E. Green St., 626-796-9501, www.maisonakira.com, Tu–F 11:30AM–2PM, Tu–Th 6PM–9PM, F–Sa 5:30PM–9:30PM, Su 5PM–8PM, Su champagne brunch 11AM–2PM)* melds the culinary riches of France and Japan. Try chef Akira Hirose's signature miso-marinated grilled Chilean sea bass. Step into a Parisian bistro at **The CrepeVine Bistro & Wine Bar (22) ($-$$)** *(36 W. Colorado Blvd., 626-796-*

7250, *www.thecrepevine.com, Tu–Sa 11AM–3PM, 5:30PM–11PM, Th–Sa till midnight, Su 10:30AM–10PM)* for sweet and savory crepes and a rich assortment of wines. **Azeen's Afghani Restaurant (23) ($$)** *(110 E. Union St., 626-683-3310, www.azeensafghani restaurant.com, M–F 11:30AM–2PM, daily 5:30PM–9:30PM)* blends Indian and Persian influences. The menu covers the basics, such as pallaw lamb stew and kabobs. Forget KFC, **Zankou Chicken (24) ($)** *(1296 E. Colorado Blvd., 626-405-1502, www.zankouchicken. com, daily 10AM–10PM)* is the place for fried chicken slathered with garlic butter.

Bars & Nightlife:

Old Towne Pub (25) *(66 N. Fair Oaks Ave., 626-577-6583, www.lochnesspub.com, daily 4PM–2AM)* presents live music on its thumbprint-size stage every night, from folk to jazz to punk. Live bands grace the stage on weekends at **Pasadena Jazz Institute (26)** *(260 E. Colorado Blvd., 626-398-3344, www.pasjazz.org, shows at 8:30PM)*. Sommelier Scott Teruya helps you sort

through a selection of more than 400 wines at **Vertical Wine Bistro (27)** *(70 N. Raymond Ave., 626-795-3999, Tu–Th 5PM–11PM, F till 1AM, Sa 4PM–1AM, Su 4PM–11PM)*. One hundred wines are available by the glass and there's an extensive wine flight program. **NeoMeze (28)** *(20 E. Colorado Blvd., 626-793-3010, www.neomeze.com, Su–W 5PM–midnight, Th–Sa 5PM–2AM)* serves late-night eats as well as a full menu of

DJs and live acts. Patrons at **Colorado Bar (29)** *(2640 E. Colorado Blvd., 626-449-3485, daily noon–2AM)* love the potent cocktails—especially the spicy Bloody Marys. The jukebox features everything from classic rock to heavy metal.

WHERE TO SHOP

Vroman's Bookstore (30) *(695 E. Colorado Blvd., 626-449-5320, www.vromansbookstore.com, M–Th 9AM–9PM, F–Sa till 10PM, Su 10AM–9PM)* the largest independent bookshop in Southern California, has a wide selection of titles and a steady stream of author events. Armchair travelers transport themselves to Distant Lands (31) *(56 S. Raymond Ave., 626-449-3220, www.distant lands.com, M–Th 10:30AM–8PM, F–Sa till 9PM, Su 11AM–6PM)* for travel needs; maps, books, clothing, luggage. Oddball variety store Lula Mae (32) *(100 N. Fair Oaks Ave., 626-304-9996, www.lulamae.com, M–Sa 10AM–8PM, Su noon–5PM)* hawks everything from wacky refrigerator magnets to punk rock tote bags and baby toys. For Mexican crafts, The Folk Tree (33) *(217 S. Fair Oaks Ave., 626-795-8733, www.folktree.com, M–W 11AM–6PM, Th–Sa 10AM–6PM, Su noon–5PM)* features Oaxacan wood carvings and papier-mâché figures among other items. Ten Thousand Villages (34) *(496 S. Lake Ave., 626-229-9892, www.pasadenavillages.com, M–Sa 10AM–7PM, Su noon–5PM)* is one in a network of over 100 fair-trade stores in North America whose proceeds help thousands of artisans by providing income for food, education, health care, and housing. Vegan shoppers fulfill animal-friendly needs at fashionable Alternative Outfitters (35) *(408 S. Pasadena Ave., Suite 1, 626-396-4972, www.alternativeoutfitters.com, M–F 11AM–4:30PM).*

WHERE TO STAY

The Langham, Huntington Hotel & Spa (36) ($$$) *(1401 S. Oak Knoll Ave., 626-568-3900, www.pasadena.langham hotels.com)*, formerly the Ritz-Carlton, has been a Pasadena landmark since 1907. The property is set on 23 acres overlooking San Marino. Take high tea in the lobby lounge, or visit **The Bar** for evening cocktails and live music. B&B **Artists' Inn (37) ($$)** *(1038 Magnolia St., 626-799-5668, www.artistsinns.com)* is a secluded property replete with rosebushes and a white picket fence. Another B&B, **The Bissell House (38) ($$-$$$)** *(201 Orange Grove Ave., 626-441-3535, www.bissellhouse. com)*, built in 1887, is located on Pasadena's Millionaires' Row. An eight-bedroom Victorian, former home of the famed philanthropist and vacuum heiress of carpet-sweeper fame, is still filled with antiques.

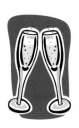

INDEX

22nd Street Landing Seafood Grill and Bar 178, 189

4100 Bar 77, 87

6150 Wilshire Boulevard . .55, 60

7 Dudley Cinema 166

7+ Fig at Ernst & Young Plaza 26, 43

8 Ball 208, 223

A Different Light Bookstore . .100, 116

A+D Architecture and Design Museum 55, 59

Aahs 128, 132

Abbey 100, 115

Abbot Kinney Festival 21

Academy Awards . .17, 102, 105

Academy of Television Arts and Science Plaza 207, 216

Ace Gallery 99, 120

Ackee Bamboo 178, 204

ACME Comedy Theater . .55, 60

Actors Forum Theatre .207, 215

Adamson House 153

Aero Theater 149, 160

AFI Fest 22

African Marketplace and Cultural Faire 20

Age of Innocence 208, 219

Ahmanson Theatre 39

Akasha 128, 144

Akbar 77, 86

Alegria Cocina Latina . .178, 195

Alegria on Sunset 77, 86

Alex Theatre 207, 221

Alex's Bar 178, 196

Alibi Room 128, 145

All' Angelo 100, 114

Alternative Outfitters . .225, 234

Ambrose 151, 164

America's Best Value Inn .78, 92

Amoeba 100, 109

Amtrak 9, 10, 30

Andaz West Hollywood . .101, 117

Angelini Osteria 55, 62

Angels Flight Railway 25, 38

Angels Gate Cultural Center 177, 188

Angels Gate Park 177, 187

Angelus Temple 90

Anonymous Clothing Company 150, 169

AOC 55, 61

Apple Pan, The 127, 138

Aquarium of the Pacific . .177, 194

ArcLight Cinemas . .18, 99, 105

Area 100, 115

Aristeia 128, 137

Armand Hammer Museum of Art and Culture Center . .127, 130

Arnold Schoenberg
  Institute 48

Art's Delicatessen 207, 212

Artists' Inn 225, 234

Asanebo 207, 211

Atomic Records 208, 223

Audrey Skirball Kenis
  Theater 130

Aunt Kizzy's Back Porch .150, 173

Auntie Em's Kitchen 78, 95

Aura 150, 163

Autry National Center . .77, 80, 94

Avalon Seafood 199

Avenues of Art & Design . .99, 112

Avila Adobe 25, 29

Axe 150, 167

Azeen's Afghani
  Restaurant 225, 232

Babe's and Ricky's Inn .178, 204

Backstage Bar & Grill .128, 145

Baked Potato, The 207, 218

Ballerina Clown 149, 167

Ballona Wetlands 149, 172

Bar Keeper 78, 88

Bar Lubitsch 100, 115

Bar Marmont 100, 115

Bar One 207, 218

Barnsdall Art Park . . .77, 79, 80

Bashan 207, 221

Baxter Stairway 77, 90

Beach Festival 20

Beach House at Hermosa . .179,
  185

Bedfellows 208, 213

Beechwood 150, 168

Behind the Scenes
  Costumes 178, 190

Beige 56, 65

Bel-Air 134-137

Belamar Hotel 179, 185

BeMe 179, 196

Bergamot Station 149, 159

Best Western Dragon Gate
  Inn 27, 36

Best Western Eagle Rock
  Inn 78, 97

Beverly Center 56, 63

Beverly Garland's Holiday Inn at
  Universal Studios . . .208, 219

Beverly Hills 119–125

Beverly Hills Civic Center Public
  Art Walking Tour 15

Beverly Hills Hotel and
  Bungalows 101, 124

Beverly Hills Trolley 16

Beverly Terrace 101, 125

Beverly Wilshire Beverly
  Hills 101, 124

Bigfoot Lodge 77, 82

Billy Wilder Theater 130

Bissell House, The 225, 234

Bistro Provence 207, 221

Black & Blue 150, 163

Black & White Photographer's
  Guild 211

Blair's 77, 85

Blessing of the Animals 17

Blonde 150, 163
blue on blue 100, 123
Blue Room 208, 222
Blue Velvet 56, 72
Blue Windows 179, 196
Blum & Poe 127, 143
Boardwalk 11 .....128, 146
Bob Hope Airport 9
Bodhi Tree Bookstore ..100, 116
BondSt 125
Book Soup 100, 116
Bordello Bar 26, 51
Bradbury Building 25, 46
Brand Bookshop 208, 223
Brass Monkey 56, 74
Brentwood Restaurant and
  Lounge 127, 136
Brewery Art Walk 49
Brewery Arts Colony 26, 49
Brick Lane 150, 169
Brite Spot 78, 91
Broad Contemporary Art
  Museum 59
Broadway Bar 26, 51
Buffalo Exchange 128, 133
Bullocks Wilshire 55, 71
Bunker Hill 37–44
Bunker Hill Steps 25, 38
Burbank 220–223
Burbank Bar & Grille ..208, 222
Burgundy Room 100, 108
Burton W. Chace Park ..149, 173
Ca del Sole 207, 217

Cabrillo Marine
  Aquarium 177, 189
Cadillac Hotel 151, 170
Café Beaujolais 78, 95
Café Boogaloo 178, 184
Café Brasil 128, 144
Café Del Rey 150, 173
Café Pierre 178, 182
Café Stella 77, 85
Café-Club Fais Do-Do ..178, 205
Calabasas 209, 212
California African-American
  Museum 25, 47
California Heritage
  Museum 149, 160
California Institute of Abnormal
  Arts (CIA) 207, 218
California Science Center .26, 49
Cameo at the Viceroy ..150, 162
Camera Obscura 159
Campanile 55, 61
Canter's Deli 55, 62
Capitol Records Tower ..99, 103
Caravan Book Store 26, 42
Carney's Restaurant ...207, 212
Carpenter Performing
  Arts Center 177, 194
Casa Bianca Pizza Pie ...78, 95
Casa del Mar 151, 164
Casa Malibu 150, 157
CasaVino 178, 196
Casino Art Gallery 199
Catalina Canyon Resort & Spa ..199

Catalina Country Club 199
Catalina Island 198–199
Catalina Island Museum 199
Cathedral of Our Lady of the
    Angels 25, 31
CBS Television City 55, 60
Celebrity Helicopters 15
Cella Gallery 207, 216
Center for the Arts
    Eagle Rock 77, 95
Center Theatre Group . . .40, 143
Century City 99, 120
Century City Towers 120
Cha Cha Lounge 78, 87
Chalet, The 78, 96
Chandler Outdoor Gallery . . .216
Charles F. Lummis Home and
    Garden 77, 94
Chateau Marmont 101, 117
Checkers Restaurant 43
Cherry Blossom Festival 17
Chevalier's Books 56, 69
Chez Mélange 178, 183
Chiat-Day Building 149, 167
Children's Book World . .128, 140
Chinatown . . .15, 16, 29, 32, 34
Chinatown Plaza 26, 35
Chinese American
    Museum 25, 32
Chinese Historical Society of
    Southern California 25, 30
Chinese New Year 16
Cholada Thai Cuisine . .150, 156

Choose Chinatown 26, 35
ChoSun Galbee 56, 73
Christopher Street West Festival
    & Parade 19
Chunju Han-il Kwan 56, 73
Cicada 26, 50
Cinema Bar 128, 146
City Hall 14, 25, 30
Ciudad 26, 41
Civic Center 28, 30
Civic Light Opera of South Bay
    Cities 182
Cliff's Edge 77, 85
Clifton's Brookdale
    Cafeteria 26, 51
Clover 78, 87
Coast Anabelle Hotel . .208, 223
Coast Long Beach Hotel .179, 197
Cobras & Matadors 55, 62
Coffee Cup Café 178, 196
Colorado Bar 225, 233
comme Ça 100, 113
Cook's Library 56, 65
Copper Room, The 178, 190
Corner Cottage 208, 222
Counter, The 150, 161
Craft 100, 122
Craft & Folk Art Museum .55, 59
CrepeVine Bistro & Wine
    Bar, The 225, 231
Criminal Courts Building .25, 31
Crowne Plaza Harbor Hotel . .179,
    191

Culver City 142–147
Culver Hotel 128, 147
Curve 100, 116
CUT 100, 121
Dakota 110
Dan Sung Sa 56, 75
Dan Tana's 100, 114
Dari 208, 213
DASH 13
Dean 78, 87
Debs Park 77, 94
Decades 100, 116
Descanso Gardens . . . 225, 228
Día de Los Muertos 22, 29
Diddy Riese Cookies . .127, 131
Dime, The 55, 63
Dining Room at the Langham,
   The 225, 231
Disney's Grand Californian Hotel
   & Spa 201
Disney's Paradise Pier Hotel . .201
Disneyland 23, 200–201
Disneyland Hotel 201
Distant Lands 225, 233
Dockweiler State Beach . .149, 172
Dodger Stadium 77, 90
Dolce & Gabbana 100, 123
Dolce Vita 150, 163
Dollyrocker 178, 184
Doo Dah Parade 16
Dorothy Chandler Pavilion . . .39
Doubletree Hotel San
   Pedro 179, 191

Downtown Commercial
   District 45–53
Downtown Financial
   District 37–44
Downtown Historic
   District 28–36
Drago 150, 161
Dragon Books 128, 137
Drawing Room 77, 82
Dresden Room 77, 82
Duke's Malibu 150, 156
Dunes Inn Wilshire 56, 69
Dynasty Center 26, 34
Eagle Rock 93–97
Eagle Rock Motel 78, 97
Eagle Rock Underground .78, 99
Eastern Columbia Building . .25, 46
Eat 207, 217
Echigo 128, 139
Echo, The 78, 91
Echo Park 89–92
Echo Park Historical Society . .15
Echo Park Lake 77, 89
Echoplex 91
Edendale Grill 77, 85
Edison, The 26, 42
Egyptian Theater 99, 105
El Capitan Theatre 99, 104
El Cholo 56, 73
El Compadre 78, 91
El Pueblo de Los Angeles
   Historic Monument . . .25, 29,
32

El Pueblo de Los Angeles
  Plaza 29

El Rey 55, 63

Élan Hotel 56, 65

Elf Café 78, 91

Elysian Park 77, 90

Emmy Awards 21

Engine Company No. 28 .26, 41

Equator Books 150, 169

Equator Vinyl 170

Eric's on the Pier 199

Eso Won Books 179, 205

Exposition Park 25, 45–53

Faire Frou Frou 208, 213

Fairmont Miramar Hotel . .151,164

Falcon Theatre 207, 221

Farmer's Daughter
  Hotel 56, 65

Farmers Market 55, 58

Father's Office 150, 162

Fernandos 178, 184

Fern's Garden 179, 197

FIDM Museum and
  Galleries 26, 49

FIDM Museum Shop 26, 53

Fiesta Broadway 18

Figueroa Hotel 27, 53

Firefly 207, 212

Fisherman's Village . . .149, 171

Flight Club 56, 65

Flock Shop 26, 36

Flounce Vintage 78, 92

FlyAway 9

Folk Tree, The 225, 233

Footsie's 78, 96

Ford's Filling Station . .128, 144

Forest Lawn Memorial
  Park 207, 220

Fort MacArthur Museum . . .187

Foundry on Melrose, The . .100,
  113

Four Points by Sheraton Los
  Angeles Westside . . .128, 147

Fowler Museum at
  UCLA 127, 130

Fraiche 128, 144

Franklin D. Murphy Sculpture
  Garden 130

Freaks Vintage Clothing . .26, 36

Fred Segal 100, 116

Fred 62 . . . . .77, 81

Frederick's of
  Hollywood 100,109

Fremont Centre
  Theatre 225, 230

Frenchy's Bistro 178, 195

Frolic Room 100, 108

Fugetsu-Do 26, 35

Fun Factory 181

Furaibo Restaurant 128, 139

Gagosian Gallery 99, 120

Gale's 225, 231

Gallery Bar 43

Gallery Plus 179, 205

Gamble House 225, 227

Gascon Theatre 143

Gate Inn 27, 36

Geffen Contemporary at the Museum of Contemporary Art 25, 31

Geffen Playhouse 127, 130

Geoffrey's Malibu 150, 155

George J. Doizaki Gallery 32

Georgian Hotel 151, 164

Getty Center 23, 127, 134

Getty House 55, 67

Getty Villa Malibu 149, 155

Ghettogloss 77, 85

Ghosts and Legends Tour . .193

Giant Robot 128, 140

Gingergrass 77, 86

Girasole 55, 68

Gladstone's Malibu 149, 155

Glendale 220-223

Glow 150, 174, 175

Go Los Angeles Card 14

Gold Room 78, 91

Golden Gopher 26, 51

Good Luck Bar 77, 82

Good Nite, The 207, 218

Grace Home Furnishings . .128, 137

Grafton on Sunset 101, 118

Grand Avenue Festival 22

Grauman's Chinese Theater 99, 104

Greyhound Bus 10

Greystone Mansion 99, 120

Griddle Café 100, 114

Griffin, The 77, 82

Griffith Observatory 77, 80

Griffith Park 23, 77, 79-83

Griffith Park Light Festival . . .22

Grove, The 56, 64

Grub 99, 107

Gushi 127, 131

HaHa Comedy Club . . .207, 216

Hal's Bar & Grill 150, 168

Hale House 94

Hama Sushi 150, 168

Hancock Park 66-69

Happy Six 128, 140

Harold & Belle's 178, 203

Harry Winston 100, 123

Harvelle's Blues Club . .150, 162

Hatfield's 55, 61

HD Buttercup 128, 146

Heist 150, 169

Heritage Square Museum 77, 94

Hermosa Beach . .177, 180-185

Hermosa Beach Playhouse 177, 182

Hermosa Cyclery 181

Hey Kookla 150, 163

Hide Sushi 127, 139

Highland Gardens Hotel 101, 110

Highland Park 93-97

Hiko Sushi 128, 145

Hilgard House Hotel . . .128, 133

Hilton Checkers Hotel . . .27, 43

Hilton Los Angeles North/Glendale & Executive Meeting Center 208, 223

Holiday Inn Express Hotels & Suites 78, 88

Holiday Inn Express West Los Angeles 128, 141

Hollyhock House 81

Hollywood 102–110

Hollywood & Highland 100, 102, 109

Hollywood and Vine .99, 102, 103

Hollywood Bowl 99, 105

Hollywood Bowl Museum . .105

Hollywood Chamber of Commerce 103

Hollywood Film Festival 22

Hollywood Forever Cemetery 99, 103

Hollywood Museum 99, 105

Hollywood Park Racetrack 177, 203

Hollywood Pro Bicycles 15

Hollywood Reservoir . . .99, 104

Hollywood Roosevelt Hotel 101, 110

Hollywood Sign 99, 103

Hollywood Toys and Costumes 100, 109

Hollywood Walk of Fame 23, 99, 103

Honda-Ya 26, 33

Hornblower Cruises and Events 172

Hostelling International— Los Angeles South Bay ..179,191

Hotel Amarano Burbank . .208,223

Hotel Angeleno 128, 137

Hotel Bel-Air 128, 137

Hotel Metropole 199

Hotel Palomar Los Angeles– Westwood 128, 133

House of Blues Sunset Strip 100, 114

House of Davids 55, 67

Hugo's 207, 212

Hump, The 150, 161

hungry cat, the 99, 106

Huntington Library and Gardens 23, 225, 229

Hyde 100, 115

Iguana Import Gallery 179, 197

Iliad Book Shop 208, 218

Imix Book Store 78, 97

Improv, The 99, 113

Indian Film Festival 18

Indie Collective 128, 146

Inn at 657 . . . . .27, 53

Inn at Playa del Rey . . .151, 175

Inn at Venice Beach . . .151, 170

Inn of the Seventh Ray . .150, 156

Inn on Mt. Ada 199

International Surf Festival . . .20

Irori Japanese Restaurant 150, 174

It's a Wrap 208, 222

Ivy, The 100, 121

Izakaya by Katsu-ya 55, 62

J Trani's Ristorante . . .178, 189

Jack's Classic Hamburgers 207, 217

Japan LA 100, 117

Japanese American Cultural and Community Center 25, 32

Japanese American National Museum 25, 31

Japanese Village Plaza Mall 26, 35

Jazz Bakery, The 127, 142

Jer-ne Restaurant and Bar 150, 173, 175

Jet Propulsion Laboratory 225, 228

Jet Rag 100, 116

Jewelry District 26, 52

Joan's on Third 55, 62

Joanne's Closet 178, 190

Joe's Restaurant 150, 167

John O'Groats 128, 139

John Wayne Airport 10

Judith Kaufman Gallery . 207, 216

Kantor/Feuer Gallery ...99, 113

Karaoke Bleu 128, 140

Katsuya 127, 136

Kenneth Hahn State Recreation Area 177, 203

Kidrobot 100, 117

Kidspace Children's Museum 225, 230

Kirk Douglas Theatre ..127, 143

Kitchen, The 77, 86

Kitson 100, 123

Knitting Factory, The ...99, 108

Kodak Theatre 99, 105

Koi 100, 114

Korean American Museum ..55, 72

Korean Cultural Center 72

Korean Friendship Bell 187

Koreatown Galleria 56, 75

Koreatown Plaza 56, 75

Kyoto Grand Hotel & Gardens 26, 36

L.A. City Tours 14

LA Louver Gallery 149, 166

LA Shorts Fest 22

LA/Ontario International Airport 10

L'Scorpion 99, 108

La Brea Tar Pits 23, 55, 58

La Cabanita 208, 222

La Cachette 100, 122

La Dijonaise 143

La Parolaccia Osteria Italiana 178, 195

La Sosta Enoteca 178, 183

LA Times Festival of Books ..18

La Ve Lee 207, 213

La Velvet Margarita Cantina 99, 108

Lamonica's New York Pizza 127, 131

Langer's Delicatessen ...56, 74

Langham, Huntington Hotel & Spa, The 225, 234

Lankershim Arts Center 207, 215

Larchmont Village 66–69

Larchmont Village Farmers' Market 56, 69

Larchmont Village Wine Spirits & Cheese 55, 68

Larry Edmunds 100, 109

Last Chance Boutique .128, 147

Last Remaining Seats 19

LAStageTIX.com 14

Le Petit Greek 55, 68

Left Coast Galleries ..207, 210

Leimert Park 202–205

Lemon Rags 208, 213

Leo Carrillo State Beach ...149, 153

Leslie Sacks Fine Art ..127, 135

Liberty Grill 26, 50

Library Alehouse 150, 162

Library Bar 26, 42

Lighthouse Café, The ..178, 183

Lily Simone 78, 96

Liquid Kitty 128, 139

Lisa Kline 100, 124

Little Bar 55, 63

Little Cave 78, 96

Little Door 55, 61

Little Toni's 207, 217

Lobster, The 150, 161

Lola's 100, 115

London West Hollywood 101, 118

Long Beach 192–197

Long Beach Airport 10

Long Beach Convention & Entertainment Center ..177, 194

Long Beach Jazz Festival 20

Long Beach Lesbian & Gay Pride Parade and Festival 19

Long Beach Museum of Art 177, 193

Long Beach Opera 194

Long Beach Playhouse 177, 194

Long Beach Symphony 194

Longfellow-Hasting House ...94

Looff Hippodrome Carousel 160

Los Angeles Ballet 182, 221

Los Angeles California Temple 127, 129

Los Angeles Chamber Orchestra 221

Los Angeles City Birthday Celebration 21

Los Angeles Conservancy ...14, 48, 72

Los Angeles County Arboretum & Botanical Gardens ..225, 227

Los Angeles County Museum of Art 55, 59

Los Angeles Fashion District 26, 52

Los Angeles Film Festival 19

Los Angeles Flower District .26, 52

Los Angeles Historic Park 29, 149, 154

Los Angeles International Airport 9

Los Angeles Marathon 17
Los Angeles Maritime
   Museum 177, 188
Los Angeles Memorial Coliseum
   & Sports Arena 25, 47
Los Angeles Museum of the
   Holocaust 55, 60
Los Angeles National
   Cemetery 127, 138
Los Angeles Opera 39
Los Angeles Philharmonic . . .39
Los Angeles Police Historical
   Society Museum 77, 95
Los Angeles Times
   Building 25, 31
Los Angeles Zoo 77, 81
Los Feliz 79–83
Lotus Festival 20
Lucky You 208, 219
Lucques 100, 113
Lula Mae 225, 233
Luxe de Ville 78, 92
Luxe Hotel Rodeo Drive . . .101,
   124
Luxe Hotel Sunset
   Boulevard 128, 137
M Café de Chaya 99, 107
M&M 204
M&M Soul Food 178, 204
MacArthur Park 55, 71
Madrona Marsh Preserve
   & Nature Center 177, 181
Magic Castle Hotel 101, 110
Maison Akira 225, 231

MAK Center for Art &
   Architecture 99, 113
Malibu 152–157
Malibu Beach Inn,
   Carbon Vista 150, 157
Malibu Bella Vista 150, 157
Malibu Country Mart . .150, 157
Malibu Creek State Park . . .149,
   153
Malibu Inn 150, 156
Malibu Lagoon Museum . . .153
Malibu Lagoon State
   Beach 149, 153
Malibu Ocean Sports . .149, 154
Malibu Pier 149, 153
Malibu Seafood Fresh Fish
   Market and Patio
   Café 150, 156
Malo 77, 86
Mama D's Italian 178, 182
Mandrake Bar 128, 146
Manhattan Beach 180–185
Manhattan Beach Pier 177,
   180
Mardi Gras 17
Marie et Cie 208, 219
Marina Bike Rentals 181
Marina Boat Rentals 171
Marina del Rey 171–175
Marina del Rey Marriott . . .151,
   175
Marina del Rey
   Sportfishing 172
Marina del Rey Water Bus . .172

Marina International Hotel and Bungalows 151, 175

Marine Mammal Care Center .187

Mark Taper Forum 39, 40

Masa of Echo Park 78, 90

Mashti Malone's Ice Cream 99, 107

Mastro's Steakhouse . .100, 122

Matsuhisa 100, 122

Max 207, 212

Max Karaoke 128, 140

Maxfield 100, 116

Meals by Genet 55, 62

Melisse 150, 161

Merkato 55, 62

Mermaid 178, 183

Merry Karnowsky Gallery . . .55, 60

Metro 12

Metro Gallery 77, 84

Metrolink 10

Mexican Cultural Institute 25, 32

Mexican Independence Day 21

Mexico City 77, 81

Mi Piace 225, 231

Michael Levine 26, 53

Mikawaya 26, 35

Mildred E. Mathias Botanical Garden 130

Milk 55, 62

Millennium Biltmore Hotel 27, 43

Mint, The 55, 63

Miracle Mile 57–65

Miracle Mile Art Walk 60

Miss T's Barcade 56, 74

Miyako Hotel 27, 36

Mobius 56, 75

MOCA Grand Avenue 25, 40

MOCA Store 40

Molly Malone's 55, 63

Mondrian 101, 117

Monkeyhouse Toys 78, 87

Montgomery Arts House for Music and Architecture .149, 155

Moonshadows 150, 156

Mother's Beach 149, 172

Mount Wilson Observatory 225, 227

Mountain Bar 26, 34

Mr. T's Bowl 78, 96

Mulholland Grill 127, 136

Muscle Beach 149, 166

Museum of African American Art 178, 203

Museum of Contemporary Art (MOCA) 112

Museum of Design Art & Architecture 127, 143

Museum of Jurassic Technology 127, 143

Museum of Latin American Art 177, 194

Museum of Neon Art 26, 49

Museum of Tolerance . .99, 121

Music Box, The 99, 107

Music Center 25, 39
Musso & Frank Grill 99, 106
Nanbankan 128, 139
Napa Valley Grille 127, 131
Nate 'N Al 100, 122
Native Foods 127, 131
Natural History Museum of Los
   Angeles County 25, 47
NBC Television
   Studios 207, 221
NeoMeze 225, 232
Nic's Beverly Hills 100, 123
Nick & Stef's Steakhouse 50
NineThirty 133
Nisei Week Japanese
   Festival 20
Nite Inn 208, 214
Nobu Malibu 149, 155
Noe Restaurant and Bar . .26, 41
NoHo Arts Center 207, 215
NoHo Gallery LA 215
Nokia Plaza 48
Nokia Theatre L.A. Live . .25, 48
Noni 56, 68
North End Caffé 178, 183
North Hollywood 215–219
Norton House 149, 166
Norton Simon
   Museum 23, 225, 228
O Hotel 27, 44
O-Bar 100, 115
Observation Bar 178, 196
Off 'N Running Tours 15

Oinkster 78, 95
Old Pasadena 225, 227
Old Towne Pub 225, 232
Olvera Street 29
Omni Los Angeles Hotel at
   California Plaza 27, 43
On the Waterfront
   Café 150, 168
One Pico 164
Oou 78, 83
Open Sesame 178, 195
Orange Drive Hostel . . .101, 110
Orbit Hotel and
   Hostel 101, 118
Organic Panificio 150, 173
Original Pantry Café, The .26, 51
Orlando, The 56, 65
Ortolan 55, 61
Osteria Latini 127, 136
Osteria Mozza 99, 106
Otheroom, The 150, 168
Paramount Studios 99, 104
Park Plaza Hotel 55, 71
Parker's Lighthouse . . .178, 195
Parkway Grill 225, 231
Pasadena 226–234
Pasadena Jazz
   Institute 225, 232
Pasadena Museum of California
   Art 225, 229
Pasadena Museum of
   History 225, 230
Pasadena Playhouse . .225, 230

Pasadena Playhouse
District 230

Patina 26, 41

Patinette Café 40

Paul Smith 100, 116

Pazzo Gelato 77, 86

Pershing Square 25, 46

Petersen Automotive
Museum 55, 59

Petros Greek Cuisine and
Lounge 178, 182

Petticoats 56, 69

Philippe the Original 26, 33

Phillips Bar-B-Que 178, 204

Phoenix Bakery 26, 34

Piccolo Ristorante 150, 167

Pickett Fences 56, 68

Pig N' Whistle 100, 108

Pike at Rainbow Harbor,
The 177, 195

Pink's Hot Dogs 99, 107

Pinkberry 127, 138

Pizzeria Mozza 99, 106

Playboy Jazz Festival 19

Playclothes Vintage
Fashions 208, 213

Point Dume State Beach . . .149,
153

Point Fermin Lighthouse . . .187

Point Fermin Park 177, 187

Point Mugu State
Park 149, 154

Point Vicente Lighthouse . .177,
186

Polka Dots & Moonbeams . .56,
64

Polo Lounge 100, 123

Poop Deck 178, 183

Popkiller Second 26, 36

Port of Los Angeles Lobster
Festival 21

Portofino Hotel & Yacht
Club 179, 185

Portrait of a Bookstore 208,
214

Ports O'Call Marketplace . . .177,
188

Prado 55, 67

Prime Time Shuttle 9

Primitivo Wine Bistro . .150, 167

Prince, The 56, 74

Providence 99, 106

Puka Bar 178, 196

Pull My Daisy 78, 87

Queen Mary Hotel 179, 197

Queen Mary Scottish
Festival 17

R & R Soul Food
Restaurant 178, 204

R Bar 56, 74

R23 . . . . .26, 33

Radisson Hotel Los Angeles
Midtown at USC 27, 53

Radisson Hotel Los Angeles
Westside 129, 147

Ramada Wilshire Center . .56, 75

Ray Charles Memorial
Library 25, 47

Re: Style 178, 184

Realm 26, 35

Red Line Tours 15

REDCAT 25, 40

Redondo Beach 180–185

Redondo Beach Performing Arts Center 177, 182

Redondo Beach Pier/Fisherman's Wharf 177, 181

Redwood Bar & Grill 26, 42

Regeneration 78, 97

Renaissance Hollywood Hotel & Spa 101, 109

Renaissance Long Beach Hotel 179, 197

Rex's Café 178, 189

Richard Riordan Central Library 25, 38

Ritz Milner Hotel 27, 44

Ritz-Carlton Marina del Rey 151,175

Riviera Village 178, 184

RMS Queen Mary . .23, 177, 193

Robert H. Meyer Memorial State Beach 149, 153

Rock'N Fish 178, 182

Rockaway Records 78, 88

RockWalk 99, 104

Rodeo Drive . .23, 99, 100, 119, 123

Ronald Reagan Library & Museum 207, 209

Rooftop Bar at the Standard 26, 42

Roost, The 77, 82

Roosterfish 150, 169

Roscoe's House of Chicken and Waffles 99, 107

Rose Bowl Stadium . . .225, 226

Roundhouse Marine Lab & Aquarium 180

Russian Foxtrot Submarine 177, 193

S&W Country Diner . . .128, 145

Saddle Peak Lodge . . .207, 212

Safari Inn 208, 223

Saints & Sinners 128, 146

Saketini 127, 135

Sam Woo Bar-B-Q Restaurant 26, 34

San Gabriel Valley . . .226–234

San Pedro 186–191

San Pedro Brewing Company 178, 189

Sanam Luang Café 207, 217

Santa Monica 158–164

Santa Monica Boulevard . .99, 112

Santa Monica Historical Society Museum 149, 159

Santa Monica Mountains National Recreation Area 207, 210

Santa Monica Museum of Art 159

Santa Monica Pier 23, 149, 158, 160

Santa Monica Pier Aquarium 149, 160

Santa Monica Playhouse . . .149, 160

Santa Monica Puppetry Center 149, 160

Santa Monica State Beach . .149, 159

Santa Monica Visitor Information Kiosk 159

Santee Alley 7, 52

Sapori Restaurant 150, 173

Satine Boutique 56, 64

Schindler House 113

Scout 56, 64

Sea View Inn at the Beach . .179, 185

Seaside Lagoon 177, 181

Sepulveda Basin Recreation Area 207, 210

Sepulveda House 25, 29

Seven Grand 26, 52

Shabu Shabu House Restaurant 26, 34

Shack, The 150, 174

Shade Hotel 179, 185

Shellback Tavern, The .178, 183

Sheraton Universal 208, 219

Short Stop 78, 91

Show Pony 78, 92

Shutters on the Beach . .150, 164

Side Door 178, 184

Silent Movie Theater, The . . .55, 60

Silver Lake 84–88

Silver Lake Film Festival 21

Sirens and Sailors 78, 92

Six Flags Magic Mountain . .217

Skaf's Grill 207, 217

Skirball Cultural Center 127, 135

Skybar 100, 115

Skyla 128, 132

Skylight Books 78, 83

Small World Books . . .150, 170

Sofitel Los Angeles 56, 65

Soleil 127, 131

Sona 100, 113

Sony Pictures Studio Tour .127, 142

Sonya Ooten Gem Bar . . .56, 69

Soot Bull Jeep 56, 73

South Bay Bicycle Trail 152

South Bay Galleria 178, 184

South Coast Botanic Garden 177, 187

South Los Angeles 202–205

Southwest Museum of the American Indian 77, 94

Spaceland 77, 86

Spago 100, 121

Spirit Cruises 16

Sponto Gallery 149, 166

Sportsmen Lodge Hotel . . .208, 214

Sprinkles Cupcakes . . .100, 122

Squaresville 78, 83

Stacey Todd 208, 213

Standard, The 101, 117

Standard, Downtown LA, The 27, 43

Staples Center 25, 48

Star Eco Station 127, 144

Starlite Room 207, 213

Stars Antique Market . .178, 185

Steakhouse 55 201

Storyopolis 207, 211

Strange Invisible
Perfumes 150, 169

Studio City 209–214

Studio Gallery, A 210

Sunset Plaza 99, 112

Sunset Strip 99, 112, 114

Sunset Tower Hotel . . .101, 118

SuperShuttle 9

Surf Academy 181

Surfrider Beach Club . .150, 157

Sushi Go 55 . . . . .26, 33

Sushi Nozawa 207, 211

Sushi Sasabune 127, 135

Sushi-Gen 26, 33

Table 8 . . . . .100, 114

Taix 78, 90

Takao 127, 135

TarFest 21

Taschen 101, 124

Taxis 11

Taylor's Steak House 56, 74

Taylrz Joynt Boutique . . .208, 214

Temescal Canyon
Gateway Park 149, 154

Temple Bar 150, 162

Ten Thousand Villages 225, 233

Ten Women Venice . . .149, 166

Tender Greens 128, 145

Tengu 127, 132

Terranea Resort 179, 191

Thinkspace Gallery 77, 85

Third Gallery 178, 184

Third Street Promenade . . .150, 163

Thompson Beverly Hills . . .101, 125

Thousand Cranes 36

Three Clubs 99, 108

Tiki-Ti 78, 87

Tiny's K.O. 100, 108

Tokyo Japanese
Outlet 128, 140

Tom Bergin's Tavern 55, 63

Tommy's Original World
Famous Hamburgers . . .56, 73

Tonga Hut Tiki
Lounge 207, 218

Tony P's Dockside
Grill 150, 174

Tony's on the Pier 178, 184

Topanga State Park . . .149, 153

Toscana 127, 136

Tournament House 225, 226

Tournament of Roses
Parade 16, 226

Toyota Grand Prix 18

Tracey Ross 100, 116

Tracht's 197

Train Shack, The 208, 223

Trattoria Amici 125

Travel Town Museum 77, 80

Traveler's Bookcase 56, 65

Traxx Restaurant and Bar . .26, 33

Troubadour 100, 114

Turret House, The 179, 197

Two Roads Theatre . . .207, 211

Two Rodeo 100, 123

U.S. Bank Tower 25, 38

Uncle Bill's Pancake
House 178, 183

Undiscovered Chinatown
Tour 15

Union Station 25, 30

Universal City 215–219

Universal CityWalk 208, 219

Universal Studios
Hollywood 207, 216

University of California,
Los Angeles 127, 129

University of Southern
California 25, 48

Urasawa 100, 121

Urban Shopping Adventures .52

Urth Caffé 100, 114

USC Fisher Museum of Art . .25,
48

V Room 178, 196

Valentino 150, 161

VC Filmfest 18

Venice 165–170

Venice Art Walk 18

Venice Beach House . .151, 170

Venice Canals 149, 166

Versailles 128, 145

Vertical Wine Bistro . . .225, 232

Vibrato Grill Jazz...etc. 127,
136

Viceroy Santa Monica 151,
164

Villa 100, 115

Villa Marina Marketplace . . .150,
174

Village Books 150, 157

Vinoteca Farfalla 77, 82

Vintage Collective, The . .179, 197

Vinum Populi 128, 145

Vision Theater 178, 203

Vroman's Bookstore . . .225, 233

W Los Angeles-
Westwood 128, 133

Wacko 78, 83

Wakasan 128, 139

Wally's Wines & Spirits 128,
141

Walt Disney Concert Hall 39

Warner Bros. Studios . .207, 220

Warner Grand Theatre .177, 188

Water Grill 26, 41

Waterside Marina del Rey . .150,
174

Watts Towers 177, 202

Watts Towers Arts Center . .203

Watts Towers Day of the Drum
Festival 21

Way We Wore, The 56, 65

Wayfarer's Chapel 177, 186

Weiland Brewery 26, 34

Well, The 100, 108

Wells Fargo History
Museum 25, 38

West Hollywood 111–118

West Hollywood Halloween and
Costume Carnival 22

West L.A. 138–141

West Restaurant and
Lounge 137

Western Valley 209–214

Westfield Century City 101,
120, 124

Westfield Fox Hills Shopping
Center 128, 146

Westin Bonaventure Hotel ...27,
43

Westlake 70–75

Westside Pavilion 128, 140

WestWeek 17

Westwood 129–133

Westwood Memorial Park ..127,
129

Whale and Ale, The ...178, 190

Whiskey Blue 127, 132

Whisky A Go-Go 100, 115

Whist 164

Will Rogers State
Historic Park 149, 154

William Grant Still Arts
Center 178, 203

Williams Book Store ..178, 190

Wilshire Ebell Theatre ...55, 67

Wilson 128, 144

Wiltern 55, 72

Woody's Bar-B-Que ...178, 204

World Stage, The 178, 205

Wrigley Memorial and Botanical
Gardens 199

Y-Que Trading Post 78, 83

Yamashiro 99, 106

Yolk 78, 87

York, The 78, 96

Yuca's 77, 81

Yummy Cupcakes ...208, 222

Zambezi Bazaar 179, 205

Zankou Chicken 225, 232

Zanzibar 150, 162

Zipper 56, 64

Zucca 26, 50

Zuma Beach 149, 152

NOTES

NOTES

NOTES

transportation
map